CMMI® Assessments

CMMI® Assessments
Motivating Positive Change

Marilyn Bush
Donna Dunaway

✦Addison-Wesley

Upper Saddle River, NJ • Boston • Indianapolis • San Francisco
New York • Toronto • Montreal • London • Munich • Paris • Madrid
Capetown • Sydney • Tokyo • Singapore • Mexico City

Carnegie Mellon
Software Engineering Institute

The SEI Series in Software Engineering

To Ronny and Charley.

To Cole, Travis, Heather, and Michelle.

*And to the community of Lead Assessors and Lead Appraisers
whose skill, commitment, experience, creativity, and
optimism have sustained us.*

Contents

Foreword

By Watts S. Humphrey

When you embark on a process improvement effort, you need four things: a framework to measure and evaluate the improvement work, seasoned advice on the approach to take, guidance on the methods to use, and a way to benefit from and build on the experiences of others. This book covers all of these topics and it provides specific and highly readable guidance on how and what to do. The book outlines the history of assessments and it shows how and why assessments have become the most effective way to launch and guide a process improvement effort. Drawing on the authors' many years of development and assessment experience, this book encapsulates the lessons learned from thousands of assessments and provides readable and practical guidelines. In addition to recommending this book, my objective with this foreword is to describe how the assessment business started, why we made the choices we made, and what lies ahead in our never-ending improvement journey.

How It All Started

In 1979, Art Anderson was IBM's Senior Vice President for Engineering and Manufacturing and he asked me to be his Director of Technology Assessment. Art was responsible for the development and manufacturing of IBM's entire product line and mine was to be a new position in his organization. His immediate priority was semiconductor manufacturing. He had just learned that IBM's chips cost more than the landed price of chips bought from Japan. I was to launch the effort to address this problem, but I was not to take a traditional top-down management approach. He told me that the effort must be guided and motivated by the development and manufacturing people themselves. He called this approach an *assessment*. We followed Art's advice and the results were extraordinary. In only about two years, IBM became the world's lowest-cost and highest-quality manufacturer of semiconductor chips.

Early Software Experiences

Shortly thereafter, Jack Kuehler, IBM's president, asked me to return to software work and to lead the company's software process improvement effort. In this new job, I decided to apply the lessons I had just learned about assessments. I asked Ron Radice and his team to define and launch an assessment program for IBM's software laboratories. Ron and I attended Phil Crosby's Quality College and modeled our approach on his five-level maturity framework. I participated in the first software assessment, which started with an all-day meeting with the Santa Theresa Laboratory Director and his management team. Although the director had agreed to the assessment, his managers were strongly opposed. We spent all day trying to convince them that this assessment was for them and that we would not report the results to anyone else. If they wanted to tell somebody else, that was up to them, but we would not. Once we did convince them of the confidential nature of the assessment, the first one we conducted was so successful that the other laboratories started calling and asking for assessments of their own. From then on, Ron and his team were very busy.

Assessment Issues

The initial assessments were universally successful, but the second and third assessments at any given laboratory occasionally had problems. At the IBM Kingston laboratory, for example, the entire organization had responded enthusiastically to the initial assessment and had done a great deal of improvement work. They eagerly anticipated the second assessment. However, when we finished it, the results looked worse than they had the year before. The organization's enthusiasm died in an instant. The problem was the assessment criteria. While Crosby's maturity model had provided a useful general assessment framework, it was not able to detect incremental software process improvements. We needed a framework that related directly to software work. The Kingston laboratory had undoubtedly improved but our guidelines were subjective and our judgments as assessors had changed. What would have looked good to us a year before no longer did.

The SEI and the CMM

On joining the Software Engineering Institute (SEI) in 1986, my first project had been suggested by Bob Kent of the Air Force's Electronic System's Command. It was to work with Col. Jack Ferguson and the MITRE Corporation to define a way for the Air Force to select software contractors. At that time, all 17 of the major software contracts the Air Force had studied were failures, with delivery times averaging four times the original commitments. After some debate, the Air Force agreed to the MITRE-SEI team recommendation to add a new evaluation of organizational capability and to leave the current proposal evaluation process alone. Our first step was to produce a set of about 100 questions that would distinguish well-run software organizations from poorly run ones.

I remember being stuck in the Atlanta airport trying to figure out how acquisition groups would actually use this list of questions in a real procurement. For a typical acquisition with a dozen bidders, and with the answers to 100+ questions for each bidder, we had to show acquisition groups how to organize and use these 1,200+ answers to rank the bidders. Then it hit me. By mapping these questions against the Crosby maturity framework, we would have the precise criteria that our earlier assessments had lacked. We would also have a way to evaluate and rank organizations. That is how the CMM began, and the principles we initially established are just as important now as they were then. You must have senior management support, absolute confidentiality, and a process model that closely relates to the technology and management system being evaluated.

CMM Development

While I was fortunate to be in at the beginning of the CMM and process assessment work, I did not single-handedly create the CMM and its assessment methods. Just like the assessments themselves, the assessment method had to be developed by the people who were to use it. This required a large team of SEI professionals plus the extended involvement of a host of people from industry and government. Broad participation increased the likelihood that the method would be accepted and properly used.

What Next?

As you use the assessment method to improve your organization, keep two things in mind. First, to paraphrase Winston Churchill, Level 5 is not the end, nor is it the beginning of the end. It is the end of the beginning. In following the maturity framework, you are building a self-improvement system. Once you get to Level 5, the next challenge is to use this self-improvement system to continuously improve your organization.

The second point is that Level 5 is not the end of the capability ladder. CMMI is a marvelously useful and comprehensive framework for process improvement, and it has now been successfully used by a wide range of groups from all over the world. However, software technology is constantly changing and, it seems, the rate of change is accelerating. There will be many new ideas and countless technical advances, and the CMMI framework must grow to keep in step. If it does not, it will no longer be a useful framework for evaluating and guiding incremental process improvement.

While it is risky to predict the future, a key area for future extension must involve the people in software organizations. Just as people are the key to process improvement, they are also the key to organizational performance. Soon, our models must address the way software people work, both individually and in teams. The models we use to guide our improvement work must also reflect how our people are developed, led, guided, and coached.

Watts S. Humphrey
Sarasota, Florida
December 2004

Preface

Assessments have for many years been at the cutting edge of the theory and practice of process improvement, but not many people understand what process improvement assessments were designed to do, how they evolved, and how they work. At the heart of these issues is a simple fact: Assessments are not audits.

Audits are reviews of an organization conducted by outsiders, and within the organization they feel like tests. Assessments are internal reviews aimed at making an organization better from the inside. Historically, audits have demonstrated only limited effectiveness, while assessments, undertaken in the correct spirit and in the right way, have proved able to transform an organization's technical and managerial culture and radically improve the quality and profitability of its products. The authors, who have been centrally involved in the creation and application of modern assessments, have written this book to help executives, managers, and engineers and even assessors themselves make intelligent decisions about why and when to schedule an assessment and how best to benefit from it.

Intended Audience for the Book

This book was written for three audiences.

Chapters 1, 2, 3, and 4 are aimed at senior executives and provide an overview of what assessments entail, how they can help, and what role a senior executive is expected to play in them. Chapter 12 concerns the senior executive's responsibilities in post-assessment improvement efforts and contains an extended case study of how one organization improved as it progressed through a four-year program of reiterated assessments from Level 2 to Level 5.

Chapters 4 through 11 take the reader through the stages of a typical assessment and contain a step-by-step guide to what needs to be done by whom at every step. The chapters include comments and examples that collectively comprise a manual for assessors, but the chapters are also designed to help potential participants.

Everyone in an organization about to undergo an assessment's prolonged ordeal can benefit enormously from knowing what takes place before, during, and after an assessment—such as what assessors are looking for, and who is responsible for what. Such knowledge can save participants mountains of time and effort. They will discover, for instance, that they are not required to be experts in translating their procedures into the language of software maturity models but need only to understand what kinds of things assessors are looking for.

Nor will assessors suffer by gaining some insight into the difficulties of the participants. The book tries to anticipate the major problems assessments most often encounter and includes anecdotal commentary drawn from our extensive working experience.

Assessments Are Part of the Larger Subject of Process Improvement

Whatever their power to facilitate organizational change, assessments are primarily tools of process improvement. Process improvement is another subject, however, and the literature about it is large and growing.

The most compact and complete model of the stages of process improvement is probably the SEI's IDEAL^{SM} model for organizational improvement [Gremba 97]. The model (see Figure P-1) provides a roadmap for the initiating, planning, and implementing activities of a process improvement program and is named for the five phases it describes: Initiating, Diagnosing, Establishing, Acting, and Learning [SEI web site 04].

Assessments fall into the Diagnosing phase of the IDEAL approach, which concerns identifying current processes, developing recommendations, and emphasizing follow-on activities.

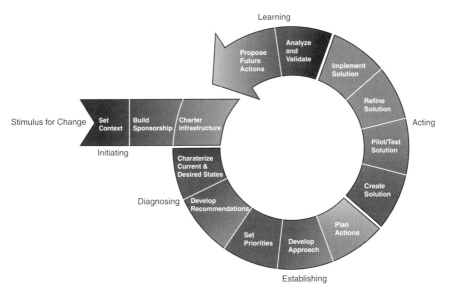

Figure P-1   *IDEAL model.*

Software Versus Systems and Hardware Process Improvement Assessments

This book is primarily concerned with software process improvement assessments. In recent years, though, the theory of software process improvement assessments has been successfully applied to project management, software engineering, hardware engineering, human resources, and service process improvement assessments as well. To describe the detailed variations between software and these non-software assessments would effectively require another book. The large picture, however, is essentially the same. The current book, therefore, should be of interest to anyone involved with project management, software engineering, hardware engineering, and other process improvement assessments, and the authors have made occasional remarks about other kinds of assessments when they have seemed relevant.

CMM/CBA IPI Versus CMMI/SCAMPI

The Capability Maturity Model Integration (CMMI) has by now almost superseded the Capability Maturity Model (CMM) as the basis of the SEI's software process improvement activities. The same can be said of the SCAMPI assessment methodology associated with the CMMI. Therefore this book primarily addresses the CMMI and SCAMPI.

However, because the CMMI and SCAMPI are in fact outgrowths of the more familiar CMM and its associated CBA IPI assessment methodology (and because the logic of both the SEI model and assessment methodologies are in some ways clearer in the CMM and the CBA IPI), the authors have treated the two programs as part of the same subject, while also indicating the important differences between the two.

Staged Versus Continuous Assessments

The most important difference between the current version of the SEI's SCAMPI methodology and its predecessor, the CBA IPI, is that the newer version provides for the possibility of an assessment based on the CMMI's Continuous Representation mode, in which segments of an organization and segments of the reference model can be assessed without addressing the maturity of the organization's capabilities as a whole.

However, because "continuous" assessments constitute a departure from the history and theory of "staged" capability maturity assessments with which the authors are primarily concerned, we have largely omitted them from the book's central focus, while being careful to describe the differences between "staged" and "continuous" assessments for anyone wishing to pursue the subject of "continuous" assessments elsewhere.

Anecdotal Histories

Wherever possible, the authors have included anecdotal histories of incidents they have encountered on actual assessments to illustrate different parts of this book. Such histories are indicated by shaded text. The identities of the principals in these incidents have been altered to Organization A, B, C, etc., and some of the details have been simplified.

A Roadmap Through the Book

Chapter 1: "Why Do Assessments?" provides an account of the function and place of assessments within a program of process improvement and concentrates on the way assessments serve as fulcrums for positive change. The last two sections of the chapter spell out the bottom-line value of assessments with the help of numbers drawn from the extended case study presented in Chapter 12.

Chapter 2: "A Brief History of Process Improvement Methodologies and Assessment Methods" explains why and how software process improvement assessment methods evolved out of audits and describes the elements of the two most sophisticated modern software process improvement models—the SEI's CMM and CMMI—along with their associated assessment methodologies, CBA IPI and SCAMPI.

Chapter 3: "Assessments: An Executive Overview" provides a brief overview of the assessment process, including questions that must be considered by senior executives before an assessment is undertaken and the role of a senior executive in the authorization and execution of a CBA IPI or SCAMPI assessment.

Chapter 4: "Planning and Preparing for an Assessment, Part 1: Senior Management Responsibilities" begins a section of four chapters about pre-onsite assessment activities and explains what senior managers must do before, during, and after an assessment.

Chapter 5: "Planning and Preparing for an Assessment, Part 2" deals with choosing a time for an upcoming assessment, formulating an assessment plan, appointing an organization site coordinator, and organizing an assessment's logistics. This chapter details the duties of both the assessment sponsor and others with special responsibilities for preparing for an assessment.

Chapter 6: "Planning and Preparing for an Assessment, Part 3" continues to describe the details of preparing for an assessment and concerns creating an assessment team, selecting projects to be assessed, selecting people to be interviewed, defining the final assessment products, and distributing questionnaires.

Chapter 7: "Planning and Preparing for an Assessment, Part 4: Assessment Team Training and Post-Training Activities" addresses assessment team training and post-training activities and completes the book's account of pre-onsite assessment activities.

Chapter 8: "Onsite Activities, Part 1" is the first of three chapters concerned with an assessment's Onsite activities. The chapter addresses the assessment kick-off meeting and other presentations and the problems of collecting and managing documents, and it focuses on problems associated with immature organizations.

Chapter 9: "Onsite Activities, Part 2: Interviewing" focuses on the selection of people to be interviewed, formulating interview questions, how the team conducts itself during interviewing, and what people being interviewed should prepare for and expect.

Chapter 10: "Onsite Activities, Part 3: The Day-to-Day Consolidation of Data" concerns how assessment teams manage and consolidate data.

Chapter 11: "The Final Stages of an Onsite Assessment: Summing Up and Presenting Results" addresses issues concerning the assessment team's final data consolidation, the preparation of draft findings, draft findings meetings at which preliminary findings are reviewed with assessment participants, and the presentation of final findings, including an optional maturity level rating, to the organization.

Chapter 12: "How to Use the Results of an Assessment Productively" concerns post-assessment improvement efforts and ends with an extended case study (including details about cost and profitability) of how one organization improved as it progressed through a four-year program of reiterated assessments from Level 2 to Level 5.

Acknowledgments

Writing a book is harder than anyone who has not done it realizes. Without the help and encouragement of others, it would have been impossible. First and foremost, this book was written with the editorial advice of Ron Bush, who gave more generously of his time than either of us would have dared ask.

The very experienced and dedicated people who have served as Lead Assessors and Lead Appraisers have inspired us with their efforts to motivate positive change in thousands of organizations around the world. Without this group of skilled professionals, no assessment method would be worth the paper it is printed on. Our thanks to all of them who have shared their experience with us.

We would also like to acknowledge the efforts of early contributors to what evolved into the CBA IPI and SCAMPI methods—especially Watts Humphrey, Carol Bothwell, Mike Dedolph, Jack Harding, Will Hayes, Dave Kitson, Steve Masters, and George Winters.

It is impossible to really understand assessments from the outside. And so the authors wish to thank the many dedicated professionals who entrusted their companies to the methods described and whose support during the assessment process and later in analyzing its benefits was invaluable. Most of them must remain anonymous, but we would like to extend special thanks to Peter Howard and Randy Varga for generously reviewing sections of this book and Eileen Rubin and Roger Wilson for providing different kinds of essential materials.

For the helpful suggestions and close reading of the text of the book, we extend very grateful thanks to Mark Paulk, Clifford Shelley, and Gary Wolf.

Peter Gordon, Kim Boedigheimer, Sarah Kearns, and Ben Lawson at Addison-Wesley provided irreplaceable assistance in producing the book. Without Peter Gordon's encouragement, patience, and expertise, the book would probably never have seen the light of day.

Closer to home, we wish to thank Ellen Wolin and Charley Bush for their support and for helpful suggestions.

Finally, there are people who are no longer with us but without whose inspiration neither we nor this book would be the same. We wish to remember Al Pietrasanta, Minnie and Louis Wolin, and Joe and Susie Kastle, whose spirit lives on.

Marilyn Bush
Oxford, Philadelphia

Donna Dunaway
Dallas

About the Authors

 **Marilyn Bush** is a leading figure in international software process improvement. After 20 years of experience as a project, systems, and software manager, she was enlisted by the SEI to provide practical and managerial perspective on the team that produced the CMM. In 1995, she became one of the co-authors of *The Capability Maturity Model: Guidelines for Improving the Software Process.* She is also an author of the SEI's Introductory Course on the CMM, and had a hand in developing the SEI CBA IPI Assessment Method and the SEI Lead Assessor Course. The head of her own consulting firm since 1992 (www.marilynbush.com), she is one of the world's most experienced CMM and CMMI Lead Assessors and has specialized in advising companies at the senior executive level.

 **Donna K. Dunaway**, Ph.D., is a pioneer in the computing industry, having taught herself to program an IBM 704 in the late '50s. After working in a number of software development organizations during her career, she joined the Process Group at the Software Engineering Institute at Carnegie Mellon University in 1992. She developed and managed the SEI Appraiser Program from its beginnings in 1994 until 2000. She served on the CMMI Product Development Team from 1998 to 2000. As head of her own consulting company, The Dunaway Group (www.dunawaygroup.com), Donna works with organizations in their process improvement initiatives to achieve greater benefits from use of the models and assessment methods.

Chapter 1

Why Do Assessments?

1.1 What Assessments Do

This is a book about the theory and practice of process improvement assessments—how assessments work and what they accomplish. It focuses on software assessments because of the industry's by now extensive experience with them, but it also implicitly addresses the kind of systems and even hardware assessments that have recently evolved along the same lines. The book is meant to help managers and engineers understand what process improvement assessments aim to do and to help them think about what assessments provide in return for a substantial cost in time and money.[1] It is also aimed at instructing them in how best to prepare for an assessment and how to get the most out of it. Finally, it is intended as a guide for working assessors in the theory and practice of conducting assessments effectively.

[1.] For an exploration of the value of assessments, see *Why Do Organizations Have Assessments? Do They Pay Off?* [Dunaway 99].

On one level, assessments can be thought of simply as tools for facilitating process improvement. They analyze the strengths and weaknesses of how an organization really works by examining its business, management, and engineering processes and their analyses and results can only be understood within the larger framework of the description of structured software development articulated by a sophisticated software improvement model. The most powerful of today's models are the SEI's Capability Maturity Model (CMM) and Capability Maturity Model Integration (CMMI), both of which emphasize the importance of detecting defects early and then preventing them. The process improvement initiated by these models involves an organizational discipline that recognizes and deals with problems early, accepts independent quality reviews, and promotes discomfort when quality procedures are missing.

But because increasing an organization's level of discipline involves changing people's expectations and motivating them to make appropriate adjustments at specific stages in the improvement process, assessments amount to more than strictly analytical procedures. They also function as instruments for organizational change. Assessments, which require an organization's active and willing involvement and which build on broad participation, are not the same as audits or external evaluations. The latter can be performed by outsiders, and they usually make insiders feel as if they are still in school and are receiving a report card.[2]

Because assessments are group efforts at self-analysis, they have the power to effect real improvement, and the crucial differences between assessments and audits have generated rules that are critical to an assessment's potential to motivate change. For example, one core aim of assessments is to fix problems, not people. Thus, assessments focus on how organizational structures work, not who did what in the past or who gave the

---

[2.] It is true that the CMM and CMMI are associated with auditing procedures for the cases that arise when an outside organization wants to evaluate the organization being audited for the purpose of, for example, deciding whether to use the organization as a contractor. These audits are called Software Capability Evaluations (SCEs) and SCAMPI/SCEs respectively and are treated briefly in Chapter 2. This book, however, is principally about assessments and will mention these other procedures only in passing.

assessors the lowdown. Interviews and the information they produce remain confidential. No statement made in an interview may be traceable to a given individual. These procedures result in a non-judgmental climate, which turns out to be crucial for helping to leverage an organization out of the dysfunctional patterns of a blame culture.

Because assessments are participant-based activities, they also help an organization "buy into" or "own" the improvement plans that come out of them. When proposals for change grow out of ideas generated by a collective effort rather than being imposed from above, people are much less prone to resist them.

But for organizations really to "own" the results of an assessment, the people in them must believe that an assessment has less to do with passing a test than with helping an organization get better at what it does. Audits evaluate organizations from without, which can be beneficial but is often discouraging. Because of the activities involved in the way they work, assessments help transform an organization into a more functional and more successful version of itself during the course of the assessment.

1.2 The Four Principal Functions of Assessments

Assessments have four principal functions: They *analyze* how an organization really works, they (often through shock) help *motivate* it toward positive change, their procedures establish precedents that help organizations begin to *transform* themselves even before the assessment is finished, and they *educate* organizations by exposing them to best practices worldwide.

These four functions are of course not independent, nor do they always work the same way. Different assessment experiences can affect companies in different ways. Less mature organizations should prepare for the shock that accompanies realizing you aren't as good as you thought you were. They will be in for a strenuous educational procedure. On the other end of the scale, highly mature organizations (many of which will have already undergone previous assessments) usually experience assessments as moments of concentration and careful self-analysis. But one never knows. No two assessments are quite the same in their impact or in their outcomes.

Example: During a follow-on assessment, two groups within Organization A reacted very differently to the assessment experience. One group had long been with the organization and had been through several previous assessments. They had once responded defensively to questions and judgments, but they had also seen the progress that the first assessments enabled (in scheduling, the quality of their products, and customer satisfaction) and a corresponding improvement in their own work situations. During the current assessment, therefore, they were eager to assist the assessment team and take on new suggestions, even probing ones. A second group, however, which had recently been merged into the organization, had never experienced an assessment and did what first-time assessees usually do—cover their weaknesses and put the best possible face on everything. They tried to keep knowledgeable people from being interviewed, and they bridled when the draft findings suggested that the organization still had work to do to achieve the maturity level it expected. (Certain managers so feared the results that they found excuses not to attend the draft findings meeting.) Finally, senior managers associated with the first group stepped in. They did their best to explain to the newcomers that their reaction was counterproductive, and they also urged the Lead Assessor to make the final findings as clear and objective as possible—telling him, "Don't hold anything back." Both groups survived, but the first group experienced a very different assessment than the second.

An assessment's success, moreover, depends as much on the understanding and skill of the assessors as on the methods they employ. Analyzing a company depends on knowing enough about technical and managerial attitudes to ask the right questions at the right times while building confidence in the assessment process and in the future of the organization. Motivating an organization toward improvement means emphasizing the positive effects of change. Educating an organization involves knowing the internal and often unspoken logic of process improvement methodologies and the international best practices out of which they grew.

1.2.1 Function 1: Assessments Serve as Analytical Tools

Assessments do not reflect the way the members of an organization *think* things work or the way the organization's paperwork says things theoretically *ought* to work. Based on separate interviews with staff at every level, they represent the way things really *do* work.

Assessments have taken the place of audits in the engineering community because audits have traditionally relied on a company's paper records of how things ought to work, whereas assessments rely on in-depth and cross-referencing interviews with practitioners that (whether or not the practitioners are happy to disclose it) get at how things really happen.

Assessments do not simply tell you the way one part of an organization works on its own. Instead they explain the way a part of the organization works within an organizational structure and an organizational culture, based on a sophisticated understanding of how the software development cycle works in the most successful companies around the world. An assessment's account of how an organization works is thus not merely descriptive. Assessment analysis depends on criteria established by a *reference model*.

Nobody likes the idea of being compared to a theoretical model. However, the models used by assessments are integrated global descriptions of how many good practices fit together, and assessments need to have a picture of the whole enterprise in mind, not just a catalogue of individual good practices. Assessment methodologies are never perfect, and they can sometimes even seem incomprehensible or perverse. But they remain the best available means of facilitating more productive, more reliable, and more profitable organizations. People apply assessments best when they understand their limitations, their logic, and their practical payoff.

1.2.2 Function 2: Assessments Function as Fulcrums of Positive Change

Assessments stimulate technical and organizational cultures to evolve. Seeing your organization as it really is can feel a little like being punched in the stomach. Managers always think their companies are better than they really are. No one is ever prepared for cold truth. But the *shock* of an assessment has priceless value because it can initiate momentum toward positive change. It dissolves complacency and enables staff to take a fresh look at how a company can be improved.

Shock alone, however, can lead to defensiveness and paralysis. Along with the shock, assessments put in place a group of mechanisms that help organizations survive the shock and work toward improvement in an open and energized way. Assessments convey the message that management is interested enough in making things better to take real action, bringing out the best in people who had become permanently discouraged. Assessments enable self-analysis to take place in a relatively penalty-free zone. Requiring broad participation, they distribute and limit exposure. Stressing that processes, not people, should be the focus of change, they diminish defensiveness. Providing a voice for change agents, they release energies that had been previously bottled up. Finally, assessments prioritize follow-on activities in an encouraging and logical way, making it easier to take the first steps toward new patterns of work.

1.2.3 Function 3: Assessments Transform Organizations by the Way They Work

When assessments work properly, the medium becomes the message and becomes self-sustaining. Assessments train and habituate organizations in continuing non-defensive self-criticism. The higher levels of maturity in assessment methodology represent nothing more than institutionalized and ongoing self-analysis. Assessments cannot work in a blame culture; therefore, for an intense moment, they condition the members of an organization to think about the pros and cons of what they do in a non-threatening way. Assessments also change people's perspective on their immediate environment and on the larger environment in which they work, and these new perspectives have a way of becoming self-perpetuating. Finally, assessments require senior management to become actively involved in the improvement process, and this involvement almost always lasts beyond the end of the assessment.

1.2.4 Function 4: Assessments Educate Organizations in Worldwide Best Practices

By exposing a large segment of an organization's personnel to the best practices embodied in an assessment's capability maturity model, assessments not only motivate companies to improve, but they also teach them *how* to improve at a time when they are most receptive to learning new techniques.

1.3 The Analytical Function of Assessments

Assessment analysis depends not only on objective procedures but also on criteria established by a *reference model*. As we mentioned earlier, models are integrated global descriptions of the way that many good practices fit together and of the stages in which different good practices should be introduced so that they can build on each other, not compete or cancel each other out. That is, rather than being a catalogue of individual good practices, they involve the notion of maturity levels—a logical process of staged improvements.

1.3.1 The Importance of Reference Models

The core appeal of capability maturity models is that they promise a structured and therefore stable procedure to implement positive changes. The most important current software improvement models have been created by integrating the best practices of the most successful software development companies around the world into a step-by-step framework for implementing process improvement. At present, this means above all the capability maturity models developed since 1984 at the Software Engineering Institute—the CMM for Software [Paulk et al, 94] and the CMM Integration [Chrissis et al, 03].

1.3.2 Assessments Stabilize Process and Prioritize Change

The crux of the SEI-based assessment reference models is a vision of how organizations stabilize themselves so that random efforts toward improvement can evolve into structured, reliable, and continuous building of strength upon strength. For both the CMM and the staged version of the CMMI (see Chapter 2 for further details), five capability maturity levels are posited: Level 1 represents a condition in which processes are unarticulated and improvements are random and sometimes contradictory. At Level 2, project management processes are stabilized and articulated so that technical developments can be approached in a predictable way. At Level 3, the best project and technical processes are identified and institutionalized in an organization-wide platform so that the organization can centrally support improvement efforts, including training. At Level 4, both projects and the central organization begin to use baseline measurements to compare the strengths and weaknesses of past and current processes and products. At Level 5, the organization and the projects are able reliably to anticipate risk and bring in new technology with a firm grasp of the consequences of change, and to initiate programs of continuous improvement in a systematic and measured way.

In short, assessments analyze not just whether organizations perform functions well but also, in reference to a process improvement model, whether they are likely to reliably generalize lessons of continued and increasing excellence out of local successes.

1.4 Assessments Function as Fulcrums of Positive Change

Assessments, though, do more than analyze. They act as fulcrums for positive change.

For process improvement to work, an organization must evolve, both technically and culturally. But change is exceedingly hard to produce. Assessments unleash important forces to move toward positive change. Consider Rosabeth Moss

Kanter's account of the change process. Laggards approach change, she suggests, with denial, then anger, then by blaming others, and finally by token efforts of acceptance, evidenced by cosmetic change. This last stage has been compared to "putting lipstick on a bulldog." It temporarily makes the bulldog look better, but it always makes the bulldog mad. The result in the long run is not substantive change but rather inevitable failure [Kanter 02].

Why do assessments succeed where other kinds of intervention fail? Assessments involve organizational staff as active participants in their company's evolution. After identifying areas of improvement, they facilitate a collaborative effort that feels like it has grown out of the collective experience rather than something that has been imposed from above or from the outside.

1.4.1 Assessments Effect Change by Involving and Motivating Organizations in Efforts of Self-Analysis

Assessment methodology requires a team to interview a broad selection of people, both managers and development staff, to provide representation across the assessed organization. Mitigating resistance, this broad participation fosters internal change.

You need to find out what's wrong with something before you can fix it. However, even in a problem-solving organization, the sudden exposure that accompanies real examination may cause people to feel frightened and stressed by having their work patterns examined: "When performance is measured objectively, you and your work can be seen by all" [Hammer 96]. It is not uncommon for this response to lead to the erection of self-protective walls, which serves as a major barrier to organizational improvement.

With the kind of broad participation required by an assessment, though, issues are shared, and turf protection either diminishes or becomes more obvious, in which case it can be dealt with directly.

Assessments also elicit specific, local response to possible avenues of improvement, reinforcing practitioners' sense that their experience and opinions are valuable. An assessment provides a chance to respond not only for the members of the assessment team but for all the assessment participants who are interviewed over a long assessment process. Staff members are given a chance to shape the way improvements are proposed. They may recognize, for example, that new practices may not be valid for certain circumstances either in themselves or in the way that they are to be implemented. Imposing such changes by fiat makes workers want to throw out the baby (the principles behind the best practices) with the bathwater (the particular circumstances in which the practices are executed) and to respond negatively to the whole project of process improvement. When workers are allowed to consider a set of "best practices" in the context of their own understanding of how to make things better, though, they stop resisting them and start thinking of ways to make them work.

A positive approach to change is strongly associated with empowerment (decisions are made by people who know most about the issue regardless of rank) and collaboration (departments and functions work actively with other groups on a regular basis) [Kanter 01].

According to Boyett, "People don't resist their own ideas. Our gurus agree that people who participate in deciding what will change and how things will change not only are more likely to support the change, but are actually changed themselves by the mere act of participation. …Participation has become the standard method for accomplishing change and is a key feature of everyone's change process" [Boyett 98].

In the words of Kotter, "Major change is essentially impossible unless most employees are willing to help, often to the point of making short-term sacrifices. But people will not make sacrifices, even if they are unhappy with the status quo, unless they really believe that a transformation is possible. Without credible communication, and a lot of it, employees' hearts and minds are never captured" [Kotter 96].

Assessments provide a forum that helps focus general but unarticulated discomfort because people are encouraged to articulate problems and because the assessment team listens to everyone's ideas empathetically and objectively. Assessments thus provide a way to examine and address problems that may be collectively perceived, but not acknowledged. Frequently, it is heard at the conclusion of an assessment that "we didn't learn anything new." What people don't realize however is that assessments allow old problems not only to be articulated but also to be addressed.

Assessments also force management to listen. Sometimes they hear what everyone except them seems to know. Sometimes they too know about problems but have no way to engage them without making them worse. Assessments require managers to acknowledge what everybody knows and to work with their employees on problem resolution. Assessments thus provide an arena for consensus between workers and management.

Finally, when an entire organization is involved in an assessment, those who have participated "own" the assessment results. Having been part of the analysis, they feel responsible for becoming part of the solution. This provides significant momentum for change.

1.4.2 Assessments Effect Change Because They Help the Workers in an Organization Understand That Processes, Not People, Need to Be Fixed

Because assessments are set up as non-threatening activities reinforced by non-attribution of information and the pledged confidentiality of everyone who participates, they say to all involved that the goal is to "fix the process, not the people." Assessments make it very clear by their principle of strict confidentiality that it is not their business to "place blame" on individuals or projects. Their goal is to improve the organization's way of doing business so that an environment is created for staff, managers, and customers that enables the production of a higher quality product.

Without confidentiality, asking organizational staff about the way they do their work could be intrusive and threatening. People could fear for their jobs and would be less than honest in expressing themselves. The entire assessment process would then be compromised.

That is why the procedures that an assessment uses to address an organization's process—not its people—need to be rigorously maintained. Strictly confidential assessment results are reported to the organization, and no specific person or project is identified with any of the assessment data collected. Each interview participant is also asked to keep confidential anything he or she may hear anyone say during the interview. The confidentiality also continues after the assessment is concluded. The assessment representative receives detailed data with all attribution removed. The assessment team members are asked to make a pledge of confidentiality, even after the assessment is over.

Sometimes concern arises that organizations need detailed identifiable data upon which to build improvement activities, but this concern is unfounded. After attribution has been removed, a large bank of highly detailed assessment data remains for improvement planning.

1.4.3 Assessments Effect Change Because They Provide a Voice for Change Agents

In any organization, there are people who have come to recognize existing problems and have tried to convince their colleagues to improve.

The organization's staff usually has a good understanding of problem areas and may have already voiced their concerns, only to have their recommendations be dismissed.

The value of assessment findings is that they synthesize and document an organization's problems, presenting them with the authority of an organization's global view of its own processes. Assessments provide a focused statement of problem areas within the organization and identify instances of best practices that can provide solutions.

Also, because management sponsors the assessment, their attention is assured. Thus, good ideas get visibility, which boosts the morale of those people in the organization who have been trying to make improvement happen.

1.4.4 Assessments Effect Change Because They Foster Follow-On Activities

Assessments prioritize improvement activities according to the prescriptions of an elaborately thought out and structured process improvement methodology (a capability maturity model such as the CMMI, for example). This makes it easier to organize the plans that follow an assessment in a logical and highly structured way.

Assessments also constitute a very visible intervention that indicates to staff that the management is interested enough in improvement to take action.

1.5 Assessments Transform Organizations by the Way They Work

Because assessments involve a broad section of the organization in a rigorous and communal act of self-analysis, they help train organizations to be systematically introspective and self-critical. The model of best practices against which the organization is evaluated provides guidance, but the ways in which best practices are introduced to the organization in the assessment create a basis for transformational effectiveness. Assessments force people to see things in more useful ways, and these new perspectives become self-sustaining: They perpetuate themselves after the assessment has been completed and make organizations more analytical and more efficient.

1.5.1 Assessments Transform Organizations by Getting Different People to See the Same Things the Same Way

A key part of the self-analysis that occurs during an assessment involves an organization's insight into how it is doing business at the moment of the assessment. This might seem like an obvious statement, but it is not, particularly in an organization that takes an ad hoc approach to improvement. When practitioners in such organizations begin to document the way they do business, they are often surprised and nonplussed. Often there is inconsistency or confusion about the way things are done. Identifying the current processes they use becomes a valuable exercise in its own right. The assessment imposes the discipline of objectivity onto a culture of wishful thinking: It examines the way things are being done at that particular point in time—not the way things should be done, or the way someone wants them to be done. The insight is the equivalent of finding your present location on a map so that you can intelligently plot a path to your goal. As Watts Humphrey once famously remarked, "If you don't know where you are, a map won't help."

1.5.2 Assessments Transform Organizations by Helping Senior Management's Efforts at Unification

Next, an assessment necessarily requires that senior management be actively involved as the sponsor of the assessment and the source of actions implemented as a result of the assessment. This also frequently constitutes a major shift in the operations of the kind of low maturity organization in which software is viewed as a mysterious process to be pawned off to a software department that may have little real authority. Without the sponsorship of senior management, grass-root efforts don't get results and become frustrating for the work force. Assessments require senior management to say that the process improvement exercise is being conducted not just for the software department's sake but also for the organization's sake.

Deming and Humphrey have indicated that major changes within an organization require leadership [Deming 82] [Humphrey 89]. Senior managers must set challenging goals and monitor their progress. Assessments require managers to establish priorities, provide resources, and monitor and support the changes in the software process. With management's hands-on involvement and support, grass-roots efforts begin to flourish. Assessments help transform an organization into a unit in which continuous management support becomes a prominent and lasting feature. Management commitment does not simply mean giving approval. It includes providing direction, having a good understanding of what and why activities are being undertaken, and providing visible active support and encouragement.

1.5.3 Assessments Transform Organizations by Softening a Culture of Blame, Permitting Staff the Freedom to Think About What Goes Wrong and How to Correct It

Another way that assessments transform organizations into better places to work is the way that they condition the members of an organization to think about the pros and cons of what they do in a non-threatening way. By insisting on the strict maintenance of confidentiality for all interviews, an assessment establishes a non-judgmental, respectful attitude toward the views of all the people who are interviewed. Non-attribution of data is essential for a free flow of information from participants in an assessment, but it also helps soften and transform organizational practices and begins to create better working environments.

Part of becoming a more mature organization involves recognizing that everyone makes mistakes and that the sooner you find the mistakes and their causes, the more profitable the company can be. As Stan Rifkin puts it, "There is no doing without mistakes. [The real question is:] What is the company's response? In the world of action mistakes are inevitable. Organizations that have closed the knowing-doing gap treat mistakes as a natural part of doing and use the mistakes as occasions for learning. Surgeons call this 'forgive and remember'!" [Rifkin 03].

1.5.4 Assessments Transform Organizations by Encouraging People to Think Across Boundaries

Assessments encourage participants to think across boundaries that may exist in the organization. Programmers learn how requirements experts think. Technical people learn how managers think. People on different projects learn how the other parts of the organization think. All in all, the experience helps everyone to feel as if he or she is part of an organization with mutual interests instead of competitors for resources or recognition. This is no small thing.

Nor is thinking across boundaries just a matter of what the other guy is doing. Different parts of the organization may have a certain way of thinking about quality, for example, even if they are doing similar jobs. The give and take of assessments helps them to question their own deeply held assumptions about what works and what doesn't work and opens them up to other and perhaps better ways to do things.

1.5.5 Assessments Transform Organizations by Consolidating a Party of Improvement

Conversely, people in different parts of an organization may have common doubts about the way things are done and common suggestions for how to make processes more reliable and more efficient. But because they are compartmentalized, their doubts are often dismissed. Assessments allow such people to confirm their own intuitions and unite to form a force for positive change. This happens not only as a product of a post-assessment action plan but also as a side effect of the assessment meetings themselves. And it can transform a culture.

1.5.6 Assessments Transform Organizations by Helping to Institutionalize Rigorous Analysis

Finally, assessments involve inculcating the plateau-sensitive logic of planned process improvement into company planning. There are many ways that an organization's action planning team can prioritize the introduction of improvements. But in immature organizations, few of them are sensitive to the knowledge contained in process improvement models about what software development processes must be in place before others can reliably function. Assessments integrate into an organization's own process of self-analysis an understanding of what software process improvement levels call *maturity levels*—that is, an awareness that unless management practices are made more predictable (the work of Level 2 in the CMMI), then sophisticated improvements in the organization's technical practices often will not work.

1.6 Assessments Educate as They Analyze, Motivate, and Transform

Assessments Educate by Giving People in Organizations a Broader Knowledge of Their Own Company and by Encouraging Organizations to Contemplate Industry's Best Practices and Compare Them to Their Own

Assessments involve perhaps dozens or even hundreds of an organization's employees, many of whom have only a vague idea of how what they do is done on other projects in the same organization, much less in other organizations around the world. When they are required to compare their own practices to the ideals of an assessment model, however, and to listen to how their fellow employees' practices also relate to that model, they begin what may be a transformative education in the field of their expertise.

The venue and framework of this educational process, moreover, is as important as its content. Assessments force people to think hard about the pros and cons of what they do. It is in the midst of this rethinking that they encounter other ways of doing the same thing—at a moment when they are uniquely receptive to alternative procedures and in an atmosphere that is structured to be non-punitive about past performance.

1.7 Why Gaming the Results of an Assessment Doesn't Help (Though Many Try)

The trigger for assessments quite often comes from an outside organization or from a higher level of the same company or corporate group. The need to achieve a maturity level frequently seems as if it has become a criterion for doing business. As a result, organizations are sometimes dragged into assessments against their will and naturally respond by an attempt to "game" the assessment—to represent the organization as functioning at a higher maturity level than is really the case.

The bulk of this chapter should have already demonstrated that this is a perversion of the assessment process—a process aimed at helping to motivate organizations to improve themselves, which can only be accomplished with an honest effort. Organizations may in the short term fool an authorizing agency, but in the long term, they only cheat themselves, in the process discouraging their quality motivated personnel and making efforts at real improvement much harder after their deception is recognized. Chapters 4 through 11 of this book contain numerous examples of how companies unsuccessfully tried to "game" better results. It can all be summed up very simply: "Gaming" leads to nothing more than frustration, and it damages more than it helps.

Organization A exerted every effort over eight years to position and distort the results of numerous assessments. It tried to dismiss every honest assessor and derail every objective assessment, and it eventually succeeded in arranging to be audited rather than assessed. It then doctored its documentation and tutored its personnel in what to say. The audit certified that it was a "Level 5 Organization," and the organization's manager was over the moon. Less than a year later, however, corporate headquarters realized that Organization A was still producing products of inferior quality—over schedule and over budget—and reassigned all of its projects. The organization wasted many years and millions of dollars that might have turned it into a first-rate software house to achieve a false certification—and ended up with nothing. The manager of Organization A is now looking for another job.

1.8 Can Assessments Really Change an Organization? A Preview of an Extended Case History to Be Found in Chapter 12

Chapter 12 supplies an elaborate case history of the way that a program of reiterated assessments not only improved the maturity level of the software division of a major defense company ("Organization Z") but also made it a more efficient, happier, and more profitable place to work. That transformation may be briefly summarized according to the four principal functions of assessments provided previously.

1.8.1 Analysis

The *analytical* power of a Level 3 assessment demonstrated real gaps between Organization Z's perception of its own processes and the way those processes really operated. For example, the assessment revealed problems with the organization's information and authority structures that involved project managers who had in effect absolved themselves of responsibility for software issues and software managers who were unaware that their engineers were not using the company's software processes. The assessment encouraged these problems to be addressed and rectified, and a second assessment encouraged Organization Z to utilize its reorganization to exploit the power of quantitative management and to create feedback loops for continuous improvement.

The force of these analyses derived not just from the assessment's power to probe issues that the organization could confront on its own, but also from an integrated vision of how software operations ought to work provided by the assessment's reference model.

1.8.2 Initiation of Positive Change

The shock of Organization Z's first assessment made its executives and project managers reevaluate the organization's management structure. That shock enabled the organization to reorganize the way one level of management reported to the next. After the first assessment, the President of Organization Z came to use his own authority to redress the organization's problems. But he did so principally because the need for the improvement was conveyed during the assessment by the organization's full ladder of personnel, middle managers, and executives. Many of these people already knew what was wrong before the assessment, but it was the assessment itself that consolidated their energies in the direction of positive change.

1.8.3 Positive Transformation

The structural transformation undertaken by Organization Z began with the procedures imposed by the assessment itself. Conducted in a way that related each project to the organizational and administrative capabilities of the entire group, the assessment launched Organization Z into a full rethinking of how its different parts and functions related to each other.

1.8.4 Education

None of these advances would have proceeded without the artificially intense education that the organization had received during a series of assessments—an education that synthesized and transmitted the current state of software practice.

Organization Z chose to change when it recognized the deficiencies of its own operation in relation to other, more successful software operations around the world. The organization's personnel had been shocked, and their ways of thinking had been transformed, but ultimately it was the taste of increased success and the lure of a more profitable operation that motivated them to improve.

1.8.5 A Continuous Program of Assessment and Improvement

Organization Z's improvement finally was facilitated not by a single assessment but by the organization's decision to begin a cyclical program of assessment and improvement. In this process, the second and each subsequent assessment and health check functioned not as wake-up calls but rather as exercises in course correction. All of them reinforced the improvements already under way at the same time that they communicated a sense that new improvements would extend initiatives undertaken in the first cycle.

1.9 Bottom-Line Profit and Cost Numbers: Assessments Pay

How much did Organization Z save by this process of reiterated assessments?

At its most basic level, process maturity creates an organizational discipline that finds and fixes defects early and then ultimately prevents them. The cost benefits of this kind of process maturity improvement may be simply calculated:

A typical software development project injects approximately 100–250 defects per thousand lines of code [Humphrey 02].

> 1 defect found early in development costs $100 to $200 to fix.
>
> 1 defect found in the testing stage costs $1,000 to $2,000 to fix.
>
> 1 defect found during operations costs $10,000 to $20,000 to fix. [Bush 02]

Today's development expectations for a Level 1 organization count on at least three to six operational defects per thousand lines of code. The fixing of these alone translates into unnecessary costs of between $30,000 and $120,00 per thousand lines of code.

Not finding or preventing defects before testing, though, can be almost as costly. A Level 1 organization is lucky to find 25% of defects before test, whereas a Level 3 organization typically finds 50% of defects before test, and a Level 5 organization finds between 75% and 80%. A Level 3 organization can thus easily save $30,000 per thousand lines of code, and a Level 5 organization can save $60,000 per thousand lines of code.

Many projects now produce programs consisting of 250,000 to one million lines of code, and the programs are getting more complex all the time.

Bottom line: Process maturity can translate into hundreds of millions of dollars of preventable costs.

Case in point—When Organization Z progressed over four years from a Level 2 to a Level 5, it reported, among other benefits, a gain in software productivity costs of 47% and an increase in customer satisfaction of 9% per year. These percentages can be easily translated into dollars by looking at the organization's history of finding and fixing defects.

At Level 2, Organization Z found 50% of its defects before testing, but after four years of assessments and improvements, that figure rose to 75%. As a result, Organization Z saved $4,542,000 in development costs over these four years, not including the positive ripple effect into other departments.

This was of course not all profit. Organization Z spent a total of $3,138,000 for software improvement costs over the four years, including assessments but also including training and new software improvement practices. ($1,956,000 of this in fact went for the cost of administering Fagan Inspections.)

The results are still startling. The numbers work out to a total return on investment of software improvement costs of $1,404,000 over four years—$350,100 per year—or in percentage terms, a return of 44.6% per year.

In a larger picture, as a percentage of Organization Z's total software development budget of $14,000,000 per year, the same figure represents a net increase in profit of 2.5%.

Nor were Organization Z's bottom line numbers extraordinary. Organization Z was a better-than-average company, producing high-quality software to its customers, though sometimes behind schedule and over budget. Companies with more problematic records benefit even more dramatically from software improvement efforts.

Interested? Read on.

Chapter 2

A Brief History of Process Improvement Methodologies and Assessment Methods

2.1 The Beginnings of Modern Software Assessment Methodology

Modern software assessments evolved out of audits. Quality audits for years have served to ensure that elements of the manufacturing process conformed to documented standards. By the late 1970s, though, there was a growing sense that examining the existence of individual processes was not enough, especially in the case of software systems. Phil Crosby, in a number of publications based on his experience at IT&T including *Quality is Free* [Crosby 79], argued that old-fashioned quality audits, even in hardware settings, neither adequately measured the reliability of an organization's development capabilities nor functioned as fulcrums for improvement. Instead Crosby proposed that quality assessments should shift their focus from individual processes to an organization's maturity grid and evaluate the extent to which individual processes were successfully integrated into an organization's institutionalized network of supporting structures. The result, he argued, would provide a sense of the real capability of a whole organization [Kasse 02]. His insight evolved into the notion of process improvement capability maturity levels. Following Crosby's and later J.M. Juran's [Juran 88] work, in the 1970s and 1980s IBM began to experiment with its own capability maturity standards for predicting software development efforts, and for several years IBM personnel, including Watts Humphrey, Al Pietrasanta, Ron Radice, Maribeth Carpenter, and Harvey Hallman, stood at the forefront of the field of software assessment.

2.1.1 The Creation of the SEI

By the 1980s, the Department of Defense (DoD) was alarmed enough by the general unreliability of software systems produced for it to create a body that could transfer the most advanced methods of software development worldwide into American practice. In 1984 the DoD chartered the Software Engineering Institute (SEI), whose first moves included employing the key players of the IBM effort and developing analytic procedures to measure the global software process capability of organizations bidding on contracts. The SEI was tasked with using the maturity framework concept to aid the DoD acquisitions process.

Following these initiatives, by 1987 Watts Humphrey had characterized the software development process within a maturity framework and then used that framework as the basis for a questionnaire designed to analyze the strengths and weaknesses of an organization-wide software process [Humphrey 87]. The questionnaire was to be distributed to and completed by representatives from various organization projects prior to the arrival of a team of assessors, who would use the information provided by the questionnaire as the start of discussions with key personnel in the company. The idea was not to rate the company on the basis of the questionnaire but rather to use the information it provided to determine which areas to explore during the assessment proper, which would eventually be conducted according to a method spelled out in a 1989 SEI publication titled "Conducting SEI-Assisted Software Process Assessments" [Olson 89].

2.1.2 Assessments Versus Evaluations

Originally, the DoD and the SEI divided their software assessment efforts between two kinds of appraisals. The first was the software process assessment (SPA) method, to be used by organizations to gain insight into their own software development capability and to prioritize actions for process improvement. The second was the software capability evaluation (SCE) method, to be used in outside evaluations of the software process of an organization competing for a DoD contract.

Note: The SEI uses "appraisal" as an umbrella term that refers both to "assessments" and audit-like "evaluations."

Evaluations such as the SEI Software Capability Evaluation (SCE) constitute investigations of an organization conducted by an *outside* business entity. SCEs are often conducted as part of a Department of Defense or other government or commercial software acquisition process and are used to help evaluate the level of a particular contractor's process maturity.

SCEs are also commonly conducted as part of the monitoring of an acquisition after a contract has been awarded or as input for an incentive/award fee decision [Averill 93].

The subsequent development of these methods, as this book argues, suggested that the second of them would prove to be burdened with many of the problems of previous audits, whereas the first would emerge as a superior alternative. But to understand why, it is necessary to understand the differences between them. SPAs and SCEs "differ in many respects, including motivation for the method, objective, ownership of results, and outcome"[1] [Besselman 92]. But the basic difference is that the SPA collaborative approach encourages an atmosphere to promote ongoing process improvement. Therefore, whereas SCE evaluations continued to be necessary for the purposes of acquisition decisions, the SPA method acquired greater and greater importance in SEI-sponsored process improvement efforts.

2.1.2.1 The Inconsistency of Early SPA Results and Its Upshot

Nevertheless, initial trials suggested that the original SPA method produced real ambiguities for assessor and assessed alike about what the categories addressed and how serious the problems were. For example, a study conducted by Joe Besselman titled "A Collection of Software Capability Evaluation Findings: Many Lessons Learned" [Besselman 92] (presented at NSIA in March of 1992) showed that there was sometimes a difference of two maturity levels between evaluation and assessment ratings of the same organization when assessed by the SPA and SCE method. Some of these discrepancies resulted from the fact that internal SPA assessment teams were not familiar with the categories guiding the process, and some arose because early SPA assessments did not require the presence of a licensed and often external Lead Assessor who could guide the assessment team in the same way as the head of an external SCE evaluation. The Besselman study concluded, however, that the benefits of the SPA method were such that the method should not be changed to be more like an audit because it would then lose the organizational benefits of the assessment process [Besselman 92]. Instead, the report ultimately prepared for two significant SPA alterations: the development of an articulated description (or model) of the software capability

---

[1.] For example, SCE teams select projects to evaluate based on their similarity to the contract being considered; SPA teams select projects that are representative of an organization as a whole.

development process so that internal assessors would have clear categories to work with, and the introduction of SEI-licensed Lead Assessors who could keep internal assessors within the same judgmental guidelines as those used in an SCE.

In regard to the first of these developments, the SEI began working on spelling out the structure implied by the original questionnaire so that the purpose and criterion for each element would be clear to all. Concurrently, Watts Humphrey elaborated the underlying principles of both the capability maturity concept and the assessment method in his 1989 work titled *Managing the Software Process* [Humphrey 89], which proved to be a landmark both in the theory of software process improvement and in the theory of software assessment. (See also [Humphrey 92].)

2.2 The SEI Capability Maturity Model

Based on Humphrey's work, the SEI evolved a capability maturity model to articulate explicitly the relationships between specific software process practices and continuous quality improvement. First in a 1993 report written by Mark Paulk, et al titled *The Capability Maturity Model for Software Version 1.1* [Paulk 93a] and *Key Practices of the Capability Maturity Model, Version 1.1* [Paulk 93b] and then in a 1995 book titled *The Capability Maturity Model: Guidelines for Improving the Software Process* [Paulk 95], the CMM emerged both as a staged plan for reliable software development process improvement and an implied template for rigorous assessment.[2]

2.2.1 Capability Maturity Levels

The SEI's capability maturity model for software (CMM) defines five distinct capability maturity levels, and it assigns certain key process areas (KPAs) that must be implemented

---

[2.] An interim phase in this history was represented by the revised maturity questionnaire [Zubrow 94] published in 1994 and tied in with the SEI capability maturity model (CMM) v1.1. The new questionnaire was again meant primarily to identify issues to be explored during the assessment proper and subsequently became a work aid associated with a newly refined SPA assessment methodology developed by the SEI.

before contingent practices can be brought under control to one of the capability maturity levels. However, the CMM as a whole also identifies (under the rubric of common features) the institution-wide activities that stabilize all key process areas. The latter include items such as measurement, training, documenting procedures, executive policies, senior management sponsorship, appropriate tools, practice verification, and continuous process improvement.

2.2.2 The Structure and Philosophy of the CMM

The CMM's five software process maturity levels are identified as initial, repeatable, defined, managed, and optimizing. The 18 KPAs distributed in Levels 2 to 5 are: 6 KPAs for Level 2, 7 KPAs for Level 3, 2 for Level 4, and 3 for Level 5. To achieve a higher maturity rating, an organization must first satisfy all the KPAs of the preceding maturity level.

The philosophy of the CMM requires that at Level 2, an organization should focus on individual projects and their management. Each project should choose methods, standards, procedures, and training.

At Level 3, the focus shifts to the organization itself. The organization now articulates and supports those standards, methods, and procedures that have worked for projects in the past and then assembles a database of metrics that projects may consult when they need to understand past projects. Thus, projects can refer to the organization's supported methods, procedures, definitions, and documents and tailor them for particular needs, rather than having to define things from scratch. At Level 3, the organization also provides more centralized support for training, which had previously been the primary responsibility of individual projects.

The focus of Level 4 shifts back to the project level and provides goals for quantitative management. Level 4 requires that projects establish (and then achieve) quality product goals and that they use past data to analyze present performance to see if it falls within established limits.

Level 5 focuses on improving the quantitative limits, both from a process and product point of view. Another name for this is continuous process improvement.

A more specific account of Maturity Levels 2, 3, 4, and 5 in an organization are summarized in Figure 2-1.

Capability Maturity

Level	Focus	Key Process Areas
5 Optimizing	*Continuous Process Improvement*	Defect Prevention Technology Change Management Process Change Management
4 Managed	*Product and Process Quality*	Quantitative Process Management Software Quality Management
3 Defined	*Engineering Processes and Organizational Support*	Organization Process Focus Organization Process Definition Training Program Integrated Software Management Software Product Engineering Integrated Coordination Peer Reviews
2 Repeatable	*Project Management Process*	Requirements Management Software Project Planning Software Project Tracking & Oversight Software Subcontract Management Software Quality Assurance Software Configuration Management
1 Initial	*Competent People and Heroics*	

Figure 2-1 *Key process areas of the SEI capability maturity model.*

The CMM document describes goals and key practices associated with each of these KPAs and coordinates each key practice with institutional capabilities, including "Commitment to Perform," "Ability to Perform," "Activities Performed," "Measurement and Analysis," and "Verifying Implementation," that must be institutionalized before the activities of a particular KPA can be accomplished.

2.2.3 Benefits from Succeeding Maturity Levels

2.2.3.1 Benefits from Maturity Level 2

Requirements are documented and controlled; work products are baselined, and their integrity is controlled. Project standards are defined, and adherence is monitored. Processes for estimating and planning are stabilized and documented at the project level, providing more predictability in planning. Commitments are understood, and people are trained. Estimates are more accurate in decreasing the differences between the actual and planned results.

2.2.3.2 Benefits from Maturity Level 3

Cost, schedule, and functionality are under control. Quality is tracked. Every project should be finding and fixing its defects before testing. An organization-wide understanding exists for activities, roles, and responsibilities of the processes in place. Management has good insight into the technical progress on the project and prepares proactively for risks that may occur. Customers can obtain accurate and rapid status updates because of greater visibility into project activities.

2.2.3.3 Benefits from Maturity Level 4

Performance continues to improve based on quantitative understanding of both processes and products. Data definition and collection are stabilized across the organization. Managers have an objective basis for decision-making. Ability to predict outcomes becomes more precise because the variability of the process is more stable.

2.2.3.4 Benefits from Maturity Level 5

The entire organization is focused on continuous process improvement. A strong sense of teamwork exists across the organization. Organized efforts are made to eliminate waste due to natural variation in processes and to prevent recurring defects. Disciplined change is a way of life for improvement of quality and productivity.

2.2.4 The CMM Assessment Method: CBA IPI

The SEI's articulation of the CMM was soon followed by a parallel articulation of Software Process Assessments, now officially called CMM-Based Appraisals for Internal Process Improvement (CBA IPI). In 1996, the SEI published a "Method Description" [Dunaway 96a] and then a "Lead Assessor Guide" [Dunaway 96b], which together spelled out the basic procedures of a CBA IPI:[3]

- **The presence of a qualified leader**—A CBA IPI assessment is led by a licensed, authorized Lead Assessor, expertly trained in the assessment method and in the CMM model and capable not only of instructing an organization in the condensed best practices contained in the model but also of making sure that the spirit is not lost in adherence to a narrow view of the letter of the CMM and the CBA IPI method.

- **The constitution of the assessment team**—A CBA IPI assessment is implemented by an assessment team that includes representatives from the organization who know the organization better than any outsider and who can transfer lessons learned back into the organization when the assessment is complete (and help lead the follow-on action plan).

- **A focus on the whole organization**—A CBA IPI assessment ascertains the capabilities of the organization as a whole by selecting representative projects to provide a cross-section of the organization's work. The use of a cross-section of existing projects ensures that the assessment measures the support and knowledge available to all projects and not just a uniquely well- or badly run project on its own.

- **A concentration on a hierarchy of maturity levels**—A CBA IPI assessment proceeds with reference to a ladder of maturity levels and their corresponding key process areas (KPAs) that "identify the issues which must be addressed to achieve [a mastery] of the maturity level" [Paulk 95]. Collectively, the full set of KPAs measures how the organization implements the necessary management and technical parts of any software development project.

[3.] For the maturity questionnaire tailored for the new CBA IPI procedure, see [Zubrow 94].

- **The importance of personal interviews**—A CBA IPI assessment does not rely simply on the verification of organizational practices through a set of paper documents (which may or may not be currently followed by the organization) but rather intensively interviews managers and practitioners to ascertain whether practices recommended by projects and the organization as a whole are properly understood and implemented. Every practice involved in every KPA at every maturity level must be verified in this way.

- **Confidentiality**—A CBA IPI assessment examines the process and does not praise or blame individual success and failure. In order to ensure that this is the case, a CBA IPI rigorously adheres to a few basic necessary ground rules concerning confidentiality and the respect of all participants. This includes the requirement that the assessment results will be kept confidential by the assessment team members [Humphrey 89].

- **Corroborated information**—The results of the assessment come directly from corroborated statements provided by organization participants and are even confirmed in draft finding meetings so that there can be no question of the results being a product of the assessment team rather than the organization.

- **Maturity level ratings**—The capability maturity level is assigned at the very end; it represents a summation of all the statements of the organization and a clear consensus both of the assessment team and of the statements from the organization on which the judgment of the assessment team is based.

- **Recommendations**—Results exist in the context of recommendations for improvement. They are not an abstract or general ranking but rather a specific set of proposals for raising software development procedures to an attainable next stage.

- **Results presented**—The results, including the capability maturity level, are announced at a final general meeting of the participants and are addressed to the participating senior manager. They therefore necessarily represent the voice of the organization spoken in a way that cannot be disregarded.

2.3 The Three Principal Advantages of a Modern Software Assessment over Traditional Manufacturing-Based Audit Procedures

The advantages of the software process improvement assessment method as described by Watts Humphrey in *Managing the Software Process* [Humphrey 89] involve the following.

(1) A Focus on the Reliability of the Organization as a Whole

An assessment does not measure how well individual projects in an organization may have performed, perhaps due to the special insight of a project manager or a happy combination of circumstances. Rather, it measures the capability of the organization as a whole to produce processes and products at a high level. Assessments therefore measure *not* how well individual projects are currently being implemented but rather the organization's global capability to replicate good work. The result of a capability maturity assessment is not a rating (like a manufacturing audit) of how well a particular set of procedures are followed, but rather of the capability or potential of the whole organization (based on its systematic implementation of core procedures) to initiate and complete projects in a measured and reliable way. A capability maturity assessment carefully selects representative projects across the breadth and depth of an organization. In Humphrey's words, "The objectives of software process management are to produce products according to plan *while simultaneously improving the organization's capability to produce better products*" [Humphrey 89].

(2) Encouraging Creativity and Initiative by Emphasizing Goals Instead of Means

An assessment evaluates the functioning of organizational practices with regard to goals, not means. This is crucial. By doing so, it encourages the kind of creativity and initiative that is not only central to the success of good work but also is a key to an organization's ability to change. The main function of old-fashioned audits, Humphrey notes, was "to ensure that the professionals follow the officially approved process." But, he notes, "typical process deviations are not motivated by greed but by a desire to get the job done as quickly and effectively as practical. The professionals often find that some aspects of the official process are outmoded and inefficient. They properly try to get the job done in spite of these bureaucratic obstacles, and their expedient shortcuts often turn out to be very effective. Thus unless it is done extremely well, an audit can actually do more harm than good, particularly if the official process is either not defined or cannot be implemented as stated" [Humphrey 89]. Assessments allow practitioners to defend and get credit for their initiative and encourage them to imagine change in terms not only of local conditions but also of their own insights into how the job might be done better. It is through such flexibility that an assessment becomes a true lever for change.

(3) An Action-Oriented Approach

An assessment is not only an analysis but also an impetus for an action plan designed for maximum immediate effect. In Humphrey's words, its "action orientation keeps the questions focused on current problems and the need to solve them." And its staging ensures that any impulse toward positive change is recognized and engaged: "Prior to an assessment the professionals generally are aware of their worst problems and often assume management…doesn't understand the issues and cannot be expected to solve them. After an assessment, this is no longer the case. An expert study has heard their concerns and suggestions for what should be done about them…After all this, any manager who does not take action will be seen by the people as either incompetent or unconcerned with their problems…In net, management must either focus on taking action or not do an assessment" [Humphrey 89].

Humphrey's name for what the SEI now calls CBA IPI and SCAMPI was originally "Software Process Assessment." In Humphrey's words, "Process assessment helps software organizations improve themselves by identifying their critical problems and establishing improvement priorities." Humphrey argues that process assessment principles must include: "1. The need for a process model as a basis for the assessment. 2. The requirement for confidentiality. 3. Senior management involvement. [and] 4. An attitude of respect for the views of the people in the organization" [Humphrey 89].

2.4 A Second Path Toward Software Process Improvement Assessments: The History of ISO-9000-3, Bootstrap, SPICE, and the CMMI

About the same time that the SEI was developing the CMM structure and the CBA IPI assessment methodology in America, European groups began to improve in their own way on the history of manufacturing audits. The most important difference between the two efforts was that in Europe, attention was focused more on small commercial organizations than on large defense-related ones. The European emphasis produced first software audits and then software assessments that diverged from the SEI model.

2.4.1 ISO 9000

In 1987, ISO (the International Standards Organization) augmented its manufacturing standards to include among other things a software component standard for products traded across international borders and specifically within the European Economic Community. The newly enlarged ISO 9000 standards were descendants, via NATO and the British Standards Institution, of U.S. DoD quality management program standards derived from pre-software experience [Bamford 93]. They were made up of "five related standards, which when combined constitute quality system" [ISO 87]. The software standard within this umbrella was called ISO 9000-3. Its philosophy was that the software development life cycle needed to be documented as carefully as manufacturing processes. Certification according to ISO 9000-3 did not involve progress up a ladder of maturity levels, nor were there incentives for process improvement. Although continuous process improvement was not precluded, it was not required or described by the standard, which addressed the control of a nonconforming product and recommended corrective and

preventive action. (IS0 9000-3 and subsequent revisions augmented software certification with an audit technique called
TickIT that attempted to copy some of the sophistication of an
early SEI Software Process Assessment.)

2.4.2 Bootstrap

Subsequently, starting in 1990, the European Strategic Program
for Information Technology, ESPRIT, adapted Humphrey and
Sweet's 1987 lead and developed what was called Bootstrap
methodology. The original Bootstrap partners were from Ger-
many, Italy, Finland, Austria, and Belgium. The project goal was
to introduce modern software technology into European industry [Kuvaja 94]. Whereas the SEI in America had focused on
large-scale and extremely complex defense-related applications, Bootstrap was designed to help European commercial
applications, and it concentrated on small- and medium-size
software systems and put more emphasis on rating individual
software practices (especially technical practices) rather than
global technical and management processes. Bootstrap combined its analytical methodology with a questionnaire aimed at
developing an action plan for process improvement. Attempting to combine the 1987 SEI questionnaire, the European Space
Agency life cycle model ESA-PS-005, and ISO 9000-3, the Bootstrap questionnaire asked more (and more specific) questions
than the 1987 SEI questionnaire. Problems remained, however,
including a limited version of a working software process
improvement development paradigm.

2.4.3 SPICE

When European groups attempted to refine their assessment
methodology by combining it with the CMM-based efforts of
the SEI, they continued to emphasize smaller commercial organizations and individual software practices. In 1991, an international effort was undertaken to refine key parts of ISO 9000-3,
Bell Canada's Trillium, and Bootstrap by incorporating perspectives from the CMM. This effort officially began at the June
1991 ISO plenary meeting of the joint technical committee of the
ISO and the International Electrotechnical Committee. Then,
beginning in January 1993, the International Organization for
Standardization   formally   created   the   Software   Process

Improvement and Capability Determination (SPICE) project to develop standards on software process. (In 1998, SPICE was converted into the model and process assessment segments of the ISO/IEC 15504 standards.)

One can most easily describe the SPICE effort by saying that it intended to modify the CMM's primary focus on total organizational capability by incorporating Bootstrap's emphasis on particular process elements. In the CMM, control over the organization's process is achieved through a step-by-step progression in which focus shifts as an organization climbs the maturity ladder from controlling an individual project's software process to controlling the system-wide organizational software processes. SPICE, however, attempted to evaluate the "capability" level of individual processes rather than the "maturity level" of the organization as a whole. The CMM states that a "maturity level is a well-defined evolutionary plateau toward achieving a mature software process" [Paulk 95]. The central SPICE document (the Base Practices Guide or BPG), however, says that a "capability level is a set of common features...that work together to provide a major enhancement in the capability to perform *a process*" (emphasis added) [SPICE 95]. SPICE called this rating of an organization's processes individually a "Process Assessment Approach," [SPICE 95] which emphasizes a "continuous" framework of assessing individual processes (as opposed to the CMM's "staged" assessment of key process areas located at specific levels of an organization's process maturity).

2.4.4 From SPICE to the CMMI: "Continuous" Versus "Staged" Assessments

Back in America, the introduction of the CMM for Software led to efforts to articulate assessment methodologies for a number of non-software areas, starting with systems. Faced with this plethora of new efforts, the U.S. Department of Defense formed a CMM Integration project to integrate three important analytical models into a single improvement framework—the CMM for Software, the Systems Engineering Capability Model (SECM, also known as Electronic Industries Alliance 731), and the Integrated Product Development Capability Maturity Model (IPD-CMM).

Because the SECM followed the SPICE "continuous" approach to process improvement, however, the CMMI sponsor decided that the new single framework, called the Capability Maturity Model Integration (CMMI), must be able to be implemented in *both* the CMM's "staged" and the SECM's "continuous" approaches to process improvement and assessment. That is, the CMMI would allow organizations to perform either "staged" or "continuous" assessments on either software- or systems-based organizations.

For the purposes of staged assessments, the CMMI methodology is very similar to that of the CMM. (Key Practices, for example, now called Specific Practices, continue to reside at maturity levels associated with levels of integrated organizational ability.) In the CMMI "continuous" version, however, a focus on large plateaus of integrated organizational ability has been replaced by an articulation of the multiple factors related to the implementation of specific practices. These factors, which take the place of what the CMM had called "common features," are called "generic practices" in CMMI—practices that concern the way that a process is institutionalized. The result is a matrix system in which individual specific practices can be evaluated according to the strength of its organizational support [CMMI Product Team 02].

2.5 The CMMI: An Enlarged Structure and Scope

Another very important difference between the "staged" versions of the CMMI and the CMM resides in the CMMI's increased scope and larger set of discriminations. The CMMI consists of 25 process areas and 510–628 practices (510 in the staged model and 628 in the continuous model), whereas the Software CMM consists of 18 key process areas and 316 practices [Chrissis 03]. There are seven more process areas in the CMMI staged model than in the CMM model because the CMMI provides "more detailed coverage of the product life cycle" and because it incorporates several new application areas including software engineering, systems engineering, integrated product and process development, supplier sourcing, and acquisition [Chrissis 03].

Figure 2-2 shows the CMMI's process areas and maturity levels; it may be compared with the chart of the CMM key process areas and maturity levels provided previously in Figure 2-1.

Capability Maturity Model Integration (CMMI)

Level	Focus	Process Areas
5 Optimizing	*Continuous Process Improvement*	Organizational Innovation and Deployment Causal Analysis and Resolution
4 Quantitatively Managed	*Quantitative Management*	Organizational Process Performance Quantitative Project Management
3 Defined	*Process Standardization*	Requirements Development Technical Solution Product Integration Verification Validation Organization Process Focus Organization Process Definition Organizational Training Integrated Project Management for IPPD Risk Management Integrated Teaming Integrated Supplier Management Decision Analysis and Resolution Organizational Environment for Integration
2 Managed	*Basic Project Management*	Requirements Management Project Planning Project Monitoring and Control Supplier Agreement Management Measurement and Analysis Process and Product Quality Assurance Configuration Management
1 Initial		

Figure 2-2 *CMMI staged model.*

2.6 A Hybrid Assessment Approach: The CMMI SCAMPI

The CMMI assessment method, known as the Standard CMMI Appraisal Method for Process Improvement, or SCAMPI, was first described by the CMMI product team in 2000 [CMMI Product Team 00] and then refined in the SEI's SCAMPI Handbook and Method Definition Document [Members of AMIT 01].

This book focuses first on CBA IPI and then on "staged" SCAMPI assessments. The two use slightly different terminology but are closely related in practice, with a few very significant differences. At the time of publication of this book, over 2,000 organizations have successfully completed a CMM or CMMI assessment. (These figures are available in published form in [Zubrow 03] and in continually updated form on the web in [SEMA 03].)

2.6.1 Differences Between the "Staged" SCAMPI and the CBA IPI Method

The most important practical difference between a CBA IPI and a "staged" SCAMPI has to do with the effect of the CMMI's (and hence, SCAMPI's) enlarged scope. On the plus side, this enlarged scope allows assessment teams not only to evaluate multiple (e.g., software and systems) functions across a whole organization but also provides them in the software area with a more sophisticated approach to requirements management and development and gives them a more fine-grained picture of the workings of Capability Maturity Levels 4 and 5 [Chrissis 03].

However, because the CMMI model (staged representation) contains over 60% more practices than the CMM for Software, SCAMPIs could require considerably more time than CBA IPIs.

To address this problem without diminishing the quality of SCAMPI, the CMMI Steering Group formed an Assessment Methodology Integrated Team (AMIT) to modify the definition of SCAMPI V1.0 and V1.1 to SCAMPI V1.2 [Members of the AMIT 01; GEIA 01]. The resulting modifications prescribed more upfront document gathering than a CBA IPI and fewer activities during the onsite period of the assessment.

For example, requirements for substantiating the existence of a necessary process were changed so that the new method of *verification*, instead of requiring two interviews or one interview and one document to substantiate a practice, required only two documents to substantiate 50% of all examined practices. The other 50% must still be substantiated by one interview and one document. Verification, however, puts additional responsibility upon the assessed organization: Documentation requirements for SCAMPI are more rigorous than for CBA IPI, and many organizations (especially less mature ones) need assistance with the gathering of the necessary documents and information. Collecting and reviewing documentation always requires knowledgeable people, and organizations should keep the necessity for their effort in mind.

Also, SCAMPI was deemed a *focused investigation* in which the practices to be substantiated by interviews could be determined by a kind of triage in which an initial review of the evidence collected (e.g., documents, questionnaires, presentations) is used to determine which questions need to be asked in the interviews. This triage or readiness review is meant to produce a set of questions and a team agreement that some practices are clearly practiced (or clearly not practiced). This does not mean that no further attention will be paid to these practices, only that questions about them do not have to be asked during the interview sessions [Armstrong 02].

Through establishing stronger focus on documentation and by reducing the person-to-person interaction of interviews, both modifications create real difficulties for assessments, as described in Chapter 1. First, they increase the risk that not enough hard information is collected from practitioners about an organization, which lowers the confidence level of an assessment. Second, in inexperienced hands, SCAMPIs can resemble audits rather than true assessments. This is true not only because of SCAMPI's reduced emphasis on interviews but also because one of the original requirements for SCAMPI was that it be designed so it could be applied either in the mode of an assessment or an evaluation (audit).[4] The result was that certain key

---

[4.] When the CBA IPI method was being written in 1994, there was discussion regarding the feasibility of having one method for both assessments and evaluations. Those who were experienced in both methods concluded that the motivations for the two appraisals were different enough to merit keeping the methods separate. Thus, CBA IPI was the assessment method [Dunaway 96], and SCE V3.0 was the evaluation method [Byrnes 96] for the CMM for Software, both published in 1996. In considering the benefits that an organization may experience during an assessment, the attributes that are at risk for process improvement during an audit are obvious. An audit is not considered to be a collegial non-threatening activity. Some important business risks are "on the line" for the organization being assessed. An audit is a very important vehicle for organizations making business decisions based on the specific results that they seek during an audit. It's important to understand that the purposes of the two types of methods are different and could yield different results for the assessed organization.

features of CBA IPIs were altered. For example, one of the main requirements of a CBA IPI is that at least one person from the assessed organization serves as a member of the assessment team. This requirement ensures that assessment results are transferred back into the organization's process improvement initiative. SCAMPI, however, has dropped the requirement so that like an SCE it can be conducted by an outside team if necessary.

It should be said in defense of SCAMPI, however, that although the changes just described can produce less satisfactory assessments than a CBA IPI, this does not necessarily have to be the case. In a SCAMPI, assessors are permitted but not required, for example, to reduce the extent of interviewing and experienced assessors will make sure to arrange as many interviews as possible and to take extra measures to include a broad cross-section of the organization in the interviewing process so that the internal benefits approximate those of a CBA IPI.

Because SCAMPI is a technically more rigorous evaluation tool than CBA IPI, moreover, SCAMPIs conducted with attention to motivating process improvement are potentially as or more effective than their predecessors. The requirement, for example, that for a goal to be considered satisfied, each of its practices must be observed on all or most of an organization's projects, means that the "wiggle room" in a SCAMPI assessment has been significantly reduced.

2.6.2 More Differences Between the SCAMPI and CBA IPI Methods

A further difference between the SCAMPI and CBA IPI methods involves the procedure for rating practices. In a "staged" SCAMPI, a document is required to substantiate every assessed practice, whereas interviews are required to verify only 50% of them (versus the CBA IPI requirement, which requires interviews for all practices and which recommends documents as a second source of verification wherever possible). SCAMPI also requires that practices within assessed process areas be rated as fully, largely, partially, or not implemented rather than (as in a CBA IPI) implemented or not implemented.

Other smaller differences between the latest versions of SCAMPI and CBA IPI can be seen in Table 2-1.

Table 2-1 *Comparison of Features of SCAMPI v1.1 and CBA IPI v1.2*

Features	SCAMPI v1.1	CBA IPI v1.2
Appraisal team	Requires each team member to receive the SEI-licensed Intro to CMMI course.	Requires each team member to receive the SEI-licensed Intro to CMM course or equivalent course defined by waiver guidelines.
	No requirement for any site members to be on team.	Requires that at least one team member be from the assessed organization.
Planning	Requires an appraisal input record signed by the sponsor.	Requires this information to be contained in the assessment plan that is signed by the sponsor.
	Requires a data collection plan to be documented including by whom objective evidence will be verified for every focus project.	Requires the plan for data collection including interviewees to be contained in the assessment plan.
	Requires items to be contained in the appraisal plan: • Appraisal input record. • Cost and schedule estimates for performing the appraisal. • Risk and mitigation plans. • Criteria to verify that 15504 requirements have been met (if requested by sponsor).	Risks are to be identified as part of the assessment plan, along with other items specified in assessment plan template.

(continued)

Table 2-1 *Comparison of Features of SCAMPI v1.1 and CBA IPI v1.2 (continued)*

Features	SCAMPI v1.1	CBA IPI v1.2
	Requires at least one readiness review to be conducted prior to assembling the team onsite for data collection.	Provides less formal method of document review conducted during the team's pre-onsite activities.
	Requires that the sponsor: • Verify the qualifications of the team leader. • Have at least one communication with team leader to ensure that minimum criteria for individual team members and the team as a whole have been met.	Provides guidance for interface between Lead Assessor and assessment sponsor; Lead Assessor has responsibility of satisfying criteria for assessment team members.
Data collection	Requires documentation (at least one direct artifact) to be obtained for all practices (specific and generic) for each focus project.	Requires data from documents for each of the KPA goals at the organizational level.
	Requires face-to-face affirmations corresponding to each goal for (1) at least one focus project for each model practice and at least one practice for each focus project, or (2) for at least 50% of entries in the project/practice matrix for the goal.	Requires corroborated observations for each practice that sufficiently covers the practice, organization, and life cycles in use.
	Requires that direct artifacts be corroborated by indirect artifacts and/or affirmations by each focus project for each model practice.	Requires data to be collected for each key practice of each process area being investigated as deemed by the team's judgment to be sufficient.

Features	SCAMPI v1.1	CBA IPI v1.2
	Requires every practice to be characterized at the project and organizational level according to a four-point scale (fully implemented, largely implemented, partially implemented, or not implemented).	No rating of practices is required; rating of satisfied/unsatisfied is permitted for practices if desired by assessment sponsor.
	Refers to validation of findings with assessment participants as "preliminary findings"; requires at least one representative from each focus project and from each associated staff function review the preliminary findings at a preliminary findings presentation.	Refers to validation of findings with assessment participants as "draft findings"; requires all assessment participants to be invited to review draft findings at one of several draft findings presentations.
Ratings	Rates the goals by considering aggregate of weaknesses associated with the goal; additionally requires that all practices associated with the goal are characterized at the organization level as either largely implemented or fully implemented for a satisfied rating for that goal.	Rates the goals by considering aggregate of weaknesses associated with the goal.
	Requires that for a ML 3 rating or higher, generic goal 3 must be rated satisfied for all applicable Maturity Level 2 process areas.	No additional goals are added for ML 2 process areas.
	Additional requirements for continuous representation in determining capability level ratings of process areas as well as determining maturity level ratings using equivalent staging.	Staged representation only.

(continued)

Table 2-1 *Comparison of Features of SCAMPI v1.1 and CBA IPI v1.2 (continued)*

Features	SCAMPI v1.1	CBA IPI v1.2
Reporting	Requires an Appraisal Disclosure Statement and an appraisal record to be delivered to the appraisal sponsor.	Assessment Acknowledgement Letter and assessment data delivered to the assessed organization is recommended but not required.
	None required.	Requires a confidence report to be delivered verbally or written to sponsor including anything that might affect confidence in assessment results.

2.7 Informal or Reduced Assessments: Class B and Class C Assessments

Organizations use assessments for different purposes. For organizations just starting on a process improvement initiative, or for those who desire a quick process area analysis (sometimes called a "gap analysis" or "health check") to monitor corrective actions that have been taken in the wake of a previous assessment, a full-scale assessment can represent an onerous and unnecessary investment of time and money.

Many organizations have chosen to define their own standards for these kinds of more limited assessment, achieving flexibility but perhaps leading to the proliferation of erroneous comparisons and claims.[5]

[5.] For one such approach, see [Wiegers 00].

This need for less sweeping and expensive assessment methods has led the SEI to introduce smaller scale assessment methods to augment a full-dress or "Class A" SCAMPI—a formal and rigorous assessment capable of culminating in a maturity level rating. These smaller "Class B" and "Class C" methodologies permit less costly procedures including smaller teams, less rigorous documentation requirements, and shorter assessment periods. However, it is important to remember that because of their smaller scope and less rigorous approach, they are not truly comparable with a full-scale Class A assessment, nor can they result in a capability maturity level rating.

An alternative for organizations that are able to spend the time and effort but do not wish to undergo the stress of an assessment that leads to an official capability maturity rating is to schedule a full Class A SCAMPI but to make it clear from the start to all concerned that a capability maturity level rating will not be derived and that the exercise can be regarded as a health check. Though it will satisfy all the requirements of a registered Class A assessment since a maturity level is optional, the exercise will produce only PA practice and goal ratings, which will not focus the organization on a capability maturity level rating. This allows for a more relaxed atmosphere while providing both an occasion for genuine self-examination and a rigorously accurate picture of interim progress. In this case, each of the practices relevant to appropriate process areas is rated, and a list of PA strengths and weaknesses is compiled, along with a set of recommendations. This counts as a Class A SCAMPI when returned to the SEI, but it will focus the organization on improvements rather than a maturity level rating.

The variations between Class A, B, and C methods for SCAMPI[6] are detailed in the SEI's *Appraisal Requirements for CMMI* (ARC) document [CMMI Product Team 01a] and are summarized in Figure 2-3.

[6.] For the equivalent document for the CMM, see [Masters 95]. For a recent review draft of an expanded "Handbook for Conducting SCAMPI B and SCAMPI C Appraisals," see [Hayes 04].

Requirements	Class A (15504 conformant)	Class A (not 15504 conformant)	Class B	Class C
Responsibilities:				
4.1.1 - Appraisal Sponsor	yes	yes	yes	yes
4.1.2 - Appraisal Team Leader	yes	yes	yes	yes
Appraisal Method Documentation				
4.2.1 - Documentation of method	yes	yes	partial (a-d only)	partial (a-d only)
4.2.2 - Guidance for identifying appraisal purpose and objectives	yes	yes	yes	yes
4.2.3 - Guidance for CMMI model scope	yes	yes	yes	yes
4.2.4 - Guidance for identifying organizational unit	yes	yes	yes	yes
4.2.5 - Guidance for team member selection	yes	yes	yes	yes
4.2.6 - Guidance for team leader qualification criteria	yes	yes	yes	yes
4.2.7 - Guidance for size of team	yes	yes	yes	yes
4.2.8 - Guidance for team member roles and responsibilities	yes	yes	yes	yes
4.2.9 - Guidance for appraisal sponsor responsibilities	yes	yes	yes	yes
4.2.10 - Guidance for team leader responsibilities	yes	yes	yes	yes
4.2.11 - Guidance for estimating appraisal resources	yes	yes	yes	yes
4.2.12 - Guidance for logistics	yes	yes	yes	yes
4.2.13 - Guidance for collecting and mapping data to appraisal reference model	yes	yes	yes	yes
4.2.14 - Guidance for creation of findings	yes	yes	yes	yes
4.2.15 - Guidance for assuring confidentiality and non-attribution	yes	yes	yes	yes
4.2.16 - Guidance for appraisal record	yes	partial (a-e only)	partial (a,b,d,e only)	partial (all except e.5)
Planning and Preparing for the Appraisal				
4.3.1 - Preparation of participants	yes	yes	yes	yes
4.3.2 - Development of appraisal input	yes	yes	yes	yes
4.3.3 - Content of appraisal input	yes	partial (all except e.5)	partial (all except e.5)	partial (all except e.5)
4.3.4 - Sponsor approval of appraisal input	yes	yes	yes	yes
4.3.5 - Development of appraisal plan		partial (a-e only)	partial (a-e only)	partial (a-e only)
Appraisal Data Collection				
4.4.1 - Data from instruments	yes	yes	At least two sources of data, one of which must be interviews	At least one source of data
4.4.2 - Data from interviews	yes	yes		
4.4.3 - Data from documents	yes	yes		

Figure 2-3   *Class A, B, and C Appraisal Requirements for CMMI (ARC) [CMMI Product Team 01a].*

Requirements	Class A (15504 conformant)	Class A (not 15504 conformant)	Class B	Class C
Data Consolidation and Validation				
4.5.1 - Consensus of team members	yes	yes	yes	optional
4.5.2 - Accuracy of observations	yes	yes	yes	yes
4.5.3 - Validation of observations	yes	yes	yes	optional
4.5.4 - Corroboration of observations	yes	yes	yes	optional
4.5.5 - Sufficiency of data	yes	yes	optional	optional
4.5.6 - Draft findings preparation		yes	optional	optional
4.5.7 - Draft findings presentations	yes	yes	optional	optional
Rating				
4.6.1 - Define a rating process	yes	N/A	N/A	N/A
4.6.2 - Basis for maturity level and capability level rating	yes	yes	N/A	N/A
4.6.3 - Rules for goal rating	yes	yes	N/A	N/A
4.6.4 - Rules for process area rating	yes	yes	N/A	N/A
4.6.5 - Rules for maturity level rating	yes	yes	N/A	N/A
Reporting Results				
4.7.1 - Report results to sponsor and appraised organization	yes	yes	yes	yes
4.7.2 - Translation for 15504	yes	N/A	N/A	N/A
4.7.3 - Appraisal results to CMMI Steward	yes	yes	optional	optional
4.7.4 - Retention of appraisal record	yes	yes	yes	yes

Figure 2-3 *continued*

Chapter 3

Assessments: An Executive Overview

Executives who are thinking of scheduling a process improvement assessment need to have answers to questions such as:

- What are my responsibilities?
- What are the first things I have to do?
- What are my staff's responsibilities?
- What are the primary activities of an assessment?
- How much time, effort, and money will the assessment require?

This chapter provides an executive overview of the assessment process and should be supplemented by a reading of Chapter 12 for a sense of what assessments can accomplish. Chapters 4 through 11 will elaborate on the details for managers, assessors, and participants.

3.1 What Are a Senior Executive's Responsibilities?

A senior executive works with his or her staff to:

- Establish the organization's business goals for the assessment.
- Choose a reference model and an assessment methodology to guide the assessment.
- Select a Lead Assessor (or Lead Appraiser).
- Select (advised by the Lead Assessor) an "assessment sponsor" (or personally serve as the "assessment sponsor").
- Define (advised by the Lead Assessor) the assessment's organizational scope (that is, the part of the company that is to be the official "organization being assessed").
- Ensure that the organization shares a common understanding of what the assessment is meant to accomplish.
  - The executive should stress that improving software development capability is the responsibility not just of engineers and project managers but of the entire organization.
  - Each person in the organization should be encouraged to accept that the structure that holds everyone together needs to be examined and improved.

3.1.1 Choosing an Assessment Methodology and Reference Model

This book is premised on the fact that the most effective and sophisticated evaluation of an organization's capability to produce quality software is a process improvement assessment such as an SEI CBA IPI or (staged) SCAMPI. An alternative is one of the several methods (including the continuous version of SCAMPI) that look primarily at individual process areas rather than the capability of the entire organization. However, as Chapter 2 has already argued, those alternatives fall outside the primary focus of this book.

Most of the information provided by what follows is applicable either for a CBA IPI or (staged) SCAMPI. There may, however, be reasons to choose one or the other depending on business requirements. As presently constituted, the CBA IPI method guarantees that the assessment will use the full power of interviews to ascertain and improve practices, whereas the SCAMPI method requires extra care to ensure the same. On the other hand, SCAMPI, which at present remains the primary focus of SEI activities, has been designed to cover not only the software but also the system elements of the development process.

An assessment commits an organization to the following objectives reflected in the assessment plan:

- To provide an accurate picture of the organization's current process strengths and weaknesses, consistent with a reference model (CMM or CMMI), and to identify key areas for improvement that provide a prioritized approach to process improvement as it relates to the business context.

- To identify any major non-model issues that impact the process improvement effort.

- To provide a set of appropriately detailed assessment findings to the organization sufficient to develop process improvement plans.

- To provide the organization with data needed to "baseline" an understanding of the organization's current capability and to track improvements over time.

- To support, enable, and encourage an organization's commitment to process improvement [Dunaway 01c; Members of AMIT 01].

3.1.2 Selecting a Lead Assessor

Selecting a Lead Assessor is one of the critical steps in beginning an assessment. Each Lead Assessor has his or her own style of approaching process improvement. The organization's senior management should try to select someone who is similar in his or her approach to the organization's culture and business goals.

The Lead Assessor functions as senior manager for the assessment. He or she must possess a set of management and interpersonal skills that will support the team in handling the problems and stresses that occur when trying to complete a complex effort that involves a number of people under significant time constraints. The Lead Assessor should have some project or line management experience at some point in his or her career.

The organization executive must choose whether a Lead Assessor should be selected from inside or outside the organization. An external Lead Assessor may have more diverse experience and a broader perspective and may be more insulated from the pressures that sometimes result from the outcome of the assessment than an internal one. An internal Lead Assessor has the advantage of intimately understanding the organization's operations.

The SEI maintains a directory of authorized Lead Assessors for CBA IPIs and authorized Lead Appraisers in the SEI Partners Directory for SCAMPIs.

3.1.3 Establishing (with the Lead Assessor) the Business Goals and the Scope of the Assessment

3.1.3.1 Business Goals

The first rule of an assessment is that an organization should make its real business objectives clear and understandable to everyone in the organization and to the assessment team.

Businesses look to assessments because they are experiencing difficulties with or have a desire to improve their levels of predictability, quality, scheduling, or costs, or because they want to distinguish themselves to the outside as having mature levels of predictability, quality, scheduling, or costs.

An assessment's business goals (which will be enumerated in the assessment plan) have a direct bearing on system/software management, development, and maintenance activities, and include attempts to do the following:

• Reduce the cost of developing and maintaining software products.
• Improve the time to market of software products.

- Improve the quality and cost of software products.
- Improve the timeliness and reliability of software development services.

3.1.3.2 Organizational Scope

The most important communications between an organization executive and the Lead Assessor involve the assessment's scope. That is, it must be decided what representative part of a company should constitute the "organization being assessed."

An assessment looks at *capability* of an *entire* division or company. However, this does not mean that it looks at all parts of the company, which in many cases would be much too large an undertaking. The idea is to examine the way company-wide institutions work within the scope of selected projects. An assessment measures how capable the whole organization has proven itself in its ability to anticipate problems and reduce the likelihood of a product having poor quality or being delivered past the promised date.

A few (usually 4–5) specific projects are selected that represent typical work being performed in the entire organization to be assessed. The projects selected depend on the company's management structure, geographic locations, and product lines being developed. The capability of organization-wide institutions is investigated by looking at support functions that span not only these selected projects but also all other projects within the organization.

Eventually, a formal assessment plan will fully identify not only the representative projects to be examined by the assessment but also the rationale for establishing the scope and the risks associated with addressing it during the assessment process.

3.1.3.3 Reference Model Scope

Another major aspect of assessment scope has to do with the reference model scope—the part of the reference model to be investigated. The reference model scope relates to the potential *maturity level* of the organization and therefore identifies the process areas to be investigated. (As a matter of practical consideration, the higher the maturity level being assessed, the more effort and time the assessment will require.)

Often senior management believes that the organization is better than it is and sets an unrealistically high standard for the maturity levels to examine. When this happens, it creates a negative and stressful experience for all concerned, rather than a positive culture-evolving experience.

3.1.4 Appointing an Assessment Sponsor from Senior Management

The second most important decision the organization executive and Lead Assessor must make is who will act as the *assessment sponsor*.

The assessment sponsor is a senior manager who not only oversees the assessment but also is responsible afterward for initiating process improvement activities and making resources available to carry them out. *It is extremely important for any process improvement effort that the assessment sponsor is of sufficient rank to lend real authority to the effort and its implementation.* Ideally, the assessment sponsor should be the president or a managing director at the top of the division that is being assessed.

When the senior executive has chosen a Lead Assessor and has helped select the scope of the assessment and the assessment sponsor, he or she should turn the assessment over to the assessment sponsor, who will guide the assessment from that point on.

3.1.4.1 The Responsibilities of the Assessment Sponsor

The assessment sponsor will strongly influence the attitude of the organization in its quest for improvement. The assessment sponsor's duties include:

- Meeting with the Lead Assessor about the scope and aims of the assessment.
- Supporting the Lead Assessor in handling any organization tensions that might arise.

- Assigning an organization site coordinator for logistical planning and execution.
- Informing executives and staff that the assessment takes precedence over most activities.
- Formally opening the assessment and announcing management's commitment to the assessment process and to the process improvement effort.
- Participating in an interview with the assessment team, if asked.
- Participating in the final findings briefing as the recipient of the assessment results.

3.1.5 Establishing Appropriate Organizational Understanding

For process improvement activities to be most effective, it is important that the assessment sponsor articulates the goals of the assessment and communicates what is intended to be accomplished by the process improvement initiative. This information helps guide the assessment team as well as the follow-on process improvement initiative. The assessment sponsor should ensure that the organization shares a mutual understanding of what the assessment is meant to accomplish.

3.2 What Are the Phases of an Assessment?

The sequence of an assessment consists of three phases:

1. **Beforehand**: Planning and preparing for an assessment. (See Chapters 4 through 7.)
2. **During the Onsite Assessment**: Onsite assessment activities. (See Chapters 8 through 11.)
3. **Assessment Conclusions**: Reporting assessment results and setting the stage for improvement. (See Chapters 11 and 12.)

These phases can be represented in Figures 3-1 through 3-4.

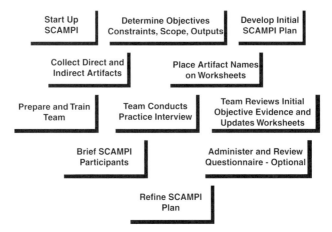

Figure 3-1   *Phase 1: Planning and preparing for an assessment.*

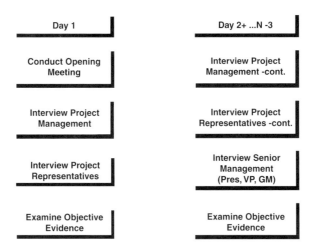

Figure 3-2   *Phase 2: Onsite assessment activities.*

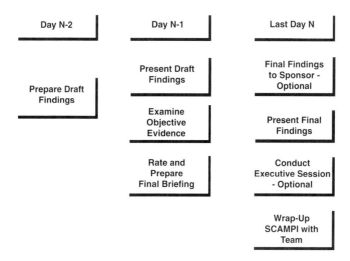

Figure 3-3 *Phase 3, Part 1: Report results.*

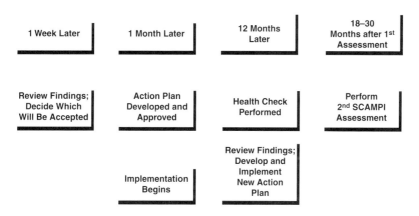

Figure 3-4 *Phase 3, Part 2: Setting the stage for improvement after assessment.*

3.2.1 Phase One of an Assessment: Planning and Preparation Activities

3.2.1.1 Choosing a Time

A time needs to be chosen to conduct the assessment, based on the answers to the questions:

- Is the organization ready?
- Will the time be intrusive in regard to deadlines and deliverables?
- Has enough time elapsed since the last assessment?

3.2.1.2 Appointing an Organization Site Coordinator

After an assessment sponsor is designated, he or she will then delegate the day-to-day practical arrangements of the assessment to someone such as a process improvement manager in the organization.

This person is known as an *organization site coordinator*, who will coordinate both the planning phase and the onsite phases of the assessment. Along with the Lead Assessor, he or she is responsible for building the assessment plan.

The Responsibilities of the Organization Site Coordinator   The organization site coordinator helps the Lead Assessor make practical choices and ensures that all team members are available and that all interviewees for the assessment are available, scheduled, and able to appear for their sessions. The organization site coordinator also ensures that rooms are scheduled, that logistic requirements are planned and completed, and so on.

Besides coordinating the assessment logistics (such as scheduling interviewees, booking appropriate rooms for assessment activities, etc.), the organization site coordinator must arrange lodging, food, and beverage for the assessment team members, obtain documentation needed by the team, and make plans to return documentation to appropriate people when the assessment is concluded. (Before the onsite assessment begins, rooms must be booked, interviews must be scheduled, lodging for non-site personnel must be arranged, food must be organized, equipment must be planned, etc.)

3.2.1.3 The Assessment Plan

The assessment plan is the organization's map through the assessment. A provisional big picture plan is generated immediately after the executive and the Lead Assessor meet and decide on what elements constitute the organization to be assessed, who will be the official assessment sponsor, and the reference model scope to be investigated. During the three phases of the assessment, this plan will be continually refined.

To begin building an assessment plan, it is necessary that the Lead Assessor understands the organization's key strategic objectives and that the assessment sponsor understands the parameters of the assessment.

An assessment plan will include answers to these questions:

- **Who** should participate in the assessment and at what stage?
- **What** are the outcomes of the assessment planning process? (For example, what outputs does the organization need from the assessment to plan further improvements?)
- **When** should the major milestones for the assessment's completion be scheduled?

An assessment plan must include documentation of the assessment's scope, the identification of assessment participants, a detailed schedule of assessment activities, and all other relevant information. The assessment plan must be agreed to and signed by the assessment sponsor, the Lead Assessor, and in most cases the organization site coordinator and the assessment team.

3.2.1.4 Creating an Assessment Team

The Lead Assessor helps create a competent assessment team, choosing key people in the organization capable of understanding organization-wide problems, concerns, and suggestions for improvement.

Generally an assessment team contains members internal to the organization as well as some from the outside. The assessment team needs to have organization-specific knowledge, but it is also necessary to have members who do not have a vested interest in the results.

The selection of assessment team members is important for the organization not only during the assessment but also after the assessment. The organizational team members are usually responsible for follow-on process improvement activities. Team members should be highly respected opinion leaders who have experience in the areas being assessed. Selecting assessment team members should not be taken lightly. Team members should not have a high personal stake in the outcome of the assessment. For an assessment to work properly, this rule needs to be followed in spirit as well as letter. People who are intimately involved with managing an activity may be too heavily involved (both technically and emotionally) with the assessment outcome and may have a difficult time listening to outside critiques. Organizations sometimes think the right people to put on the team are quality assurance staff because they are trained in performing audits. This, however, is only a part of the truth. Assessments are not audits, and assessment interviewing also requires considerable interpersonal skills.

An assessment team is composed of from four (a required minimum for SCAMPI and CBA IPI) to ten members. Fewer than four does not provide enough "group think" to provide a valid consensus. More than 10 members becomes difficult to manage, difficult to schedule, and difficult to bring to consensus. Seven, including the Lead Assessor, is an ideal size.

Assessment team members must understand that being part of the assessment team is a full-time job during the course of the onsite period.

3.2.1.5 Defining the Final Assessment Products

The precise outputs of the assessment need to be defined in the assessment plan. A final findings presentation, for instance, may or may not produce a formal maturity level rating, depending on the choice of the sponsor. A final report may or may not be requested by the sponsor.

3.2.1.6 Selecting Projects to Be Assessed

An assessment can realistically make an in-depth sampling of only three to five projects. However, it is possible to interview selected personnel from other projects to augment the in-depth part of the assessment. Projects being considered by the in-depth part of the assessment, however, must be represented at all the interview sessions. That is, after a project has been selected for an assessment, its project manager and all appropriate project members must be available to participate in interview sessions.

3.2.1.7 Selecting People to Be Interviewed

The most time-consuming responsibility of the assessment team is interviewing organization participants. These include individual or group interviews of project, middle, and senior managers. In group interviews, practitioners representing different parts of the development cycle provide breadth of coverage. For example, one group interview might include people who develop and refine requirements, a second group might include people who design products, another group might include testers, and so on. Group interviews allow people on different projects that do the same job to hear how others do their task in other parts of the organization. It is best to include as many individuals involved in the chosen projects as possible in the appropriate interview sessions. They will come away with a sense that they have been allowed their say and that they form part of the long-term improvement process.

Representatives of senior and middle management connected with the software development process also should be interviewed. They are usually interviewed as a group in order to get a management perspective on the organization, its problems, and desired improvements.

All assessment participants should ideally attend an assessment participants briefing, which will explain why the organization has undertaken an assessment, the basic principles behind process improvement, and what usually happens before, during, and after an assessment. (This is especially important for a first-time assessment.)

3.2.1.8 Distribution of Questionnaires

For a CBA IPI, the project managers from the projects chosen for in-depth investigation (in conjunction with selected project team members) must fill out a maturity questionnaire. These need to be distributed and their results summarized for the assessment team's use. They will later guide the assessment team's questioning during interviews.

3.2.1.9 Assessment Team Training

The Lead Assessor will train the assessment team members in the logic and phases of the assessment process. The team members must already be familiar with the reference model and should have already taken required courses of instruction. Assessment team training addresses the CBA IPI or SCAMPI assessment procedures, the assessment plan, site-specific organizational data, and the tools and techniques to be used during the assessment. Assessment team training also plays an important part in team building and establishing team norms.

3.2.1.10 The Assessment Team's Last Pre-Onsite Activities

After the assessment team members have been trained, they need to review appropriate questionnaire responses. These responses are used to identify patterns and help focus interview questions.

The assessment team also inventories and examines initial documents. The organization site coordinator or team librarian is responsible for beginning to put these into a library. They are then reviewed for the purposes of establishing context and determining areas to probe.

For a SCAMPI, the organization is expected, prior to the assessment, to collect an entire set of documentation for review. Finally, before the official assessment begins, the Lead Assessor, the organization site coordinator, or one of the internal team members stages an assessment participants briefing to prepare assessment participants for what is to come.

3.2.2 Phase Two of the Assessment: Onsite Activities

Onsite activities include the following:

- Opening meeting
- Other presentations
- Interviews
- Recurrent team meetings for the consolidation of information, including document reviews

The onsite phase of the assessment prepares for phase three of the assessment: the preparation of draft and final findings, and the staging of draft and final findings presentations.

3.2.2.1 The Kick-Off Meeting and Other Presentations

A kick-off or opening meeting always begins an onsite assessment. The assessment sponsor explains to his (or her) organization (at a minimum, all the people who will be interviewed) why he has authorized the assessment and what he expects from his people. He must make it absolutely clear that he fully supports the assessment and the subsequent improvement efforts. He must make sure that the assessment is one of the organization's top priorities for the week and insist that people who are scheduled to be interviewed be available at the scheduled time. At the kick-off meeting, the sponsor should encourage the participants to be open and forthcoming and explain why honesty is important. He should also explain that all assessment information is confidential, that no reports will be made about who says what, and that no one will be penalized for what they say. The Lead Assessor will introduce the team and explain what will happen during the assessment—what kind of questions will be asked, what material should be brought to the interview (and what need not be brought), and so on.

Other initial presentations made by the organization to the assessment team are also useful. Some examples include 30- to 60-minute briefings by project managers to explain the nature of their projects, demonstrations by project teams of what they produce, and briefings by department managers about how they run their departments or how they interact with other departments. Executives also might want to brief the team about their current perceptions of the organization's strengths and weaknesses and its future plans.

All of these presentations help set the stage for the assessment team and help managers and developers put on record what they regard as important.

3.2.2.2 Collecting and Managing Data

Four primary sources of data are collected during an assessment:

- **Questionnaires**—Usually administered prior to the onsite period to a small number of key individuals.
- **Documents**—Documentation at the organizational level, project level, and implementation level is collected starting before the assessment begins and is added to and consolidated during the entire course of the assessment.
- **Interviews**—Project, middle, and senior managers and practitioners (sometimes called functional area representatives, or FARs) are interviewed during the onsite period of the assessment.
- **Presentations**—Project presentations given to acquaint the assessment team with the organizational work; draft finding presentations that validate the information heard and seen by the assessment team.

The assessment team makes notes based on each kind of data. The information from each source establishes an organization context, reveals areas that need probing, corroborates other data, provides information relative to appropriate practices in the model, and answers specific questions about the processes in use by the organization.

In an ongoing process of *review*, the assessment team *consolidates* its notes onto worksheets organized by specific practices in each of the model's KPAs/PAs. The team discusses each observation created and arrives at consensus about the validity of the information.

3.2.2.2.1 Interviews   Interview questions are meant to help the team connect the dots in regard to how the organization actually implements its engineering and management processes. (People cannot describe a process in detail if they do not use it.) They also help identify areas that people believe can and should be improved in the organization, explain how work is performed, and aid the team in understanding relationships between organization- and project-level processes.

Interviews educate by explaining the reason behind processes that practitioners may only know about but not actually use.

Interviews are the most important component of an assessment, both for the purposes of analysis and cultural transformation. Employees should be encouraged to tell the team anything and everything—both technical and cultural—about the organization. Interviewees are not to take notes in deference to the confidentiality requested for other interview participants. The assessment team takes copious notes so that subsequent discussions of what was said and heard can be recalled accurately.

During interview sessions, it should seem to all concerned that an interesting and useful discussion is taking place. Employees should be able to go away from the interview feeling that they have learned something new and useful.

3.2.2.2.2 Consolidating Data from Interviews and Other Sources   An assessment team consolidates data at the end of each day's interviewing. This activity consumes by conservative estimate approximately one-third of the onsite period. (Any way that teams can automate this process while retaining the accuracy and team consensus is encouraged.) The assessment team members are dealing with a large amount of information from many different sources. Their job is to synthesize this information into precise statements that can be agreed to by the assessment team as a whole.

The three primary objectives of consolidation are to summarize the information obtained during the interviewing and document reviews and consolidate it into a manageable summary, to determine whether there is enough data for the team to make a rating judgment, and to determine if further revisions are needed to the schedule to get more information.

"Observations" are created that represent the assessment team members' understanding of information either seen or heard during the data collection activities. An observation is an assertion about a practice implementation (or lack thereof) developed by team members and agreed upon by the entire team using the consensus process. An observation addresses some aspect of the extent to which a practice is or is not implemented. An observation may be unrelated to the reference model, but it identifies an issue that has a significant impact on process capability or organizational maturity.

The assessment team is responsible for collecting data for each practice for each process area within the assessment scope. Observations must be corroborated by multiple independent sources. The set of observations must, in the judgment of the assessment team, provide sufficient coverage of the extent of implementation of each of the practices, be considered representative of the organization being assessed, and represent the life-cycle phases in use within the organization.

Observations do not record any project name or individual's name in order to preserve confidentiality, which is crucial to the assessment method.

3.2.3 Phase Three: Summing Up and Presenting the Results

After interviews and document reviews are concluded and their data are consolidated into observations, a set of draft findings is synthesized. These draft findings are publicly presented to all participants to give them an opportunity to comment on the findings' validity. After the draft findings presentations, the team conducts another consolidation meeting, where it prepares its final findings and (if desired by the sponsor) a maturity rating. A final findings presentation is then mounted for the sponsor, all assessment participants, and whoever else the sponsor chooses to invite.

3.2.3.1 Consolidating Draft Findings

"Draft findings" constitute a preliminary description of the strengths and weaknesses of the organization's assessed processes. Draft findings are keyed to KPA/PA category and usually record on average three to four important strengths and weaknesses in that category. At this stage in the assessment, it is important for the team to start summarizing the key points of its analysis. The wording of each statement of a draft finding is crucial. It must be framed in objective, easily understandable terms, and must exclude both jargon and animus. Ratings are not considered during draft findings meetings.

3.2.3.2 Draft Findings Meetings

A full set of draft findings is presented in a meeting to all the assessment participants. It is the first time the staff members who have been interviewed will have a chance to see whether the team has understood what they have been shown and told. Draft findings serve to correct misinterpretation and to gain acceptance by the assessment participants.

An assessment team usually stages two draft finding presentations—one for practitioners and one for managers. The assessment sponsor is not present at these meetings to provide a chance for assessment participants to reflect on what they have actually said and what they want to say to senior management. Participants are actively encouraged to express their views as to the accuracy of the findings.

Draft findings are considered to be part of the data collection process and therefore preliminary to rating discussions.

3.2.3.3 Final Findings Consolidation and the Establishment of Ratings, Usually Including a Capability Maturity Level Rating

The assessment team consolidates data obtained during the draft findings presentations and during follow-up interviews and document reviews. When the team certifies that full coverage of the reference model has been achieved, the rating and final findings process begins.

Final findings are arrived at in consolidation meetings after the draft findings meetings and subsequent follow-up and revision. The final findings represent the strengths and weaknesses observed during the assessment for each KPA/PA in the assessment scope plus any other issues outside of the reference model that are relevant to the organization's development processes.

Ratings are different from final findings because they involve translating the strengths and weaknesses of the organization into the analytical categories of the model, and they require a thorough understanding of what does or does not correspond to the model's requirements.

Each goal for each process area in the assessment scope is rated based on consensus of the entire assessment team. For each goal, the team reviews all weaknesses that relate to that goal and asks: "Are these weaknesses in aggregate significant enough to have a negative impact on the goal?" If the answer is yes, the goal is rated "unsatisfied." If the team decides that the weaknesses in aggregate do not have a significant negative impact on the goal, the goal is rated "satisfied." For a SCAMPI, the rules are less subject to team judgment—all practices must be rated either largely implemented (LI) or fully implemented (FI) and the aggregation of weaknesses must not have significant impact on goal achievement.

A process area is rated "satisfied" when all the goals for the process area are rated "satisfied." If one or more goals for the process area are unsatisfied, the process area is rated "unsatisfied." Those process areas outside of the assessment scope are indicated in the final presentation as "not rated." (One process area that is sometimes indicated as "not applicable" is the one relating to subcontract management when an organization does not subcontract any of its work.) All other process areas are shown as either "satisfied," "unsatisfied," or "not rated" to indicate the complete scope and rating results of the assessment.

Assignment of a maturity level rating is optional at the discretion of the sponsor, but a decision about whether to record one has been made at the beginning of the assessment process. All

KPAs/PAs within and below a given maturity level must be satisfied for a particular maturity level rating to be achieved. For example, if an organization is rated at Maturity Level 3, all Level 2 and Level 3 KPAs/PAs are investigated during the assessment and need to be rated "satisfied" by the assessment team.

3.2.3.4 Presenting Final Findings Informally to the Assessment Sponsor (Optional)

Managers in general do not like to be surprised. At this point in the assessment, it is a useful courtesy to show the final findings and/or ratings to the assessment sponsor. Obviously, no changes are made at that time, and confidentiality is maintained.

3.2.3.5 The Final Findings Presentation

The final findings are presented to the assessment sponsor at a meeting that includes not just the assessment participants but (depending on the sponsor's wishes) perhaps the entire organization being assessed. This meeting represents a message of the organization as a whole to its executive manager and constitutes the final result of the assessment.

The final findings presentation usually includes not only a chart of the KPAs/PAs that have been satisfied but a more general analysis of the organization's overall strengths and weaknesses and of the health of the organizational culture.

In addition to this analysis, the assessment team during the final findings presentation can also make global recommendations as to activities the organization could usefully focus on over the next year. These recommendations can be a powerful aid in pointing an organization toward real progress.

The final findings presentation represents the sponsor's opportunity to thank the team, thank the assessment participants, and present his or her support for follow-on improvement activities.

The assessment sponsor then "owns" the assessment results and is free to use them as he or she sees fit.

3.2.3.6 Post-Final Findings Meeting Executive Session (Optional)

An executive session provides an opportunity for the assessment sponsor to clarify any issues with the assessment team and to receive guidance about the possible focus, timing, and priorities of recommendations and follow-on activities. Confidentiality continues to be in effect.

3.2.3.7 Assessment Team Wrap-Up

In a brief session after the executive session, the Lead Assessor collects feedback from the assessment team members. Assignments are made for the writing of a final report, if one is required. One person in the organization is asked to be the steward of all assessment observations (with attribution removed). This detailed assessment information may be used for follow-on action planning by the organization. The assessment team also prepares required feedback forms for the SEI that indicate how the assessment process might have been improved.

3.3 Cost: How Much Time and Effort Does an Assessment Require?

The following data were reported in feedback from Lead Assessors in 260 CBA IPI assessments conducted between July 1998 and December 2000 [Dunaway 01a].

3.3.1 Time and Effort

Approximately two to three months are needed to perform assessment-planning activities and to train the assessment team. Planning activities usually begin six to eight weeks prior to the scheduled onsite period. Training the team members requires a total of five to six working days (two and a half to three days of training in the reference model and two and a half to three days of assessment team training).

Most Lead Assessors combine assessment team training with other planning activities, such as questionnaire response analysis, document review, and developing interview scripts. These activities are most usefully done two to three weeks prior to the onsite period so that all work may be finished before the onsite period begins.

Most onsite assessments take the better part of 10 days (32.7% of onsite assessment activities required 5 days, but these represented very small organizations; 48% of assessments report an onsite period of 6 to 10 very long—perhaps 12-hour—working days). (An SEI recommendation holds that the Lead Assessor should limit the length of working days to ten hours per day, but this is frequently very hard to do.)

A range of the number of hours recorded by CBA IPI assessment teams is provided below (see Figure 3-5). Although these numbers must be correlated with organizational size and assessment scope to be truly useful, it is worth saying that these assessment teams spent a median number of 37 clock hours working together on pre-onsite activities and a median number of 62 clock hours working together for onsite activities, making a combined median number of 96 clock hours for an assessment team. Again, the range of hours reported is probably more significant than the median numbers.

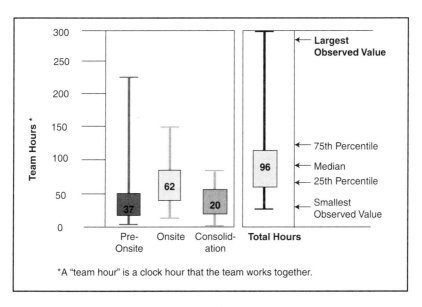

Figure 3-5 *Hours to perform CBA IPI activities.*

Another measure of the time required by an assessment is that each participant being interviewed should count on devoting five to eight hours to briefings, interviews, and meetings.

3.3.1.1 Resources and Time Estimates for SCAMPI

Resource and time estimates for SCAMPI are based on experience reports of the pilot SCAMPI assessments [Kitson 01].

Phase One: Planning and Preparing for a SCAMPI
Assessment Team Training (Delivered by Lead Appraiser)
• SCAMPI Lead Appraiser: 6–9 days
• SCAMPI assessment team members: 3–5 days
• Training facility costs
Organization Planning and Preparing
• Assessment sponsor: 3–4 days
• Organization site coordinator: 10–20 days
• SCAMPI Lead Appraiser: 10–20 days
• Assessment team members: 3–5 days
Phase Two and Three: **Onsite Activities and Summing Up and Presenting Results**
• Assessment sponsor: 4–6 hours
• SCAMPI Lead Appraiser and assessment team members: 5–10 days each
• Organization assessment participants: 1.5 days
• For 4 projects, expect between 25–92 people to be interviewed

Months Involved in Preparing and Conducting an Assessment and Preparing and Implementing an Action Plan Before Next Assessment
Overall Time
• Months 1 and 2—Assessment team training and planning
• Month 3—Onsite assessment
• Month 4—Action plan review
• Months 5–24—Action plan implemented
• Month 12—Health check appraisal
• Months 18–30—Follow-up SCAMPI

3.3.2 Summary

The demands of an assessment will vary according to the size of the organization and the reference model scope to be covered and must be figured to include time expended over a 9–12 week period by the following people:[1]

Lead Assessor	21–40 days
Assessment team members	11–20 days per member
Assessment sponsor	7–10 days
Organization site coordinator (including team training)	15–30 days
Organization participants (interviewees)	1–2 days

[1.] More actual data on time consumed during assessments is contained in *Analysis of CMM-Based Appraisal for Internal Process Improvement (CBA IPI) Assessment Feedback* [Dunaway 01a].

Chapter 4

Planning and Preparing for an Assessment, Part 1:

Senior Management Responsibilities

Now that we have examined what is *supposed* to happen during an assessment, it is time to look at what actually happens and how to make it happen. This and the following three chapters consider the nitty-gritty of what an organization needs to do from the time it commits itself to the assessment to the time when the assessment actually begins.

These chapters presume that a company has selected the CBA IPI or "staged" SCAMPI method as the basis for a software improvement assessment.

Responsibility for preparing the initial steps of such an assessment falls on a senior executive, who must:

4.1 Select a Lead Assessor.

4.2 Establish (with the advice of the Lead Assessor) the assessment's organizational and reference model scope and articulate the assessment's business goals.

4.3 Choose a senior manager to be the assessment sponsor.

4.4 With the help of the assessment sponsor, establish appropriate organizational attitudes toward the assessment.

It is presumed that an effort as large and costly as an assessment will be initiated by a high-level senior executive. Although the impetus for the assessment may come from outside (corporate headquarters or a contracting agency), only a senior executive has the means and authority to focus a company's desire to improve and to take the necessary steps to put it on the right path.

Therefore, although many accounts of the improvement process start with the actions of a software or subordinate manager, we take the view that to succeed, the decision to undertake an assessment and a subsequent program of improvement must begin at a higher level.

4.1 Selecting a Lead Assessor

Selecting a Lead Assessor is one of the most important decisions in preparing for an assessment. The Lead Assessor's style and experience should match an organization's culture and goals. Does the organization want a Lead Assessor who can talk to and influence its senior management? Or does the organization want a less senior Lead Assessor trained primarily to speak to the technical staff?

The Lead Assessor should have a strong technical background in software and systems development and management so that he or she can provide an intellectual context for the chosen model and assessment. However, the Lead Assessor also needs to understand the "real world" issues that face an organization and should have enough experience to be regarded by the organization being assessed as a credible expert.

The Lead Assessor functions as the senior manager for the assessment. The Lead will be dealing with all levels of people in the organization, from the most junior engineer to the most senior manager. In the findings that come out of the assessment, the Lead needs to be diplomatic but at the same time frank about the maturity status of the organization. The Lead must be able to translate the findings into a language the organization will understand and ultimately motivate an organization to implement improvements.

Above all, the Lead Assessor must possess a set of management and interpersonal skills that will support the team in handling the problems and stresses that inevitably occur when trying to produce a quality product that involves a number of people under significant time constraints.

A really good Lead Assessor will have some project or line management experience at some point in his or her career. It is immensely useful for the Lead Assessor to have the kind of easy rapport with senior management that only comes from having previous senior management experience.

Because trust is a fundamental component of the entire assessment process for both the organization and the team, the Lead Assessor must be a model of trustworthy behavior and must understand how to develop trust within the team and within the organization. To maintain such trust, the Lead Assessor must be perceived as someone who will respect all parties, listen carefully, tell the truth, and uphold the ground rules set in the relationship.

The Lead Assessor is also expected to manage the group dynamics of the team, particularly when the team loses focus or finds itself divided by conflict. A Lead Assessor inexperienced in handling group dynamics—including collaboration, negotiation, and conflict resolution—may find himself or herself unable to manage a situation that has gotten out of control. The recovery time and loss of trust can have a dramatic impact on both the outcome of the assessment and the follow-up improvement effort.

An SEI-authorized Lead Assessor must lead an assessment if the organization wants the assessment to be recorded and included in the Process Appraisal Information System (PAIS). The Lead Assessor must be knowledgeable about the conceptual basis of the CMM or CMMI model and of the assessment flow. Table 4-1 lists the minimum requirements for becoming an SEI-authorized Lead Assessor.

Table 4-1 *Minimum Requirements for Becoming an SEI-Authorized Lead Assessor*

The following minimum requirements have been set by the SEI for selecting an SEI-authorized Lead Assessor. He or she must have:
• Participated as an assessment team member in at least two SEI assessments and have been observed as a Lead Assessor in a third.
• Successfully taken the SEI "Introduction to the CMM" or the SEI "Introduction to the CMMI" course. (For a SCAMPI assessment, the Lead Assessor needs to have also taken the required SEI Intermediate "Concepts of the CMMI" course. For both a CBA IPI and SCAMPI, the appropriate SEI "Lead Assessor Training" course must be completed.)
• Extensive experience in software development and/or maintenance, in areas such as requirements analysis, software design, software quality assurance, configuration management, and testing (or ten years of project management and engineering experience in systems).
• A minimum of two years experience managing technical personnel (SCAMPI requires the two years to be part of the ten).
1. A master's degree in an appropriate technical area or equivalent experience together with a bachelor's degree.
2. Good oral and written communication skills.
3. The ability to interact with technical and management personnel.
4. Demonstrated knowledge of the systems and software process.

| 5. Full understanding of process definitions and process/product measurement. |
| 6. Good presentation skills for technical and instructional training. |
| 7. Substantial consulting experience. |
| 8. An ability to work effectively in a team environment; knowledge of group facilitation and team building techniques. |
| 9. Knowledge of Total Quality Management and quality improvement techniques. |
| [Dunaway 01c] [SEI 01] |

If the Lead Assessor is experienced in conducting assessments and is thoroughly grounded in the model, overseeing the assessment activities will be relatively straightforward. Problems with logistics, the activities flow, interpretation of data, and development of findings are likely to be familiar, and the Lead Assessor will be able to make judgments based on that experience.

Inexperienced Lead Assessors on the other hand may have insufficient judgment to navigate confidently through critical or highly ambiguous situations.

The possibilities for team members and participants to behave in ways that impede the assessment are limited only by human imagination.

Although in theory Lead Assessors can be selected anytime during the planning phase, selecting one soon after the organization has committed itself to an assessment means that the Lead can help in shaping the assessment's purposes and outlines. At a minimum, the Lead Assessor must review and (with the assessment sponsor) approve the assessment plan, ensure the adequate training of the assessment team, and help arrange the steps of the assessment.

4.1.1 Should a Lead Assessor Be Selected from Outside or Inside the Organization?

An external Lead Assessor is likely to have the advantage of greater assessment experience and the kind of perspective that arises from having conducted assessments across a broad spectrum of organizations and group dynamics. He or she also has the advantage of an arm's-length distance that helps to ensure objectivity and can help ward off challenges to the validity of the assessed results. Nevertheless, an external Lead is obliged to establish both credibility and trustworthiness with the organization's management structure, the assessment team, and assessment participants. (An organization should try to select an external Lead that feels comfortable with the organization's characteristics and culture.) He or she also needs to know how to gather knowledge of an organization quickly from the organization members on the team.

A Lead Assessor from inside the organization has the advantage of intimately understanding the organization's operations. The internal Lead Assessor knows or can easily identify the key players who can ensure a successful assessment, what politics are likely to affect the assessment's conduct, and how to apply or tailor the assessment method to make it most useful to the organization.

However, an internal Lead Assessor may not realize the potential for bias that comes with inside knowledge, as well as the possibility of pressure or even subtle threats about how he or she might be treated if the organization is unhappy with the assessment's outcome [Dunaway 01c].

It is extremely difficult for an internal Lead Assessor to be objective because his or her salary may depend on the senior manager that he or she is assessing. In some cases, difficult issues have to be discussed with the president of the organization, and that is easier to do if one's job is not on the line.

The risks of an internal Lead Assessor are easily illustrated. For example:

An assessment team had come to consensus, and the internal Lead was to present the agreed findings. When he had to present the findings in front of the organization's president, however, he felt compelled to sugarcoat the results. In fact, he gave a report that substantially contradicted the projected results on the screen in front of him. The result was that the president never received the hard message he needed to hear, and process improvement at his company was set back indefinitely.

4.2 Determining the Business Goals and the Organizational and Reference Model Scope of the Assessment

The senior executive should start with a sense of the business goals to be addressed by the assessment and its follow-on process improvement plan. What comes out of an assessment will have a direct bearing on the organization's system/software management, development, and maintenance activities by reducing the cost of developing and maintaining software product; improving quality, cost, and time to market of software products; and by improving the timeliness and reliability of software development services.

4.2.1 Organizational Scope (Choosing a Division or Cross-Section of the Company to Be Assessed)

Assessments look at the managerial and technical capabilities of companies by examining the way the whole interacts with a chosen sample of divisions or parts of the company. The sum of these parts is called the "organization being assessed." It is necessary to choose as "the organization being assessed" parts of the company that are both representative and critical to the company's success. This is done by selecting a sample of projects that represent the typical type of work being done in the organization.

Choosing the projects to comprise the "organization being assessed" is of course a big decision. The obvious factors that have to be considered are management structure, geographic location (if the organization is in more than one physical location), and product lines being developed.

It is also important to identify the part of the organization that is at the center of the process improvement initiative. This usually means a group of managers who are genuinely interested in allocating resources to process improvement (and to an assessment).

In identifying the assessment scope, both the breadth and depth of the organization should be considered.

The depth of the organization has to do with a selection of suitable size (usually four or five specific projects) in the organization's business base. The breadth of the organization refers to a cross-section of practitioners who work across the organization.

Factors that are eventually considered in setting the organizational scope of the assessment include:

- The feasibility of including multiple geographic locations (generally no more than two locations are recommended).
- The feasibility of including multiple divisions/business units (Are the units committed to the development of common procedures?).
- The feasibility of including multiple product lines or process focuses (e.g., do they have equal impacts on the organization's business goals?).
- Exclusion of outlier projects (e.g., projects that use less-mature processes and where improvements will have little cost benefit to the organization).

However, the company senior executive does not need to define all the details of this selection beforehand. They will be finalized in an assessment plan to be prepared by the organization site coordinator along with the Lead Assessor and then approved by the senior executive. The assessment plan will identify the full organizational scope of the assessment, the rationale for establishing the scope, and the risks associated with addressing it during the assessment process. This is discussed in Chapter 5.

4.2.1.1 The Special Problem of Matrix Organizations

CMM/CMMI assessments are designed to evaluate the management structure of an entire organization as it is embedded in given projects of the organization. Special care needs to be taken, however, when an organization operates through a matrix structure: That is, when all of engineering (including software engineering) is in one division, program management is in another, contracts are yet in another, and so on. In such cases, it makes no sense to define the organization as being the software engineering directorate only. An assessment that looks only at this one area does not address the responsible structure (the president, managing director, and executive staff) or the real authority on the projects—the individual project managers and program managers. With both the CMM and CMMI, it is clear that project management and senior management have specific roles to play, and an assessment cannot ignore them and pretend to offer reliable evidence about a company's strengths and weaknesses.

On one assessment, Company A wanted to determine if it was at Level 3. The company was organized in a matrix. On previous assessments, they had always reviewed only the software division as the "organization." When the assessment was planned, the Lead Assessor explained to the president that the entire company needed to participate, with the president being the sponsor because he was the point where the authority for all groups merged. This allowed project managers, software engineers, executive VPs, and so on to participate. What was found in this assessment was that the software engineering directorate had been isolated, not only in previous assessments but also on projects. Although software engineering processes were theoretically in place, they were not actually functioning properly. The project managers were not involved; they knew little about the software portion of the project. When something failed, it was believed to be only the software engineers' fault, not the project managers'. As a result of this assessment, the president saw the problem and directed that at every monthly program meeting, the project manager was to report to him on the status of the entire project and specifically on the status of the software. Within six months, the company's quality culture had improved radically.

Companies who regard assessments as tests to be passed often prefer to consider one small and successful project as the organization. By having a single project assessed, the companies hope to demonstrate that they are better than they really are. But the culture of an organization is pervasive. Although some projects may be better than others, the same management or mismanagement decisions tend to drive the project managers and their project teams, and this culture can only be identified by sampling a broad range of projects.

Another problem with assessing a small group is that it is extremely difficult to preserve confidentiality during and after the assessment.

An example of a division that inappropriately tried to have one project represent the "organization" involved Company B, a very large company. The division at issue in Company B was made up of about 200 people, but it only wanted to have one pilot project (about 10 people) assessed. The Lead Assessor had to explain to the managing director of the division that this was not in the company's best interest because one project can easily give a distorted view of a company or organization and also because it is nearly impossible to maintain confidentiality (one of the primary elements of an improvement effort) when only a few people are involved. The division, which was certain that the pilot project was superior to its other projects, disagreed for obvious reasons. They managed to get their way, and the assessment was almost undermined by confidentiality issues. Ironically, though, the methodology proved resilient enough that the distorting effect of good individuals did not entirely decide the rating. Even the pilot project suffered from institutional problems that affected the other projects to a greater degree, and the division, though it learned more than it wanted to about its procedures, did not "pass the test."

4.2.1.2 The Special Problem of Small Organizations

The question is frequently asked whether it is feasible to assess small organizations. Data collected by the SEI from Lead Assessors have reported that 22% of the organizations assessed have 20 to 50 software developers [Dunaway 01a]. These types of organizations can be assessed with relatively little difficulty.

For organizations with fewer than 20 software developers, however, the reference model is not ideal. The CMM and the CMMI focus on project-level management and development practices at Maturity Level 2. At Maturity Level 3, they ask organizations to consolidate their best practices from individual projects into an organization-wide set of practices. These issues have reduced relevance when there are no more than 20 people in an organization. (Having said this, it should also be said that a number of organizations with fewer than 20 software developers have reported that conducting CMM or CMMI assessments proved of real instructional benefit to them.)

4.2.2 Reference Model Scope: Which Maturity Levels Should Be Assessed?

Although deciding on the objectives of the assessment sounds straightforward, it is not always easy to gauge what maturity levels and process areas the assessment team should appropriately examine. These consequences are significant, especially in a first assessment. If an organization thinks it is Level 3 when in fact it is really Level 1 or 2, a CMM assessment will need to look at 13 KPAs instead of 6 and a CMMI assessment at 21 PAs instead of 7. The difference translates into an added week onsite.

Just as important is the risk to the organization's morale. It is common for senior management to think that the organization is better than it is, and when an unrealistically high standard has been selected, they may send a direct or indirect message to their people that says "Don't fail us." The interviewees are then afraid to say the wrong thing, reverting to "audit mode." That is, they only answer the questions that are asked and don't participate in an honest effort to examine their procedures. Thus, they get little out of the assessment other than the sense of confronting an enemy. So instead of the assessment being a positive culture-evolving experience, it ends up being a negative and stressful experience for all.

If senior managers think the organization is Level 3 and it is really Level 2 or even Level 1, the shock of looking into an assessment's mirror can be painful. In many cases, the organization never recovers from the shock.

To ascertain what part of the model should most beneficially guide an assessment, the organization may ask the Lead Assessor to spend one, two, or three days talking to people informally. This exercise may even be elaborated into a full health check or mini-assessment.

The costs of not heeding these preliminary indications can be dire.

A managing director was sure that Company C was Level 2. When he was told both at the beginning of the assessment and during the assessment that there were areas in which no data substantiated this assumption, he *still* insisted that his organization was Level 2. When the final results showed that his organization was only at Level 1, at the moment when senior managers usually thank the team and the organization for their hard work, he told the audience that he did not believe the results. He then asked if anyone in the organization really believed what they just heard. Slowly the developers in the back row started to stand up, until two thirds of them were on their feet. The managing director, abashed, could only turn to his direct report managers and ask why they hadn't listened to their developers. The next week the managing director was removed from his post. Seven years later, the organization was still Level 1.

4.3 Choosing an Assessment Sponsor

Choosing the Assessment Sponsor (Ensuring the Hands-On Role of Senior Management)

The executive who has made a decision to schedule an assessment must choose whether he or she will be the official assessment sponsor or whether another senior manager will act in that role. *It is extremely important that the assessment sponsor be of sufficient rank to lend real authority to the assessment effort follow-on process improvement implementation. Ideally the assessment sponsor should be the president or a managing director of the division whose organization is being assessed.*

The assessment sponsor's job is to demonstrate the company's genuine commitment to the assessment and to process improvement by words and support and to provide guidance to the Lead Assessor and the assessment team regarding both the organizational and reference model scope of the assessment—that is, the projects to be included for in-depth analysis and the maturity level of the reference model to be investigated—and the selection of an assessment team. The sponsor participates in planning meetings, the opening kick-off meeting, and the final findings presentation. Evidence of the sponsor's support of the assessment activities is an important aspect of creating an open, non-threatening atmosphere in the assessed organization. The sponsor funds the assessment activities as well as the follow-on activities that result from the assessment.

4.4 Establishing Appropriate Organizational Understanding

For process improvement activities to be most effective, the assessment sponsor must articulate to the entire organization his or her goals for having the assessment and be clear about what the assessment and the process improvement initiative are expected to accomplish. This clarity helps guide the assessment team as well as the organizational staff and will also shape the follow-on improvement initiative.

- The assessment sponsor should ensure that the organization shares a mutual understanding of what the assessment is meant to accomplish.

- The assessment team, the assessment sponsor, and the assessment participants all must clearly understand the organization's commitment to process improvement.

- Managers and assessment participants must view the assessment as a collaborative effort between the assessment team and the organization, between management and practitioners, and between customers and suppliers.

- Senior managers must have a common understanding of assessment goals, scope, constraints, and outputs.

- Assessment participants must have a basic understanding of software process improvement concepts.

- Organization managers and participants must agree that the assessment findings will constitute key process issues that need to be addressed.

- The organization must commit itself to taking action based on the assessment findings.

Chapter 5

─────────

Planning and Preparing for an Assessment, Part 2:

Choosing a Time.
Formulating an
Assessment Plan.
Appointing an Organization
Site Coordinator and
Organizing Logistics.

After an assessment sponsor is chosen, he or she along with the Lead Assessor is intimately involved in the process that transforms the decision to undertake an assessment into strategic and tactical decisions about how the assessment is actually conducted.

The three primary parts of this stage of the assessment's preparation involve the following:

5.1 Choosing a **time** for the assessment

5.2 Formulating an **assessment plan**

5.3 Appointing an **organization site coordinator** to help fill out the practical details of the plan and to organize the assessment's logistical preparations

5.4 Ensuring the organization is **ready** for an assessment

5.1 Choosing a Time for the Assessment

An organization must consider a number of factors when selecting a time for the assessment, the primary among them being: "Is the organization ready for an assessment?"

An assessment should also take place at a relatively unintrusive time. There probably is never an ideal time for an assessment, but certainly the weeks before a delivery to a customer is *not* a good time.

For follow-on assessments, the organization needs to consider whether enough time has elapsed since putting in place improved processes needed or recommended by the last assessment. Scheduling a second assessment without allowing time for improved practices to be implemented tends to be extremely frustrating for the assessment team and the organization. One rule of thumb is that an organization needs to demonstrate that the improved processes have been in place (and practiced on at least one project) for at least six months.

Many organizations have found that alternating health checks and assessments on a yearly basis works well. A yearly check on progress helps organizations maintain a focus on quality.

Some companies have found an Assessment Readiness Survey useful in helping them answer this question (see "Assessment Readiness" at the end of the chapter).

5.2 The Assessment Plan

5.2.1 How Far in Advance to Begin Formulating the Assessment Plan

An assessment constitutes something of an ordeal. How could it not when it involves an outside analysis of one's own work and an intrusion that disrupts normal business for anywhere from three weeks to three months? Because an assessment involves coordinating many people (for Level 3 assessments, as many as 75 people in the organization) and considerable resources, serious planning is an essential step.

On average, the organization should assume that it takes a minimum of three months from the time an assessment is scheduled to prepare and execute a workable plan so that the on-site assessment can be efficiently staged.

5.2.2 How (and by Whom) the Assessment Plan Is Written

In the first phase of assessment planning, the Lead Assessor studies the organization's key strategic objectives and advises the assessment sponsor about the parameters of the assessment.

The Lead Assessor works first with the senior executive and then with the assessment sponsor to define the boundaries for the assessment plan. The Lead Assessor and senior management must have a clear understanding of the assessment context, its goals, and its objectives. They must agree on the scope, outputs, and any constraints on the assessment process (cost, schedule, and participants), and the Lead Assessor must be given written authorization to proceed with the assessment.

When all this is agreed upon, the Lead Assessor gives the organization site coordinator (see Section 5.3) the general contents (template) of the assessment plan. The organization site coordinator fills in the details of the plan. The Lead Assessor reviews and revises as necessary.

5.2.3 General Features

The assessment plan is an organization's map through an assessment. It is also an important way for the organization and Lead Assessor to document mutually agreed upon assumptions, establish and maintain sponsorship, track and report the performance of the assessment process, and reinforce commitments at key points in the assessment process.

The plan is continuously refined. Typically scope-related decisions, a planned list of assessment outputs, and an evaluation of resources are finalized early on, along with risk and risk-mitigation plans. Cost, schedule, and logistics are finalized later. By using the organization information found in the Organizational and Project Questionnaires and the Project Selection Matrix (see Chapter 6), the Lead Assessor can refine the scope of the assessment.

After their initial discussions, the Lead Assessor and the assessment sponsor meet to nail down the scope of the assessment—that is, which parts of the organization are to be assessed, what maturity level of the organization is to be assessed, and the characteristics and mix of people who will make up the assessment team.

At its most basic, an assessment plan initially reflects: 1) which portion of the selected model will be investigated, and 2) the bounds of the organization for which the results can be considered valid (e.g., a project, a product line, an operating division, a business unit, or an entire global enterprise), and the rationale for selecting these projects. After these are determined, the assessment plan then proceeds to refine the scope of the assessment by prescribing more specific goals—principally the specific process areas (PAs) to be assessed.

The characteristics of an assessment team must be agreed upon (how many in all, how many from inside and how many from outside the organization, at what ranks, with what specialties, etc.), and assessment team members must be appointed and have their names and qualifications recorded in the plan. A schedule for when the assessment team must meet for training, presentations, review of questionnaires, data management, and so on also must be constructed.

The plan prescribes that prior to the beginning of the assessment, the Lead Assessor and all members of the assessment team will sign a confidentiality agreement. (It is also good policy to have the assessment sponsor sign the agreement.)

The plan must provide a list and rationale for all those to be interviewed (interviewing too few people, or not interviewing the right kind of people, may lead to major problems) and must provide a schedule for the interviews that are to be conducted. (A list should also be made of who else should be interviewed if people named on the first list should have to travel. The plan should anticipate the risks these decisions are likely to incur.)

Decisions must be made about which data collection, analysis, and validation approaches will be utilized, including supporting work aids and tools. This is an issue for the assessment team, whose members must decide what mechanisms will be used to control the data being collected. Which parts will be computerized and which parts will be manual? What combination of questionnaires, document reviews, interviews, and presentations will be used? What rules will be used to corroborate the findings, and how will the team validate the findings with the organization?

Besides indicating *who* should be involved in the assessment and at what stage, an assessment plan must specify *when* the major milestones for the assessment's completion are due and *what* outputs from the assessment are needed by the organization to be able to plan further improvements.

The assessment sponsor and the Lead Assessor must approve the final assessment plan. Having the entire assessment team sign the plan is an even better arrangement because it helps team members buy into an assessment. Formal approval of the plan demonstrates executive and team commitment and ensures a mutual understanding of the assessment goals, constraints, outputs, responsibilities, and confidentiality.

5.2.3.1 The Assessment Plan: Identifying Confidence Factors and Risks in the Coming Assessment

One part of the assessment plan not yet discussed has to do with identifying risk and confidence factors beforehand for the coming assessment.

Defining confidence is a way of stating whether the assessment's characterization of its representative projects can predict the capabilities of similar projects throughout the organization.

A rigorous assessment correlates with a high confidence factor. The quality of the assessment can be affected by:

- The adequacy of the composition of the assessment team, taking into consideration:
  - Qualifications of individual team members
  - Team size
  - Potential biases of organization site team member(s)
- The model coverage planned and achieved:
  - The extent to which the data maps to the (key) process areas within the scope of the investigation
  - The extent to which the data collected covers the organization's defined life cycle activities
- The organization coverage planned and achieved:
  - The number of projects and the extent to which they are representative of the organization being assessed
  - The cohesiveness of the appraised entity in terms of its management structure, geographic location, and product line
  - The extent to which the participants are forthcoming concerning shortcomings in the organization processes
  - The number of people interviewed and the extent to which they are representative of the organization being assessed
  - The extent to which data and observations are corroborated by the selected participants
- Use of data collection techniques planned and achieved:
  - The combination of techniques used to obtain objective evidence (instruments, document review, interviews, presentations)
  - The extent to which the data collected is corroborated through use of the selected techniques

- Validation of findings:
  - The rules of corroboration used in validating findings
  - Validation of findings by the organization assessed
- Time spent (the amount of time spent per assessment)
- Adherence to the assessment plan [Dunaway 01c]

The assessment plan should identify circumstances that could diminish confidence in the accuracy and completeness of the assessment results and should include prescriptions for mitigation in case risk factors begin to threaten the quality of the assessment. The assessment sponsor should be kept abreast of risk factors throughout the assessment. At the end of the assessment (either verbally or in the Final Report), an assessment confidence statement must be provided to the assessment sponsor.

5.2.4 While the Details of the Assessment Plan Are Being Finalized: A List of Interim Tasks

While the plan is being written and before its completion, the following tasks will be accomplished:

- Analyzing the project questionnaires
- Reviewing the organization site information packet
- Refining the scope of the assessment if necessary within the constraints established during the beginning of the assessment
- Identifying the goals for how projects and interviewees will be selected
- Selecting the projects and interviewees for the assessment
- Preparing a detailed assessment schedule
- Selecting assessment team members
- Identifying the list of documents for document review and coordination (objective evidence)
- Identifying logistics requirements, which included booking rooms, transportation, accommodations, and managers
- Preparing assessment participants' briefing and opening briefing

5.2.5 A Full-Scale Template of a Working Assessment Plan

The following represents a useful SCAMPI Assessment Plan Template.[1] (The same format can be used for planning CBA IPI assessments.)

Angular brackets '<>' denote where text replacement will be required.

**SCAMPI Appraisal Plan for
<name of organization>**

Date: <planned duration of SCAMPI>

Approved by (Sponsor) : <name of sponsor>

SCAMPI PLAN TEMPLATE
Contents
<Table of Contents>

1. **SCOPE OF ORGANIZATION TO BE APPRAISED**
2. **RESPONSIBILITY FOR PLAN**
3. **CONFIDENTIALITY**
4. **SPONSOR'S RESPONSIBILITIES**
5. **SCOPE OF APPRAISAL**
   5.1 Appraisal Goals
   5.2 PAs to Be Assessed
6. **APPRAISAL TEAM**
   6.1 Leader of the Appraisal
   6.2 Appraisal Team Members (ATMs)
   6.3 Appraisal Team Member Experience/Qualifications
   6.4 Appraisal Team Member Roles
7. **MATURITY QUESTIONNAIRES**
8. **PARTICIPANT SELECTION MATRIX**
9. **PROJECT SELECTION/CRITERIA MATRIX**
10. **TASKS TO BE ACCOMPLISHED PRIOR TO START OF APPRAISAL**
11. **APPRAISAL SCHEDULE**
12. **RISKS & CONSTRAINTS**
13. **APPENDIX A**

[1.] With thanks to Roger Wilson. In the following template, in accordance with SEI usage, the word "appraisal" is used to denote a formal SCAMPI assessment.

1.0 Scope of Organization to Be Appraised

The organizational scope of the appraisal will be:

<Details and scope of the organization being appraised. Include details of any elements of the organization (e.g., sites/projects/ business areas/software development areas/IT/firmware/ ASICS/system modeling and simulations) excluded from the appraisal.>

<Include details of the size of the organization being appraised, such as the total number of staff in the organization and the total number of software engineers (indicate permanent staff/contractors). The number of software engineers identified in the organization should be the same number reported in the quarterly report. >

2.0 Responsibility for Plan

The Lead Appraiser along with the site coordinator will be responsible for producing the SCAMPI Appraisal Plan in conjunction with the ATMs, sponsor, and others.

3.0 Confidentiality

Prior to a SCAMPI appraisal, the Lead Appraiser and all members of the appraisal team should sign a confidentiality agreement.

4.0 Assessment Sponsor's Responsibilities

In approving this plan, the sponsor accepts responsibility for:

1. Committing the necessary resources for assessment team members, project leaders, and functional area representatives and ensuring their full and unchallenged participation in this assessment.

2. Endorsing the principals of confidentiality and honesty during and after the assessment.

3. Attending the opening meeting and final findings presentation and taking ownership of the assessment results.

5.0 Scope of Appraisal

5.1 Appraisal Goals

The primary goal of this SCAMPI is to identify improvement opportunities and acknowledge improvements achieved.

<Details of any secondary goals or aims of the assessment>

5.2. PAs to Be Assessed

The PAs to be appraised are as follows:

<List the PAs to be appraised providing any details associated with those PAs being partially assessed and not to be rated.>

6.0 Appraisal Team

6.1 Lead Appraiser (LA)

Name

SEI SCAMPI Registration Number:

6.2 Appraisal Team Members (ATMs)

6.2.1 Organization Team Members

The following identifies the name and home organization of each team member from within the organization to be assessed:

Name	Role/Division
<names>	<roles>

6.2.2 External Team Members

The following identifies the name and home organization of each team member external to the business group and organization to be assessed:

Name	Role/Organization
<names>	<positions>

6.2.3 Appraisal Team Member Experience/Qualifications

The following chart reflects the individual and combined credentials of the team members to participate in the SCAMPI:

Name	Engineering (Systems, Software, Hardware) (yrs/mos)	Project Management (Including Software) (yrs/mos)	SEI CMMI Course	Other Process Improvement Training	Previous Assessments (e.g., CBA IPIs, SCAMPIs)
<name>	<details>	<details>	<details>	<details>	<details>

6.2.4 Appraisal Team Member Roles

6.2.4.1 Mini-Team/PA Assignments

The following identifies specific PAs assigned to team members:

	Team 1	Team 2	Team 3	Team 4
Members	<names>	<names>	<names>	<names>
PAs	<assigned PAs>	<assigned PAs>	<assigned PAs>	<assigned PAs>

6.2.4.2 Additional Responsibilities

The following table identifies specific roles assigned to team members:

Librarian	<name>
Timekeeper	<name>
Logistics	<name>
Other	<name>

7.0 Maturity Questionnaires (if used)

The following table identifies the distribution of the Maturity Questionnaires:

<The minimum requirement shall be all project managers of the projects being assessed.>

Maturity Questionnaire Distribution

Name	Role
<name>	<position in organization>
<name>	<position in organization>
<name>	<position in organization>
<name>	<position in organization>

8.0 Participant Selection Matrix

Individuals and Groups to Be Interviewed	Projects/Business Areas				
	<Project A>	<Project B>	<Project C>	<Project D>	<Other, Sampled Projects>
Project Managers	< name>	< name>	< name>	< name>	< name>
Software Managers	< name>	< name>	< name>	< name>	< name>
System Managers	< name>	< name>	< name>	< name>	< name>
Group 1 Team Leads (System and Software)	< name>	< name>	< name>	< name>	< name>
Group 2 Require-ments (System and Software)	< names>	< names>	< names>	< names>	< names>

	Projects/Business Areas				
Individuals and Groups to Be Interviewed	<Project A>	<Project B>	<Project C>	<Project D>	<Other, Sampled Projects>
Group 3 Architects	< names>	< names>	< names>	< names>	< names>
Group 4 Detailed Design (System and S/W Engineers)	< names>	< names>	< names>	< names>	< names>
Group 5 Implementation	< names>	< names>	< names>	< names>	< names>
Group 6 Testing (System, Software, Integration, and Acceptance Test Engineers)	< names>	< names>	< names>	< names>	< names>
Group 7 Configuration Management (System and Software)	< names>	< names>	< names>	< names>	< names>
Group 9 Quality Assurance (System and Software)	< names>	< names>	< names>	< names>	< names>
Group 10 Causal Analysis Team	< names>	< names>	< names>	< names>	< names>

(continued)

(continued)

	Projects/Business Areas				
Individuals and Groups to Be Interviewed	*<Project A>*	*<Project B>*	*<Project C>*	*<Project D>*	*<Other, Sampled Projects>*
Group 11 Engineering Process Group (System and Software)			<names>		
Group 12 Middle Management (e.g., Program Directors, etc.)			<names>		
Group 13 Executive Management (e.g., Vice Presidents)			<names>		
President			<names>		

9.0 Project Selection/Criteria Matrix

All Projects in Organization	*<Project A>*	*<Project B>*	*<Project C>*	*<Project D>*
Business Areas (type)	<details>	<details>	<details>	<details>
Age and Duration of Project <years/months>	<yrs/mos>	<yrs/mos>	<yrs/mos>	<yrs/mos>
Present Life Cycle and Life-Cycle Phase (Bid Phase, Requirements Design, Code, Unit Test System Test, Integration Acceptance, or Maintenance)	<details>	<details>	<details>	<details>

All Projects in Organization	*<Project A>*	*<Project B>*	*<Project C>*	*<Project D>*
Current Business Value (determined by sponsor) High, Medium, or Low	\<H/M/L\>	\<H/M/L\>	\<H/M/L\>	\<H/M/L\>
Future Business Value (determined by sponsor) High, Medium, or Low	\<H/M/L\>	\<H/M/L\>	\<H/M/L\>	\<H/M/L\>
Project Team Size (denote full-time or part-time team members and indicate contractors) (Number of Project Staff, Systems, Engineers, Software Engineers, Test Engineers, etc.)	\<details\>	\<details\>	\<details\>	\<details\>
Development and Target Platforms (PC Workstation, Embedded)	\<details\>	\<details\>	\<details\>	\<details\>
Size and Language of Product (e.g., Number of Req., Source Lines of Code [SLOCS], etc.)	\<details\>	\<details\>	\<details\>	\<details\>
Software Safety Criticality (Safety Significance)	\<details\>	\<details\>	\<details\>	\<details\>

10.0 Tasks to Be Accomplished Prior to Start of Appraisal

<Details of tasks to be accomplished by appraisal team or site coordinator prior to start of onsite period of the SCAMPI.>

Examples:

Task	Assigned to
Review Maturity Questionnaires	\<names\> \<target completion date\>
Finalize APB	\<names\> \<target completion date\>
Finalize OPB	\<names\> \<target completion date\>
Arrange Interview Rooms	\<names\> \<target completion date\>
Arrange OHP, etc.	\<names\> \<target completion date\>
Arrange Food/Drinks for Team	\<names\> \<target completion date\>
Identify Stationery Needs	\<names\> \<target completion date\>
Complete Initial Document Review	\<names\> \<target completion date\>
Obtain Company HQ Approval of This Plan	\<names\> \<target completion date\>
Obtain Sponsor's Approval of This Plan	\<names\> \<target completion date\>
Hotel Arrangements for ATM	\<names\> \<target completion date\>
Other	\<names\> \<target completion date\>

11.0 Appraisal Schedule

\<Initial appraisal schedule may be updated during the pre–onsite SCAMPI period. This should be updated to reflect the actual schedule of events (including additional/follow-on interviews—see example below).\>

The following schedule indicates the interviewees in addition to the LA and ATMs, and when they are required:

Detailed SCAMPI Schedule
Onsite Assessment

DAY 1

Arrive at site	08:00–08:30	
Opening Meeting	**08:30–09:15**	Sponsor and all participants

Team briefing/discussion	09:15–09:30	Site coordinator	
Interview 1: Project Manager (1)	**09:30–11:00**	<Participant>	<roles in org>
Consolidation period	11:00–11:30		
Interview 2: S/W Manager (1)	**11:30–13:00**	<Participant>	<roles in org>
Consolidation period	13:00–13:15		
Lunch Break	13:15–14:00		
Interview 3: Project Manager (2)	**14:00–15:30**	<Participant>	<roles in org>
Consolidation period (Day 1)	15:30–20:00		

DAY 2

Arrive at site	08:00–08:30	<Participant>	<roles in org>
Interview 4: S/W Manager (2)	**08:30–10:00**		
Consolidation period	10:00–10:30		
Interview 5: Project Manager (3)	**10:30–12:00**		
Consolidation period	12:00–12:15	<Participant>	<roles in org>
Lunch Break	12:15–13:15		
Interview 6: S/W Manager (3)	**13:15–15:45**	<Participant>	<roles in org>
Consolidation period (Day 2)	15:45–20:00		

DAY 3

Arrive at site	08:00–08:30		
Interview 7: Reqmnts FAR (System & S/W)	**08:30–10:15**	<Participant>	<roles in org>
Consolidation period	10:15–10:45		
Interview 8: S/W Team Leaders FAR	**10:45–12:15**		
Consolidation period	12:15–12:30		
Lunch Break	12:30–13:30		

| Interview 9:
Design & Code FAR | 13:30–15:00 | <Participants> | <roles in org> |
| Consolidation (Day 3) | 15:00–20:00 | | |

DAY 4

Arrive at site	08:00–08:30		
Interview 10: Configuration Management (System and S/W)	08:30–10:15		
Consolidation period	10:15–10:45	<Participants>	<roles in org>
Interview 11: S/W Subcontract Management	10:45–12:30		
Consolidation period	12:30–12:45	<Participants>	<roles in org>
Lunch Break	12:45–13:45		
Interview 12: QA Interview (Systems and Software)	13:45–15:30		
Consolidation (Day 4)	15:30–20:00		

DAY 5

Arrive at site	08:00–08:30		
Interview 13: Test FAR (Acceptance, System Integration, Software)	08:30–10:15	<Participants>	<roles in org>
Consolidation period	10:15–10:45		
Interview 14: Causal Analysis Team	10:45–12:00	<Participants>	<roles in org>
Consolidation period	12:00–12:15		
Lunch Break	12:15–13:15		
Interview 15: SEPG and/or EPG	13:15–15:00	<Participants>	<roles in org>
Consolidation (Day 5)	15:00–20:00		

DAY 6

| Arrive at site | 08:00–08:30 | | |
| Interview 16:
Middle Managers | 08:30–10:00 | <Participants> | <roles in org> |

Consolidation period	10:00–10:30	
Interview 17: Executive Managers (VPs)	**10:30–12:00**	
Consolidation period	12:00–12:15	
Lunch Break	12:15–13:15	
Interview 18: Assessment Sponsor (President)	**13:15–14:15**	
Consolidate	14:15–16:00	
Begin preparing draft findings	16:00–20:00	

DAY 7

Prepare draft findings (continued)	08:00–18:00	

DAY 8

Present Draft Findings (Session A Practitioners)	**09:00–10:30**	Participants; practitioners
Consolidate data	10:30–11:00	
Present Draft Findings (Session B Management)	**11:00–12:30**	Participants; senior management
Lunch Break	12:00–13:00	
Consolidate, rate, and prepare final findings	13:00–20:00	

DAY 9

Arrive at site	08:00–08:30	
Prepare final findings (continued)	08:30–11:00	
Present Final Findings	**11:00–12:00**	Sponsor and all participants
Lunch Break	12:00–13:00	
Executive Briefing	**13:00–14:00**	Sponsor and selected execs
Team wrap-up	14:00–16:00	

12.0 Risks & Constraints

<Identify any risks or constraints that may impede the execution of the SCAMPI. >

Risk Description	Risk Management Strategy	Status	Assigned Monitor	Resolution

13.0 Appendix A

Confidentiality Agreement
(To be signed by all team members)

With the objective of identifying improvement opportunities for the organization, I agree to keep an open mind, to receive and review all information received during the SCAMPI without bias or prejudice, and to at all times remain focused on moving the organization forward.

All SCAMPI results and associated data (e.g., Interview Notes, Final Findings Presentation, Final Assessment Reports) are proprietary to the organization and may not be distributed or discussed in any forum outside the appraised organization without the approval of the sponsor(s).

Understanding the need to keep all of the information obtained during the appraisal confidential without attribution to individuals or projects, I agree to not disclose information obtained during the course of the appraisal.

The Lead Appraiser and team members reserve the right to report any deviations/concerns associated with the conduct of SCAMPI process itself directly to the sponsor.

The undersigned agree to these provisions.

<u><Assessment Sponsor></u> <Print name>	<u><Organization Site Coordinator></u> <Print name>
<u>< Lead Appraiser></u> <Print name>	<u><SEI registration></u> <Print name>
<u><Team Member></u> <Print name>	<u><Team Member></u> <Print name>
<u><Team Member></u> <Print name>	<u><Team Member></u> <Print name>
<u><Team Member></u> <Print name>	<u><Team Member></u> <Print name>
<u><Team Member></u> <Print name>	<u><Team Member></u> <Print name>
<u><Team Member></u> <Print name>	<u><Team Member></u> <Print name>

5.2.6 The Assessment Plan: Managing Resources and Estimating Costs

Resource management is typically not included in the assessment plan document. A separate, more confidential plan must be constructed to provide estimates of the effort and time to be invested by the organization and the assessment team in preparation, including pre-onsite data collection and analysis and the on-site assessment. This plan is formulated by the assessment sponsor with the help of the organization site coordinator.

While planning, the organization develops and includes a top-level cost breakdown and schedule. General activities include estimating:

* The duration of key events as a basis for deriving a comprehensive schedule.

- The hours likely to be required of the people participating in the assessment.
- The costs associated with using facilities and equipment (as appropriate).
- The costs for incidentals (e.g., travel, lodging, meals) as appropriate.

5.3 Managing Logistics: Appointing an Organization Site Coordinator

The assessment sponsor delegates the day-to-day management of the assessment to a subordinate (sometimes the process improvement manager). This subordinate is known as an organization site coordinator. The organization site coordinator helps organize both the planning phase and the two onsite phases of the assessment. He or she along with the Lead Assessor is responsible for arranging the practical details of the assessment plan and organizing all the logistics of the assessment.

5.3.1 The Logistical Responsibilities of the Organization Site Coordinator and Associated Staff

The organization site coordinator spends a great deal of time (at a bare minimum of 100 hours) prior to and during the onsite assessment. He or she first helps the Lead Assessor make practical choices and then ensures that all team members are available and that all interviewees for the assessment are available, scheduled, and able to appear for their sessions. The organization site coordinator also ensures that rooms are scheduled and that logistic requirements are planned and completed.

As part of coordinating the assessment logistics, the organization site coordinator must arrange lodging, food, and beverage for the assessment team members, obtain documentation needed by the team, and make plans to return documentation to appropriate people when the assessment is concluded.

Particular attention must be given to:

- **Scheduling**—A high-level schedule should be established early in the assessment process and refined as projects and participants are selected. Schedules should be coordinated with assessment participants as soon as they are selected. Detailed schedules must be provided to participants during the assessment participants briefing. Schedules should limit the assessment workday to a ten-hour maximum.

- **Facilities**—Required facilities should be established early and rooms reserved as soon as a high-level schedule is available (rooms for team training, briefings, questionnaire administration, interviews, and assessment team work room).

- **Tools and materials**—Tools and materials should be identified and a complete list documented in the final assessment plan: projectors, screens, flip charts, white boards, copiers, computers, software, supplies, and so on.

- **Transportation and accommodations**—Transportation and accommodations should be arranged for assessment team members as soon as they are selected. Any additional arrangement for other assessment participants should also be arranged as soon as they are identified.

- **Catering**—Arrangements for catering should be made prior to finalizing the assessment plan.

- **Support**—Support for the production of presentations should be arranged [Dunaway 01c].

The logistical aspects of assessment planning need attention early in the assessment process and must be monitored effectively.

5.3.2 A Sample Logistics Checklist

The checklist below can be used as a guide for the organization site coordinator to ensure that all needed tasks are accomplished. This list is not prescriptive and should be tailored to the particulars of the organization and the assessment.[2]

[2.] Checklist with thanks to Eileen Rubin.

Item	Details	Done
PLANNING PHASE		
Date of assessment		
CBA IPI or SCAMPI or health check		
Scope		
Maturity questionnaire		
Team gifts		
Gather supplies gradually to avoid chaos as the assessment approaches		
Schedule "team room" at least one day in advance to do setup and testing—it really takes one full day		
Generate new schedule		
Determine FAR groups		
Generate plan		
Determine who is on assessment team		
Name of Lead Assessor (lead)		
Name of ATM 1		
Name of ATM 2		
Name of ATM 3		
Name of ATM 4		
Name of ATM 5		
Name of ATM 6		
Obtain ATMs qualifications for chart		
Date sent to ATMs		
Received from ATMs—who—track until all received		
Name of assessment coordinator		
Plan to assessment coordinator—six weeks before—what is final date?		
Approval at least two weeks before		
Plan needs current organizational charts		

Item	Details	Done
Send out copies of the appropriate policies to the ATMs		
Send out copies of the appropriate processes with supporting information to the ATMs		
Check into travel considerations—hotel, car, transportation to/from airport, other needs; preferred hotel		
Send out hotel confirmation numbers		
Send out rental car confirmation numbers, if applicable		
Provide maps—airport to hotel, hotel to site		
Notify security of team members and working hours—need badges		
Need charge number for internal team members		
Dinner out with assessment team—coordinate with Lead Assessor		
On first day—meet team at the hotel and escort to plant		
If available, have a sign in lobby to welcome ATMs—check spelling of names		
Set up distribution lists for internal ATMs, external ATMs, interviewees as a group, and possibly FARs. This makes emails easier.		
Send out schedule in Outlook		
Send out preliminary schedule to interviewees to determine if any conflicts exist		
Reminders for pre-meeting		
Reminders for opening meeting		
Reminders for draft findings		
Reminders for interviews		

(continued)

(continued)

Item	Details	Done
Reminders for final findings		
Pre-assessment meeting if desired		
Review briefings (PMs, Directors, etc.) prior to presentation		
Get presentation copies to put on PC and to make backup slides		
Make copies of presentations and load on computer—bring disk just in case network is down—if network is down, need to have presentations on standalone system. May want to do that the day before—just in case (because most PCs run PowerPoint off the network).		
Make electronic copies of processes and associated material and put on disk just in case network is down		

Opening meeting with assessment team
    Sponsor must be there
    Need PC/projection capability
    Need large room		

Draft finding meeting
    Need PC/projector capability
    Need large room		

Final findings meeting
    Sponsor must be there
    Need PC/projection capability
    Need large room		

Team room—for the duration		
Stationery—all sorts		
Phone with international capability		
Voice mail account—and message		
Room layout		
Five computers—four with network capability, one not on network. One not on network needs office.		

Item	Details	Done
Two printers—fast LaserJet and color printer		
Zip drive—if possible		
Need userid/password for any external people		
Need internal people to be able to read their email		
At least two keys to room—one for site coordinator and one for team member		
Get two keys to meeting rooms		
Copier codes and location of nearest copier		
Make sure everything works and that computers all have needed software and helper applications set up		
Make sure that other needed applications are installed—MS Project, etc.—MS Project is not part of Office		
Check if lights on timers—need lights on 7:00 a.m. to 12:00 midnight		
Breakfast/lunch for team		
Check dietary requirements beforehand		
Cheese, vegetables, fruit		
Get menus		
Morning and afternoon refreshments in team room		
Morning and afternoon refreshments in conference room		
Dinner?		
Newspapers		

(continued)

(continued)

Item	Details	Done
Check with cafeteria every day to adjust as schedule changes		
Two conference rooms for interviews		
SUPPLIES		
Copies of last assessment—three-hole punched—one for every ATM		
Loose-leaf binders—2" (preferably with slot to slide in cover)		
Cover pages—individual		
30 dividers each		
Loose-leaf paper		
3.5" disks		
Computer overhead projector		
Overhead projector		
Transparencies with pens		
Three-hole punch		
Paper clips		
Scotch tape		
Masking tape		
Post-It (small, medium, large)		
Post-It colored tabs		
Scissors		
Garbage cans (large)		
Tell maintenance/custodians not to remove equipment/materials from room—post sign		
Easel—in third-floor training room		
Pens/pencils (0.5 mm with extra lead)		
Erasers		

Item	Details	Done
Stapler (with staples)		
Staple remover		
Paper pads		
Markers		
Highlighters		
Board erasable markers		
Two boxes (to store materials that require shredding)		
Two filing boxes to archive documentation		
File folders		
Mouse pads		
Any other material identified by the Lead Assessor or other assessment team members		
CLEANUP ACTIVITIES		
Assessment coordinator invited to attend final finding—also send to him/her		
Detailed action plan due four weeks after assessment		
Detailed action plan reviewed with Lead Assessor within two weeks after completion (total = six weeks)		
Copy of detailed action plan reviewed; sent to assessment coordinator		
Clean up assessment room		
Put finding brief and "sanitized ratings sheets" on 3.5" floppy or other transportable electronic media		
Remove everything from C-drive and recycle bin		
Return all original documents		

(continued)

(continued)

Item	Details	Done
Ensure other materials are shredded		
Plan dinner out on last day if desired		
Maps to locations where the assessors are going		
Have international telephone removed		
Have email accounts closed and all email forwarded		
Thank-you note to participants		
Thank-you note to support personnel		

5.4 Assessment Readiness[3]: When Is an Organization Ready for an Assessment?

Sponsorship: The senior manager responsible for the assessment ideally should be:

- Dissatisfied with the current state.
- Willing to demonstrate the type of public support necessary to convey strong organizational commitment to the assessment.
- Willing to commit resources to the assessment and to follow-up improvement activities.
- Willing to support improvement plans through enough resources and power.
- Willing to assure that progress and problems will be tracked during follow-up improvement.
- Aware of the personal, organizational, and political costs of the technical and cultural changes that flow from assessments and constitute the first step of long-term improvement.

[3.] Credit should be given to John Maher, Ph.D., and Betty Deimel for creating the first version of this survey. We have made our own revisions to their original version.

Resistance-Free: Assessments should be undertaken when the organization is informed and prepared for the assessment effect. Ideally:

- Practitioners see a need for improvement.
- Managers at all levels see a need for process improvement.
- Communication between management and practitioners is clear and direct.
- Management understands the costs of process improvement in time and personnel to be reasonable.
- Practitioners are confident that management will provide support (i.e., time, money, personnel not expected to do the job in their spare time) to help improve processes.
- Management understands the anticipated impact initially on cost and schedule of projects and supports process improvement.

Synergy:

- Groups in the organization can communicate with each other.
- Managers are prepared to listen to and deal with differences in opinion.

Organizational Issues:

- Not all projects are in a fire-fighting mode so that the organization can manage changes that come as a result of the assessment.
- The organization has clear lines of responsibility and authority.
- The organization provides employees the latitude to make mistakes and encourages risk-taking.
- When changes are introduced, there are negative consequences for failing to support the changes.
- When management announces a strategic directive, the organization acts on it.
- Managers don't resist making changes when turf or control may be at stake, because the corporate goal always has priority over the goals of individuals.

Score each question:

1. Hardly at all
2. To a mild extent
3. To a moderate extent
4. To a great extent

Total each section's scores. Then list the total score for each section. A Sponsorship score of 9 or lower, a Culture score of 3 or lower, a Resistance score of 17 or lower, a Synergy score of 5 or lower, and an Organizational Issues score of 12 or lower means the organization should reconsider the time for an assessment.

High marks in the categories of Sponsorship and Culture are critical for conducting an assessment. The sponsor, whether it is the president, managing director, or general manager, must be willing to commit resources not only for an assessment but also for the follow-up improvement activities. Otherwise, the considerable expense of any assessment will be wasted.

Resistance, Synergy, and Organizational Culture are also critical criteria for initiating and implementing a process improvement program. If these areas are rated low, and Sponsorship and Culture are rated high enough to indicate that the time is right for an assessment, the organization would want the assessment team to look into these areas as well as the reference model. How entrenched is the organization in a "blame culture?" Are people afraid to tell the next level of management there is a problem? Is the process improvement effort considered completely distinct from the organization's business? Does it suffer when there is a choice? Do managers feel that process improvement is not their own but rather a developer's problem? Are the people leading the process improvement effort seen as necessary experts or as people without another job?

The organization can request that the assessment team suggest how the organization should proceed after the assessment.

Chapter 6

Planning and Preparing for an Assessment, Part 3:

Creating an Assessment Team. Selecting Projects to Be Assessed. Selecting People to Be Interviewed. Defining the Final Assessment Products. Distributing Questionnaires.

The next steps in preparing for an assessment involve sorting out who is on the assessment team and which people from which projects they will be interviewing. It is also necessary to define what the organization wants out of the assessment by enumerating a list of final assessment products. Then questionnaires are distributed if required.

The important parts of this stage of the assessment's preparation involve the following:

6.1 Selecting the assessment team

6.2 Selecting projects to be assessed

6.3 Selecting people to be interviewed

6.4 Defining final assessment products

6.5 Distributing questionnaires

6.1 Selecting the Assessment Team

When selecting the assessment team, the organization needs to take into account the knowledge, skills, and abilities of both the assessment team as a whole and of individual team members.

Being part of the assessment team is a full-time job during the training and onsite period. The team members must be freed from their daily work to perform these duties. They cannot be expected to attend project meetings, write documents, or travel, for example, during the assessment week.

6.1.1 How Big Should the Team Be?

An assessment team is a cohesive group of experienced individuals that assesses the process capability of an organization. The team as a whole must have the collective knowledge, skills, and ability to conduct the assessment for the organization. Team members are selected so that their combined experience and skills match what is required for a particular assessment. (All team members must have successfully completed assessment team training and CMM training for a CBA IPI or the SEI-licensed introduction to the CMMI course, delivered by an instructor who is authorized by the SEI.)

Teams usually consist of no fewer than four members including the Lead Assessor. For SCAMPI, the team should have no more than nine members, and for CBA IPI no more than 10. Smaller teams may have difficulty in performing extensive document review and in achieving accuracy in interviewing activities. Larger teams require a great deal of time and coordination in order to come to consensus on collective judgments.

A team of seven seems to work well for an average organization for most assessments. If the team is larger, interview sessions can be intimidating to the interviewees.

6.1.2 Insiders Versus Outsiders

Generally an assessment team contains members internal to the organization as well as members who are from other organizations in the division or other divisions in the company.

It is often useful to have some members from other parts of the division or other divisions in the company so that they can learn how their counterparts are performing their tasks. These "crossings" help break down barriers between divisions and bring different parts of a company together.

The most important part of the team, however, will consist of personnel from the organization being assessed who are not directly involved in the representative projects to be interviewed and therefore do not have vested interests in the results. (This means that no manager whose direct reports are to be interviewed in the assessment should be on the team.) For the assessment team to have organization-specific knowledge, local representatives must be on the team. It is also highly desirable for the sake of future developments that local representatives be present to pass on the larger view of the assessment. Later they will help the organization to internalize the assessment results and move forward with the improvement effort.

Insiders should represent different engineering disciplines and have knowledge of a number of projects. Both project managers and line managers should be included.

If an organization has trained its own Lead Assessors, it is important to have some of them on the team along with the outside Lead Assessor. This gives internal Lead Assessors an opportunity to work with and learn from other leads. It is also useful to have people who aspire to be Lead Assessors on the team.

Having insider project managers on the team who are not from one of the projects being assessed has long-term advantages.

Although they may not be intimately familiar with the assessment model, being on the team introduces them to best practices and helps them be better managers. Often, they emerge as new improvement advocates when the assessment is over.

Insider team members must satisfy certain criteria specified in the assessment method. They also should be highly respected opinion leaders who have experience in the areas being assessed and who can objectively collect assessment data and accurately reflect the results [Dunaway 01a].

When an assessment is over, the assessment team members will know more about the organization than any other individual, sometimes including the president. If team members are not from the organization, they disappear after the assessment, as does their accumulated knowledge.

6.1.3 Official CBA IPI and SCAMPI Team Member Selection Guidelines[1]

When selecting team members for assessments, the organization needs to consider their experience:

- **In the engineering field**—For a CBA IPI, the average experience for individual team members should be at least six years, with no team member having fewer than three years of software field experience. The team should have a minimum of 25 years of combined field experience. For a SCAMPI team, members may also need systems engineering experience. The SCAMPI team members as a group must have an average of at least six years of engineering field experience, and the team as a total must have 25 total years experience in each of the disciplines to be covered in the assessment.

- **In management**—For both the CBA IPI and SCAMPI, it is expected that the team as a group has a total of at least 10 years of management experience, and at least one team member must have at least six years of experience as a manager.

---

[1] [Dunaway 01c] and [Members of the AMIT 01].

- **In life-cycle phases and functional activities**—For a CBA IPI, 75% of the team members must have experience in at least one third of the organization's software life-cycle phases and their associated functional activities. One team member must have experience in a minimum of 80% of the organization's software life-cycle phases and associated activities. At least two team members must have had experience in each life-cycle activity. For SCAMPI, the team should in total have representative experience in the life cycles used within the organization. It is expected that for any given life-cycle phase, at least two members of the team should have experience as a practitioner.

- **In organizational environment, applications, and existing software processes**—At least one team member must be knowledgeable in both the organization's environment and application domain. Organization team members are important to the team; however, these team members must not have a vested interest in the assessment results.

- **In software process improvement concepts**—All team members must be knowledgeable in software process improvement concepts.

- **In the CMM and CMMI**—Each team member must have knowledge that includes the ability to explain the assigned KPAs or PAs and their intent and to provide examples relevant to the organization being assessed. The Lead Assessor will have knowledge of each of the KPAs and PAs in the reference model. The Lead Assessor functions as the assessment team's model authority.

- **In process assessment**—The Lead Assessor, being authorized as such, will have experience in conducting process assessments. Other team members with previous experience in conducting assessments will provide additional strength to the team. For a SCAMPI, it is desirable that at least half of the assessment team have previous assessment experience.

- **In team skills**—Each team member must have good written and oral communication skills, the ability to facilitate the free flow of information, and the ability to perform as team players and to negotiate consensus.

- **In credibility**—Each team member should have credibility with senior management, respect within the organization, and the ability to influence people.

- **In motivation and commitment**—Each team member must demonstrate the motivation to improve the software process, the commitment to act as change agents, and the willingness to do what it takes to achieve assessment goals.

6.1.4 Selecting Assessment Team Members: Sensitive Areas

Selecting assessment team members is a crucial decision that should not be made lightly. The CMM/CMMI assessments specify that team members should not be managers of one of the selected projects or be within the direct supervisory chain of any of the anticipated interviewees.

The idea here is that team members should not have a high personal stake in the outcome of the assessment. For an assessment to work properly, this needs to be followed in spirit as well as letter. The point of the exclusion is that people being interviewed may feel uncomfortable talking about problems in front of a manager responsible for their work. People who are intimately involved with managing an activity have a difficult time listening to outside critiques.

Team members who are in any way directly impacted by the outcome can be distracted by the potential consequences of their decisions. Objectivity and credibility of assessment results depends on the objectivity and credibility of the team. Biased teams produce biased assessment results.

Some organizations put process improvement managers (sometimes known as software engineering process group managers or SEPG managers) on the assessment team because they have been intimately involved in the improvements to date or will be intimately involved in the future. This, however, should be done with caution. Process improvement managers can provide substantial help in organizing an assessment. They may act, for example, as the senior manager's representative in planning the assessment. However, because of their role in the organization, process improvement managers sometimes have a difficult time maintaining objectivity. They have been heavily involved in the improvement process and can be defensive if projected improvements for some reason have not been sufficiently implemented. On the other hand, they are invaluable as interviewees.

On one assessment, the process improvement manager who had been on a previous assessment a year before and who was excellent at that time as a team member (he had not been assigned the role of PI manager yet) had asked not to be on the team for the second assessment because he wasn't sure he could be objective. Other team members were selected. However, at the start of the assessment, an assessed division's team member became ill and the PI manager needed to fill in. After the first day of the assessment, the PI manager argued about every point. He said people being interviewed didn't know what they were saying. At the beginning of the second day, the Lead Assessor spoke to the PI manager, explained what his behavior was doing to the assessment, and suggested that he decide if he could continue as a team member. By the end of the second day, the PI manager asked to be removed.

On another first-time CMMI assessment, the Lead Assessor allowed the process improvement manager, who incidentally was also the quality assurance manager and the configuration manager, to participate as a team member. It had been explained that this person was the driving force behind the process improvement program and had a realistic view of where the organization was. For most of the assessment, the process improvement manager came to consensus with the team on individual practices. However, on the next to last day of the assessment, after the draft findings but before the team was to rate the organization, the process improvement manager said he would not rate the organization at lower than Level 2. Nothing could be said to change his mind, even though this clearly was not indicated from the draft findings, for all PAs showed that there were a number of weaknesses, of which several were significant. The managing director was called in.

Another sensitive area concerns the appropriateness of having someone from the QA organization on the team. These people are sometimes overly invested in the outcome of the assessment, especially a follow-on assessment.

A number of QA departments are primarily set up to defend the organization during audits. An assessment is meant to have the organization take a hard and tough look at what the organization is not doing well. In-house auditors are often trained to put the organization in the best possible light, and such instincts are hard to break.

> During an assessment of Company R, problems occurred early when the quality assurance team members argued vehemently over every statement that, in their opinion, was not "positive." An organization can satisfy a PA /KPA even with weaknesses as long as the team does not consider the weaknesses significant, but the organization's quality assurance people resisted this strenuously, causing the team consolidation period to last at least twice as long as it should have.

On the other hand, QA personnel who are not defensive may be extremely useful on an assessment team because they have a deep knowledge of the organization's documents and processes.

> Two members of a team assessing Company Q were from the QA department. (One was the head of SEPG.) Both of them had been strong internal voices for improvement and were eager to present an accurate picture of the company's prospects to senior management. Not only did they not resist the assessment's analysis, but they also were able to offer invaluable information about not just how the company worked but also why it worked that way—not in a negative spirit but rather in order to facilitate the positive change that many people in the organization desired.

A last category of sensitive cases involves the temptation to select people as assessment team members because they are not busy. However, not being busy could mean not being interested, which is a strong indication that such a person should not be on the team.

6.2 Selecting Projects to Be Assessed

An assessment can realistically make an in-depth sampling of only three to five projects. However, it is possible to interview selected personnel from other projects to augment the in-depth part of the assessment. Projects being considered by the in-depth part of the assessment, however, must be represented at all the interview sessions. That is, after a project has been selected for an assessment, its project manager and all appropriate project members must be available to participate in interview sessions.

Selection of projects is critical to helping the organization move forward. The criteria involved for selecting representative projects include:

- Do they produce typical products?
- Are the processes they use representative?
- Do the projects represent a quality mix? (Some should represent the organization's best-managed projects, others should be average, and one project should represent a project that is or has been in trouble.)
- Are they important in the current and future business of the organization?
- Are they representative in terms of their product size, staff size, and project length? (Normally the projects selected should not have durations of fewer than six months. Selected projects should be at varying points in the life cycle, with emphasis on later stages.)
- What kind of application types and domains do they involve?
- What kinds of technology do they employ?

Assessed projects should represent the kind of business the organization has and expects to have in the future. Project selection should also take into account the impact of the project on the business in terms of revenue, profit, and strategic value. Factors to consider are not only the current business value but also future business value, size, and safety criticality. Looking at a project in a business area that is not strategic for the organization will not necessarily benefit the organization. It is better to include a project that represents the future direction of the organization because the assessment team can help the organization determine if the processes chosen will work on future projects.

Projects selected should be at different stages of their life cycles (or development) because the team needs to understand the processes used throughout development and have the project members think about whether they would use the same processes again or how they would improve those processes. A typical mix might include one project that has almost completed its development and is in the last stages of testing (or in the maintenance phase), a second project at the beginning of its life cycle in, say, system requirements or software requirements, and a third project in the middle of its life cycle. (A project at the beginning of its life cycle can be improved by learning positive and negative lessons from projects currently being assessed.)

The portion of the assessed organization represented by the projects (this may be calculated in terms of the number of projects assessed or by the number of staff involved in the projects assessed) affects the confidence of the assessment results.

6.2.1 Project Selection Matrix Checklist (See 5.2.5)

The following table provides a useful guide to help determine which projects should be selected for an assessment:

All Projects in Organization	<Project A>	<Project B>	<Project C>	<Project D>
Business Areas (type)	<details>	<details>	<details>	<details>
Age & Duration of Project <years/months>	<yrs/mos>	<yrs/mos>	<yrs/mos>	<yrs/mos>

All Projects in Organization	*\<Project A>*	*\<Project B>*	*\<Project C>*	*\<Project D>*
Present Life Cycle and Life-Cycle Phase (Bid Phase, Requirements Design, Code, Unit Test, System Test, Integration Acceptance, or Maintenance)	\<details>	\<details>	\<details>	\<details>
Current Business Value (determined by sponsor) High, Medium, or Low	\<H/M/L>	\<H/M/L>	\<H/M/L>	\<H/M/L>
Future Business Value (determined by sponsor) High, Medium, or Low	\<H/M/L>	\<H/M/L>	\<H/M/L>	\<H/M/L>
Project Team Size (denote full-time or part-time team members and indicate contractors) (Number of Project Staff, Systems, Engineers, Software Engineers, Test Engineers, etc.)	\<details>	\<details>	\<details>	\<details>
Development and Target Platforms (PC Workstation, Embedded)	\<details>	\<details>	\<details>	\<details>

(continued)

(continued)

All Projects in Organization	*<Project A>*	*<Project B>*	*<Project C>*	*<Project D>*
Size and Language of Product (e.g., Number of Req., Source Lines of Code [SLOCS], etc.)	<details>	<details>	<details>	<details>
Software Safety Criticality (Safety Significance)	<details>	<details>	<details>	<details>

6.3 Selecting People to Be Interviewed

The best assessments generally interview a large and diverse group of people. Those interviewed range from new hires, practitioners, and team leaders to middle managers and senior executives.

Some interviews are with individuals, and some are group interviews. Generally individual interviews are limited to project managers and the president of the organization. Most other interviews are done in groups.

For a CBA IPI, the whole team must be present at all first-time interviews. For a SCAMPI, this is desirable but not required.

6.3.1 Selecting People to Be Interviewed: Senior and Middle Management

Managers above the rank of project manager with some (but not direct) connection to the projects to be assessed are not technically required to be interviewed by the CBA IPI / SCAMPI rules, but interviewing them anyway is highly desirable because subsequent process improvement efforts depend on senior and middle managers' understanding of assessment results and on their sense of having been part of the assessment process. They are interviewed not to obtain technical information but rather to understand the context of the organization's operations and improvement efforts.

Examples of managers who might be interviewed are finance, human resources, contract, engineering, or program executives.

Senior managers should be interviewed in one group and middle managers in the other, and these interviews should take place near the end of the assessment so that they have a chance to discuss trends that have already been reported. (But a manager and his subordinate should not be interviewed together.)

It is recommended that a president, managing director, or general manager be interviewed individually.

6.3.2 Selecting People to Be Interviewed: Project Managers

Project managers from representative projects need to be interviewed. This means most obviously the managers of the projects that have been selected for in-depth evaluation, but others may be included as well.

The project manager of each project is interviewed separately. In no case should he or she be interviewed with subordinates.

Also it is important to interview those who function as project managers as well as those who actually have the title. On large, complex projects, the project manager may be removed from the day-to-day management of the development, and development responsibilities may be distributed between several lower-level managers, who must also be interviewed. In still other cases, it may be necessary to interview functional managers as well, such as the software manager, systems manager, configuration manager, test manager, quality assurance manager, and so on.

6.3.3 Selecting People to Be Interviewed: Technical Groups

Technical employees performing the same job on different projects should be interviewed together as a group. (It is also good to include some individuals from non-assessed projects.)

Generally each group interview should have four to six participants.

In planning for the assessment, it is best to include as many individuals involved in the chosen projects as possible in the appropriate interview sessions. As a result, more people will feel that they have been given a chance to have their say. Also the organization will get a broader and more objective view of what its employees perceive.

The side benefit of putting people from different projects together (e.g., requirements developers) is that they have a chance to learn how other projects in different parts of the organization are handling common issues.

When there is a possibility of interviewing more than one individual from a given project, the following criteria apply. Interviewees ideally should:

- Be practitioners, not managers or staff.
- Include opinion leaders.
- Have the interpersonal skills required to facilitate the free flow of information.
- Be representative of types of people in the organization.
- Not include any two individuals that have a reporting relationship.

6.3.4 Selecting People to Be Interviewed: A Checklist Matrix (See 5.2.5)

The following provides a useful guide to help determine which interviewees should be considered in an assessment:

	Projects/Business Areas				
Individuals and Groups to Be Interviewed	*<Project A>*	*<Project B>*	*<Project C>*	*<Project D>*	*<Other, Sampled Projects>*
Project Managers	< name>	< name>	< name>	< name>	< name>
Software Managers	< name>	< name>	< name>	< name>	< name>
System Managers	< name>	< name>	< name>	< name>	< name>
Group 1 Team Leads (System and Software)	< name>	< name>	< name>	< name>	< name>
Group 2 Requirements (System and Software)	< names>	< names>	< names>	< names>	< names>
Group 3 Architects	< names>	< names>	< names>	< names>	< names>
Group 4 Detailed Design (System and S/W Engineers)	< names>	< names>	< names>	< names>	< names>
Group 5 Implementation	< names>	< names>	< names>	< names>	< names>
Group 6 Testing (System, Software, Integration, and Acceptance Test Engineers)	< names>	< names>	< names>	< names>	< names>

(continued)

(continued)

Individuals and Groups to Be Interviewed	Projects/Business Areas				
	<Project A>	<Project B>	<Project C>	<Project D>	<Other, Sampled Projects>
Group 7 Configuration Management (System and Software)	< names>	< names>	< names>	< names>	< names>
Group 9 Quality Assurance (System and Software)	< names>	< names>	< names>	< names>	< names>
Group 10 Causal Analysis Team	< names>	< names>	< names>	< names>	< names>
Group 11 (Engineering Process Group— System and Software)	<names>				
Group 12 Middle Management (e.g., Program Directors, etc.)	<names>				
Group 13 Executive Management (e.g., Vice Presidents)	<names>				
President	<names>				

6.4 Defining Final Assessment Products

Different assessments have different final products. Some, for example, will end with a maturity rating for the organization, while others will not. Such decisions must be made early in the assessment planning, and they will result from discussions between the Lead Assessor, the assessment sponsor, and possibly the senior executive.

For a CBA IPI, final products include all or some of the following:

- Final findings presentation (required)
- Confidence report (verbal or written)
- Recommendations briefing (optional)
- Final report (optional)
- PAIS report to the SEI (required)
- Assessment data (optional)
- Assessment plan and schedule (required)
- Feedback forms (required) for sponsor, Lead Assessor, and team member
- Requirements checklist (required)

For a SCAMPI, the products required to be delivered by the assessment team are:

- A final findings presentation, which transmits to the sponsor:
  - Final findings, including statement of strengths and weaknesses documented by the team for every PA investigated (similar to CBA IPI)
  - All ratings planned for and generated by the team
- A copy of the plan's section on "assessment input"
- Assessment disclosure statement (to the SEI)
- PAIS report (to the SEI)

The following final products are optional but may be requested by the organization:

- Maturity level and/or capability level ratings
- PA satisfaction/capability profiles

- Practice ratings
- An option to use "partially satisfied" as a rating assigned to a PA
- 15504 process profile
- Discipline-specific ratings (e.g., systems engineering or software engineering)
- Project-level findings or ratings
- Assessment final report
- Recommendation for taking action upon the assessed results
- Process improvement action plan

For an SCE, only an assessment plan and schedule and the final findings briefing are required to be delivered to the assessment sponsor.

After the final products are delivered, the assessment sponsor officially owns the assessment results and can disclose them (or not) at his or her discretion.

6.5 Distributing Questionnaires

In the past, software process assessments always began with the distribution of a maturity questionnaire. Recognizing their deficiencies, today's assessment methodologies use them not as the basis of the assessment but rather primarily to identify issues to be explored further during the onsite period and to be corroborated through document review and interviews. (In SCAMPI, questionnaires are optional. If a SCAMPI questionnaire is to be used, that fact needs to be identified in the SCAMPI Data Collection Plan.)

The CBA IPI maturity questionnaire is required to be distributed to participants before the start of an assessment [Zubrow 94]. As it includes a glossary of terms and KPA descriptions, the questionnaire partly serves as an aide to CMM terminology. It covers all 18 KPAs of the CMM, addressing each KPA goal in the CMM but not all of the key practices. Limited to six to eight questions per KPA, the questionnaire can usually be completed in one hour.

The use of questionnaires to gather written information from members of the organization represents a relatively low-cost way to collect data when done well. Questionnaires typically require yes or no answers. (Respondents are given an opportunity to comment if they wish.)

Questionnaire data, however, may be problematic. Because the questionnaire has specific CMM language in it, those who fill out the questionnaires sometimes don't understand the questions. The questionnaire therefore needs to be administered by someone familiar with the model in case explanations are needed.

When the team evaluates questionnaire responses about whether a particular process is or is not present, a determination needs to be made as to whether the respondent has understood what he has been asked. The team should also consider whether the respondent has answered yes to something merely because he thinks that a loyal response is better than a truthful one.

It is the task of the organization site coordinator to summarize the responses to a given question on the questionnaire. Such summaries give the team a quick overview of what respondents think are the company's strengths and weaknesses, but they should be treated by the team with some skepticism because of the difficulties just described. Answers to questionnaires are most useful in preparing interview questions about specific technical areas.

The widespread distribution of questionnaires may be more trouble than it is worth. It is recommended that the questionnaire be filled out by four to ten people—ideally by each participating project manager. In addition, key technical personnel or functional managers for the organization may be asked to fill out the questionnaire as well.

Whenever possible, the organization site coordinator should collect the documents mentioned in questionnaire responses so that the team can review them early in the process.

6.5.1 Specimen Section of the CBA IPI Maturity Questionnaire (Section for the Requirements Management KPA)

Maturity Questionnaire (version 1.1.0) Page 1 of 42
[Zubrow 94]

Software Process Maturity Questionnaire

Capability Maturity Model, version 1.1
April 1994

This document contains questions about the implementation of important software practices in your software organization. The questions are organized in groups of key process areas such as software project planning and software configuration management. A short paragraph describing each key process area precedes each group of questions. Unless directed otherwise by the person who administers this questionnaire, please answer the questions based on your knowledge and experience in your current project. To help us better interpret your answers to the questions about software process in your organization, this document begins with questions about your own background in software work.

Please read and answer all of the questions. If you wish to comment on any questions or qualify your answers, please use the comment spaces provided. Your answers will be held in strict confidence by the appraisal team. Specific answers will not be identified within your organization, nor in any other manner. Your name will be used for administrative purposes only: to guide the appraisal team during response analysis and help them contact you for any needed clarifications.

Thank you for your help.
Software Engineering Institute
Carnegie Mellon University
Pittsburgh, Pennsylvania

Page 2 of 42 **Maturity Questionnaire (version 1.1.0)**
2 CMU/SEI-94-SR-7

Filling in Your Answers
Definitions of Terms
Respondent Identification
(Please specify)

YOUR NAME:
TODAY'S DATE:
PROJECT NAME:
WORK TELEPHONE:

We will be using optical scanning technology to enter your answers, so please print or write neatly throughout the questionnaire.

- Feel free to use the margins if you need more space for your written answers or other comments, but please don't write over the check boxes or crosshair (+) symbols.
- Please keep your marks within the check boxes. Any mark will do: ✓
- You should use a pen with dark blue or black ink.

The Capability Maturity Model on which this Maturity Questionnaire is based uses a number of terms which may be used differently in your organization.

- **Organizational terms** are defined on the blue placard. You may wish to review it now, and refer to it as necessary as you complete the questionnaire.
- **Technical terms** are defined on the pages where they are used.

CMU/SEI-94-SR-7 3
Maturity Questionnaire (version 1.1.0) Page 3 of 42

Section I Respondent Background

1 Which best describes your current position? *(Please mark as many boxes as apply)*

PROJECT OR TEAM LEADER MANAGER
TECHNICAL MEMBER SOFTWARE ENGINEERING PROCESS
GROUP (SEPG) MEMBER
OTHER (Please specify)

2 On what activities do you currently work? *(Please mark as many boxes as apply)*

SOFTWARE REQUIREMENTS SOFTWARE QUALITY ASSURANCE
SOFTWARE DESIGN CONFIGURATION MANAGEMENT
CODE AND UNIT TEST SOFTWARE PROCESS IMPROVEMENT
TEST AND INTEGRATION OTHER (Please specify)

3 Have you received any CMM-related training? NO YES *(Please describe)*

4 What is your software experience in: *(Please specify for each category)*

Your present organization? .... YEARS
Your overall software experience? .... YEARS

5 Have you participated in previous forms of Software Process Assessments, Software Capability Evaluations, and/or other forms of software process appraisals? *(Please mark one box)*

NO
YES How many? *(Please specify for each category)*

OF SPAs (Software Process Assessments)
OF SCEs (Software Capability Evaluations)

OF OTHER SEI-BASED METHODS (*Please describe briefly: e.g., mini-assessments or instant profiles*)
BASED ON NON-SEI PROCESS IMPROVEMENT WORK
(*Please describe briefly:* e.g., ISO 9000/9001 audit)

Page 4 of 42 Maturity Questionnaire (version 1.1.0)
4 CMU/SEI-94-SR-7

Section II Software Practices
Instructions

1 To the right of each question there are boxes for the four possible responses:
Yes, No, Does Not Apply, and **Don't Know**.

Check **Yes** when:

• The practice is well established and consistently performed.

- The practice should be performed nearly always in order to be considered well-established and consistently performed as a standard operating procedure.

Check **No** when:

• The practice is not well established or is inconsistently performed.

- The practice may be performed sometimes, or even frequently, but it is omitted under difficult circumstances.

Check **Does Not Apply** when:

• You have the required knowledge about the project or organization and the question asked, but you feel the question does not apply to the project.

- For example, the entire section on "Software Subcontract Management" may not apply to the project if you don't work with any subcontractors.

Check **Don't Know** when:

• You are uncertain about how to answer the question.

2 Use the **Comments** spaces for any elaborations or qualifications about your answers to the questions.

3 Check one of the boxes for each question. Please answer all of the questions.

• This Page Intentionally Left Blank •

CMU/SEI-94-SR-7 5
Maturity Questionnaire (version 1.1.0) Page 5 of 42

Page 6 of 42 **Maturity Questionnaire (version 1.1.0)**
6 CMU/SEI-94-SR-7

The purpose of **Requirements Management** is to establish a common understanding between the customer and the software project of the customer's requirements that will be addressed by the software project. Requirements Management involves establishing and maintaining an agreement with the customer on the requirements for the software project. The agreement covers both the technical and non-technical (e.g., delivery dates) requirements. The agreement forms the basis for estimating, planning, performing, and tracking the software project's activities throughout the software life cycle. Whenever the system requirements allocated to software are changed, the affected software plans, work products, and activities are adjusted to remain consistent with the updated requirements. **allocated requirements** (system requirements allocated to software)—The subset of the system requirements that are to be implemented in the software components of the system. The allocated requirements are a primary input to the software development plan. Software requirements analysis elaborates and refines the allocated requirements and results in software requirements that are documented.

policy—A guiding principle, typically established by senior management, which is adopted by an organization or project to influence and determine decisions.

software plans—The collection of plans, both formal and informal, used to express how software development and/or maintenance activities will be performed. Examples of plans that could be included:
software development plan, software quality assurance plan, software configuration management plan, software test plan, risk management plan, and process improvement plan.

software quality assurance (SQA)—(1) A planned and systematic pattern of all actions necessary to provide adequate confidence that a software work product conforms to established technical requirements.
(2) A set of activities designed to evaluate the process by which software work products are developed and/or maintained.

software work product—Any artifact created as part of defining, maintaining, or using a software process, including process descriptions, plans, procedures, computer programs, and associated documentation, which may or may not be intended for delivery to a customer or end user.
Does Not Apply
Don't Know
Yes
No

1 Are system requirements allocated to software used to establish a baseline for software engineering and management use?............

Comments:

2 As the systems requirements allocated to software change, are the necessary adjustments to software plans, work products, and activities made? ....

Comments:
Does Not Apply
Don't Know
Yes
No

CMU/SEI-94-SR-7 7
Maturity Questionnaire (version 1.1.0) Page 7 of 42

3 Does the project follow a written organizational policy for managing the system requirements allocated to software?

Comments:

4 Are the people in the project who are charged with managing the allocated requirements trained in the procedures for managing allocated requirements?
....

Comments:

5 Are measurements used to determine the status of the activities performed for managing the allocated requirements (e.g., total number of requirements changes that are proposed, open, approved, and incorporated into the baseline)? ....

Comments:

6 Are the activities for managing allocated requirements on the project subjected to SQA review? ....

Comments:

Page 8 of 42 **Maturity Questionnaire (version 1.1.0)**
8 CMU/SEI-94-SR-7

Chapter 7

Planning and Preparing for an Assessment, Part 4:

Assessment Team Training and Post-Training Activities

The last phases of preparation before an assessment actually begins have to do with the assessment team's training, its pre-onsite activities (reviewing documents and other kinds of material evidence, formulating interview questions and a data collection plan), and briefing the organization participants about the upcoming assessment.

The important parts of this stage of the assessment's preparation involve the following:

7.1 Assessment team training

7.2 The assessment team's pre-onsite organization and activities

- Delegating team member responsibilities
- Establishing teamwork guidelines

- Reviewing documents
- Reviewing other kinds of material evidence
- Formulating interview questions
- Developing a data collection plan

7.3 Briefing organization participants

7.1 Assessment Team Training

Assessment team members must have training in the CMM or the CMMI model and in the CBA IPI or SCAMPI assessment method. They must also be briefed about the particulars of their assessment's goals and objectives, the status of the ongoing assessment plan, and the Lead Assessor's plans for managing the assessment.

7.1.1 The Lead Assessor's Team Training and Leadership Responsibilities

The Lead Assessor is responsible for training team members in the logic and the sequence of the assessment process. Team members must already be familiar with the reference model (CMM or CMMI). The Lead Assessor needs to confirm this and then instruct the team in the assessment's norms, goals, and objectives, the assessment methodology (CBA IPI or SCAMPI), the particulars of the assessment plan, techniques for managing organizational data, and the tools and techniques to be used during the assessment.

The Lead Assessor not only briefs team members but also conducts team building. He or she should initiate a program of exercises intended to develop facilitation skills and create team unity.

Above all, the Lead Assessor must inculcate in all team members the importance of observing strict rules for confidentiality, protecting proprietary or sensitive data, and making sure that statements are never attributed to specific participants. A nondisclosure statement or confidentiality agreement is often used to formalize these understandings. (This agreement is discussed in Chapter 5, "Planning and Preparing for an Assessment, Part 2," which also provides a specimen agreement.)

7.1.2 Training the Assessment Team in the Reference Model

For a CBA IPI or SCAMPI, prior to assessment team training, team members need to have received training in the CMM or the CMMI model. These models are central to the assessment process, and it is difficult to understand the assessment methodology without understanding the model upon which it is based.

The SEI requires that team members on a CBA IPI assessment either take the official SEI-licensed Introduction to the CMM course (a three-day course teaching the basics of the CMM model), take an equivalent commercial CMM training course, or be trained by the Lead Assessor using an SEI-provided CD-based CMM course.[1] For a SCAMPI, the SEI requires that

---

[1.] **CMM Waiver Guidelines**

At the discretion of the Lead Assessor, an assessment team member might be waived from taking CMM training prior to serving on an assessment team if the team member can document that they have taken training that is at least equivalent to the three-day SEI Introduction to CMM course and that covers the following topics:

1. CMM Concepts and Terminology: Understand and be able to explain fundamental concepts such as:
   - Process, capability, and maturity
   - Process management
   - Process change
   - Capability versus performance
2. CMM Structure: Explain how the CMM is structured and be able to use that structure:
   - The five maturity levels and the key process areas associated with each level
   - The purpose of and terminology associated with each key process area (e.g., requirements management, SQA, organization standard software process, organization process database, process performance baseline)
   - The common features of the CMM
3. Applying the CMM: Be able to apply the CMM with intelligence:
   - Interpret the key practices in different contexts
   - Identify immature and mature software organizations
   - Explain why the organization cannot skip maturity levels
   - Identify, locate, and explain some of the common themes that run throughout the CMM
   - Locate information in the CMM
4. Benefits from use of the CMM: Relate the benefits of improvement to the value of the CMM:
   - Return of investment for software process improvement
   - Impact on quality and productivity
   - Impact on cost and schedule
5. Ownership and plans for the CMM: Explain the SEI's role in CMM evolution and related work:
   - Who owns the CMM
   - Related maturity modeling work going on at the SEI
   - Related standards work

[Dunaway 01c]

team members receive CMMI model training solely via the SEI-licensed Introduction to CMMI course, delivered by an SEI-authorized instructor.

The Lead Assessor is responsible for ensuring that each team member's understanding of the CMM or CMMI model is up to date and for requiring team members to take additional instruction if necessary.

On Level 4 or Level 5 assessments, team members must also be familiar with advanced topics, such as statistical process control.

7.1.3 Training the Team in the CBA IPI and SCAMPI Assessment Methodologies

As part of their SEI authorization, Lead Assessors are taught how to train an assessment team and conduct associated team building. The Lead Assessor walks the assessment team through every step of the assessment process and explains the

---

[2.] If one or more team members have had assessment experience and have received CBA IPI Team Training within the past six months, they can be waived from all or part of the team training at the Lead Assessor's discretion.

[3.] Team training delivered to groups of potential future team members covers the complete set of tailoring options and allowable variations for the method to prepare them for a range of situations they are likely to encounter on future assessments.

SCAMPI assessment team training materials should be tailored to fit team needs and objectives of the assessment. Tailoring provides opportunities to:
- Provide insight into the context, objectives, and plans of the particular assessment
- Communicate team members' assigned roles and responsibilities
- Identify tailoring of SCAMPI for the upcoming assessment
- Acquaint the team with the organization characteristics and documentation
- Focus on skills that may be more critical to the upcoming assessment, such as the ability to facilitate interviews or the ability to identify alternative practices

SCAMPI team training must be provided within 60 days of the assessment. The Lead Assessor typically provides method training. Regardless of how method training is delivered to the team members, opportunities for team building should be provided to bring the team together and up to speed on the specifics of the assessment planned.

SCAMPI team training and team building provide good opportunities to establish team familiarity with the assessment plan. This includes such items as assessment objectives, organizational scope, reference model scope, and the schedule, resources and constraints for conducting the assessment. Team member input can be obtained to refine or complete the contents of the assessment plan.

team's duties and how they are to be performed. Training includes instruction in what kinds of questions to ask and how to ask them, the scheduling of practice interviews, data-consolidation exercises, and so on.

Team training usually takes two and a half to three days and emphasizes situations that are likely to be encountered by team members. (With an experienced team, less time may be required.) CBA IPI and SCAMPI team training are both usually provided at the beginning of a specific assessment.[2] However, the SEI allows SCAMPI training to be taken in one of two ways, in no case earlier than 60 days before the start of the assessment:

- Team training specific to the assessment
- Team training delivered to a large group of potential future team members who are not currently engaged in an assessment[3]

Analysis of the objective evidence provided by the assessed organization, such as questionnaires, responses, or worksheets summarizing objective evidence, can follow or can be part of assessment team preparation and training.

Team members will become familiar with the instruments to be used during the assessment (e.g., questionnaires, process implementation indicators [PII] database). Exercises using the data collection tools and methods planned for the assessment should be used to provide assessment team members with an opportunity to practice techniques for data recording, verification, and analysis. This may include mechanisms such as wall charts, spreadsheets, or data reduction tools. The more familiar and comfortable the team is with these tools before the assessment, the easier the assessment will be.

The SEI Appraiser Program specifies additional requirements about delivering training to people who are not already members of an assessment team.

Team members who have participated in previous assessments are not automatically qualified to participate on subsequent ones without first attending SCAMPI team training. In such cases, the Lead Assessor is required to understand the nature of the training delivered previously and the adequacy of that training for the assessment at hand. This requires that the previous assessment be compared with the planned assessment. For example, if the team member assessment focused only on software engineering, using the continuous representation, and the planned assessment is focused on SE/SW/IPPD using a staged representation, there may be some important new concepts to cover.

[Members of the AMIT 01]

There are significant advantages to having all members of an assessment team undergo team training together. Team training offers significant opportunities for team building. Also, team training courses can be tailored for the particular assessments.[4] If the training of some team members is waived because they have had prior assessment experience, other team activities should be scheduled for team-building purposes and to bring the team up to speed on the specifics of the particular assessment being planned. At a minimum, there must be at least one event where the team gathers as a group for the purpose of establishing team norms and operational decisions about how the team will work for the upcoming assessment [Members of the AMIT 01].

Some organizations have established a capability to perform assessments with very limited preparation effort through the use of a pool of trained assessment team members. Drawing from an established group of experts who are accustomed to working together clearly provides a savings over time for organizations that conduct frequent assessments.

Team training provides a time to review the assessment plan with team members. They should be sent the plan in advance of their arrival so that they can think about their roles.

---

[4] **Tailoring CBA IPI Team Training**
When training is provided to an assessment team for the purpose of performing a particular assessment or series of assessments, the Lead Assessor will tailor the training to the team's needs. Modifying the team training exercises is the primary tailoring technique. Some exercises might even include data that relates specifically to the organization being assessed, although a separation of training material and actual assessment data collection must be maintained.
    In tailoring team training, the Lead Assessor uses training to:
    - Provide insight into the context, goals, and plans of the organization's assessment that the team will undertake.
    - Assign team member roles and responsibilities in the upcoming assessment process.
    - Identify the manner in which the Lead Assessor has tailored the CBA IPI assessment method for the upcoming assessment.
    - Acquaint the team with the assessed organization's characteristics and documentation.
    - Focus on skills that have a greater criticality in the upcoming assessment (such as the ability to facilitate group interviews or the ability to identify alternatives to CMM key practices that satisfy KPA goals).
Many teams have found it useful to follow team training in the same week with examination of questionnaire responses, initial document review, and scripting of interview questions.

[Dunaway 01c]

Experienced teams usually use the early stages of training to assess the organization's readiness for the assessment and to validate the reasonableness of assessment estimates. Where organizational artifacts such as procedures, plans, and so on exist, they should be used in the training. Just-in-time training can also be used at appropriate points in the assessment process to re-emphasize method concepts.

During team training, it is useful to arrange an interview with a project manager whose project is not expected to be selected for the assessment. In theory this is a practice interview, but as all projects reflect the organization's management practices, the interview also contributes real information.

For most assessment teams, the first interview is the most difficult, partly because the team is not used to working together and partly because the team doesn't know what to expect from the organization personnel. Will they be overly chatty or try to not answer the questions? Will they only answer the questions they are asked? This practice session shows the team what to expect during actual assessment interviews.

The risks of too little assessment team training are obvious. Consider Organization X, which requested a Level 3 assessment after several years of preparation. The organization had never experienced an assessment. During the assessment, although it became clear that the organization had fulfilled a few Level 3 goals, real concerns surfaced concerning many Level 2 areas. In the consolidation period, the team attempted to identify interview responses to help it demonstrate the performance of necessary Level 2 and Level 3 activities. Much arguing ensued. At that point, it became clear that not all team members understood what Level 2 or Level 3 were about. It was therefore necessary for the Lead Assessor (starting at 10:00 p.m.) to conduct an on-the-spot tutorial about the CMMI. In the end, the organization was rated at Level 1. Better pre-assessment training would not only have cut down on the stress of the assessment but also might have helped the organization to schedule a more appropriate assessment in the first place.

7.1.4 Topics Covered During an Assessment Team Training Course

The following gives an overview of the topics covered during an ordinary sequence of team training:

> Introduction
>
> Assessment Overview
>
> Team Development
>
> Pre Onsite Assessment Activities
>
> Onsite Assessment Activities
>
> - Part 1: Opening Meeting
> - Part 2: Interviews (Individual and Groups)
> - Practice Interview
> - Part 3: Review of Objective Evidence
> - Part 4: Prepare and Present Draft Findings
> - Part 5: Rate and Prepare Final Findings
> - Part 6: Present Final Findings, Wrap-Up, and Next Steps

7.1.5 Assessment Team Training: Team Building

Team members can be competent in performing assessment activities as individuals, but if they fail to work together as a team, the assessment will fall apart. The Lead Assessor must therefore foster crucial non-technical team skills, including communication, negotiation, collaboration, and conflict resolution. In part, this is a question of managing the allocation of responsibilities.[5]

[5.] **Planning for Team Member Roles During an Assessment**
The Lead Assessor assigns and explains team member roles and responsibilities to be performed during the assessment. Typical assessment roles include:
- **Organization Site Coordinator**—The organization site coordinator handles on-site logistics and provides technical, administrative, and logistical support to the Lead Assessor. This usually includes activities such as coordinating schedules, notifying participants, arranging adequate facilities and resources, obtaining requested

Teams whose members have not previously worked together will usually need to spend significant time on team development. The process does not stop with training, however. The team must explicitly focus on its working relationship during preparation and then learn to sharpen those skills during the first set of assessment activities. The investment will pay off during the onsite assessment's aggressive schedule. Although the Lead Assessor is expected to facilitate team-building activities, all members at some level should share this responsibility.

A team where the majority of members have worked together previously on an assessment will need to review the ground rules and work to incorporate new team members.

Team dynamics can change dramatically with small alterations. When one member of the team is changed, even if all other members remain the same, the entire working relation of the team can change. If team members are working well, a new team member can feel like an outsider, so extra effort needs to be made to incorporate that person into the team.

documentation, and arranging catering. The OSC coordinates or provides clerical support to the team. This role is often assigned to one or more members of the organization. The OSC may be one of the team members, or this role may be assigned to other site personnel (see Chapter 5).
- **Librarian**—The librarian manages the inventory of the documents provided for the assessment, coordinates requests for additional documentation, and returns documents at the end of the assessment.
- **Mini-Teams**—Mini-teams take the lead for data collection in assigned Process Areas (or KPAs). They ensure that information collected during a data gathering session covers their PAs or KPAs, request additional information needed relative to their PAs or KPAs, and record the work performed by individual assessment team members in their PA or KPA area.

   Mini-teams typically consist of two or three members. Mini-team assignments can be made based on several factors, including:
   - Related PAs or KPAs (e.g., PA categories)
   - Composition mix of mini-team members (e.g., discipline experience, assessment experience)
- **Facilitator**—The facilitator conducts interviews, asking questions of interview participants or facilitates other team members asking questions.
- **Timekeeper**—The timekeeper is responsible for tracking time and keeping the Lead Assessor informed of possible schedule constraints during interviews and other activities.
- **Observer**—Due to the confidentiality required during an assessment and the cohesiveness needed to participate in assessment activities, observers are not permitted to participate in the assessment. The only exception is an observer who is authorized by the SEI to observe a candidate Lead Assessor's performance as Lead Assessor or to perform an audit as part of the quality audit function of the SEI.

[Members of the AMIT 01]

Team Partnership: Sensitive Areas

A number of horrors can result if the Lead Assessor and team members are not working well together and do not realize it. One of the biggest issues has to do with that moment at the end of an assessment when teams must come to consensus about whether PAs/KPAs are satisfied. A team that remains at logger-heads at this point usually indicates one of two things—either the team has not collected enough data during the course of the assessment, or it has not sufficiently discussed problematic issues during the daily consolidation periods. A team must be aware of potential disagreements during the assessment and be able to express and work them through *before the ratings session.*

Some team members will be naturally shy or hesitant to bring up problems. However, they must learn to bring out their concerns early instead of waiting until time has grown very short.

Another kind of problem is team members who believe they know it all and try to dominate discussions and even interviews. This tactic intimidates the rest of the team, and in the short run, the dominant person seems to get his way. However, these circumstances almost invariably lead the team as a whole to feel that it has not come to consensus. Even if the dominant member wins the day during ratings, after the assessment is over, the other team members may complain publicly that they do not agree with the results of the assessment. *Assessments are about building a consensus about real problems and a collective will to solve them. No one wins if an artificially high (or low) rating is imposed by one individual.*

7.2 The Assessment Team's Pre-Onsite Organization and Activities

7.2.1 Managing and Facilitating Responsibilities for the Tasks Ahead

Even after the team has been assembled and trained, the Lead Assessor remains accountable for ensuring that its processes remain on track.

As team manager, the Lead Assessor assigns and helps negoti-ate roles and responsibilities for various assessment activities.

Ideally, team members make these decisions collectively, including who will monitor which KPA or PA, who will ask which question, how the consolidation time will be organized, and so on. When the team reaches an impasse, however, or when no one agrees to take on a particular task, it is the role of the Lead Assessor to take responsibility for seeing that a decision is reached.[6]

The Lead Assessor also serves as team facilitator and addresses the processes by which the team works together to perform the

---

[6] **Team Management Skills**
The following seven areas are the cores of team management skills.
- **Planning**—Mapping out the sequence of activities and their interdependencies is a key skill for managing the assessment method. Planning is much more than scheduling because it involves being able to estimate with some confidence all resources required, and to identify, coordinate, and negotiate with key stakeholders.
- **Decision-Making**—The team needs to identify and agree to both a set of decision rules and a process for arriving at decisions that is consistent wit the purpose of the assessment and the needs of the team. While the recommended decision-making strategy during the assessment is consensus, the team needs to consider what latitude rests with the Lead Assessor in making a decision when the team is either unavailable or is at an impasse and refuses to negotiate.
- **Ground Rules**—The team needs to create a set of ground rules for how it will work together. Although certain ground rules are implicit in the assessment method (e.g., confidentiality and consensus), it is important that the team explicitly agree to guidelines for what they expect from one another and how they will handle various situations that may arise.
- **Communication**—Communication has two components: sending and receiving. The team is expected to provide high-quality written and oral communication during the assessment, adhering to the principle of neutral (i.e., non-judgemental) feedback. The team is also expected to listen carefully to participants and to control their own biases as much as possible so that it can hear and understand the participants' perspectives.
- **Collaboration**—The assessment method places a high value on recognizing that each team member and each participant has expertise to share. You can enact this by conducting all meetings as peer activities and giving multiple opportunities for team members and participants to provide input. Within the context of this value, however, some boundaries need to be set in the interest of time, especially during the closed team meetings. Although guidance is provided, the team needs to identify where it needs to collaborate and where it is appropriate for team members to work independently.
- **Negotiation**—The assessment method involves a large number of people and activities that require careful coordination. Line managers, participant, and the assessment team all must understand and agree to the schedule, the resources committed, and their roles and responsibilities so that the assessment is conducted effectively. The Lead Assessor has dual responsibility for securing those agreements as well as being explicit about his or her needs during the assessment.
- **Conflict Resolution**—Each team member brings a unique perspective and set of experiences to the assessment activities, which by definition creates the potential for conflict. These different perspectives should be welcomed because they offer a more complete picture of a situation. The problems arise when differences harden into non-negotiable positions or when they are perceived as personal attacks.

[Dunaway 01c]

assessment. Effective performance is based on a shared understanding of and commitment to the ground rules and a shared commitment to the neutrality of the outcome. These issues are initially covered in the team building sessions during assessment team training, but they need reinforcement starting from the first activities of the assessment.

Facilitation keeps the team focused on the desired outcome of each assessment activity, especially when situations arise that divert the team from its expected course.

Teams often find that designating an individual to act as process facilitator keeps them focused on working together effectively, especially under the stress of the late hours and frequent deadlines that are part of the assessment onsite period. This role may be traded off throughout the assessment so that it does not become a burdensome addition to the responsibilities of team members.

In the final analysis, though, the Lead Assessor must be the ultimate arbiter. When there is conflict between two or more team members, the Lead Assessor is responsible for sorting it out. (It is quite common in fact to have situations where two team members cannot get along—one will always disagree with whatever the other says.)

The Lead Assessor must also continually monitor confusion about what the assessment is trying to accomplish or differing expectations about how an activity has been or will be conducted. Many of these confusions are based on misunderstanding the model, and they lead to arguments about what the model says (or should say). The Lead Assessor, as the facilitator, must anticipate these situations and negotiate a way through them, in part by on-the-spot instruction about the model.

The Lead Assessor needs to watch carefully for differences that can escalate into conflict and raise them in team discussions. (It may be helpful to establish ground rules for this early.) Focusing on objective data rather than on opinions, inferences, and conclusions is a good way to turn an argument into a discussion.

To the extent that team members keep focused on assessment principles, the risk that conflicts will sidetrack the team or split it into factions will be lessened.

7.2.2 The Assessment Team Examines
Questionnaire Responses

The bulk of the assessment team's pre-onsite work is to examine the responses to questionnaires, review collected documents, and prepare for the upcoming interviews by scripting
questions and becoming experts on appropriate parts of the
model.

Questionnaires are now used only for CBA IPIs. When examining the responses, each team member:

- Makes notes of any response patterns that are significant.
- Highlights any comments that are judged to be relevant.
- Makes note of any comments alluding to documents or
  other potential sources of information.
- Makes summary notes about his area of responsibility.

The Lead Assessor conducts a brainstorm session for each area:

- The mini-teams take notes on the information brought out
  in the session.
- Mini-teams consolidate information for the areas they are
  assigned.
- The whole team reviews what information is still needed.

7.2.3 The Assessment Team Begins to
Review Documents

The Lead Assessor and the assessment team should now begin
to review documents. Document review constitutes one of the
principal efforts undertaken during the assessment, and the
techniques and criteria used by the team will be considered in
depth in Chapter 8, "Onsite Activities, Part 1 (which is the first
chapter devoted to significant onsite assessment activities). For
present purposes, it is important to emphasize how the Lead
Assessor and the team cooperate with the organization to
assemble the documents to be reviewed, whether they are
reviewed before or during the onsite assessment proper.

By the time the team has been assembled, the organization
needs to have collected a "library" of documents to be used as

evidence of the model practices it believes it has implemented. The Lead Assessor will have specified a particular format or level of detail needed for these documents, which are particularly important for a SCAMPI assessment, where documents carry more weight than they do for a CBA IPI.

The "library" of documents that the organization supplies may take the form of hard copy or electronic copy. The organization does not need to make copies of the documents but can loan them to the team. The organization should remember that the documents will continue to remain available when the assessment team is not using them. (The documents will remain in the team workspace until after the assessment is completed.)

Company confidential or proprietary information requires care. In general, all team members not from the assessed organization need to complete non-disclosure agreements prior to the assessment. However, at least one person on the team must be able to review the classified information.

Someone from the organization (sometimes the organization site coordinator) is designated the team's "librarian." This person is responsible for compiling not only the documents but also a master document index, which comprises the assessment's initial document inventory—its initial data set. The index contains a list of documents and also refers to related documents and to personnel who can provide relevant information. (Some organizations experienced in process improvement may already have collected this type of data to track their own progress.) A document index refers to all development and management activities both from the central organization and from each project to be assessed. The Lead Assessor may wish to verify the document inventory in advance, prior to the assessment team's arrival.[7]

---

[7] **The SCAMPI Instruments Used During an Assessment**
Although SCAMPI does not require the SEI questionnaire, it does allow and encourage any instruments (e.g., surveys, questionnaires, or an objective evidence database) that help the organization characterize their process and support showing how the organization has put CMMI model practices in place. There is no need to provide the same information in two or more formats; one will do.

[Members of the AMIT 01]

The team's librarian is responsible for explaining how the documents (hard copies, soft copies, or web hyperlinks) have been indexed and arranged. The librarian briefs the team about the organization's library management procedures during the initial team meeting.

The documents typically compiled and reviewed by the assessment team include:

- Organization policies mentioned in the model used
- High-level standard procedures in use across the organization
- Copies of project-level procedures
- Project development plans
- Samples of standard management reports
- Descriptions of the life cycle(s) used
- Descriptions of the process architecture
- Copies of defect records
- Training material
- Checklists

As Chapter 8 will elaborate, the team review process is intensive. When documents are reviewed, team members flag critical sections for future reference. (Team members who are part of the organization are extremely useful to answer other team members' questions about the documents.) Before the assessment is finished, the team will need to verify objective evidence for "each instance of each practice" within the scope of the assessment.

It is desirable for the team to compile a complete set of Process Implementation Indicator (PII) database worksheets, one for each PA/KPA, before the onsite assessment begins. If the document database is incomplete, the onsite assessment will take more time.

The following illustrates a sample PII worksheet page of a kind typically filled out by the assessment team. The page in this case refers to part of the requirements worksheets, one for management PA.

Sample PII Worksheet Page

Goal ID	Practice ID	Goal/Practice	PIID Strengths	PIID Source Type A, B, C	PIID Weaknesses	Model Practice FI, LI, PI, NI	Information Needed
SG 1		Manage requirements. Requirements are managed and inconsistencies with project plans and work products are identified.					
	SP 1.1	Develop an understanding with the requirements providers on the meaning of the requirements.					
	SP 1.2	Obtain commitment to the requirements from the project participants.					
	SP 1.3	Manage changes to the requirements as they evolve during the project.					
	SP 1.4	Maintain bi-directional traceability among the requirements and the project plans and work products.					

Note: PIID—Process Implementation Indicator Description

SG—Specific Goal   SP—Specific Practice   A—Direct Artifact
B—Indirect Artifact   C—Affirmation   FI—(practice) Fully Implemented
LI—(practice) Largely Implemented   PI—(practice) Partially Implemented   NI—(practice) Not Implemented

During the pre-onsite phase of the assessment, the assessment team begins its document worksheets, one for review. First, individual team members or mini-teams identify the information needed to verify each KPA/PA practice. Documents are then assigned and selected for review. The Lead Assessor may make specific review assignments or may let experienced team members select their own documents for review.

Whether collected via questionnaires, document review, presentations, or interviews, the data used for an assessment is organized in categories related to the practices of the model. For every practice and for every instance of each practice, objective evidence must be found to determine the extent to which the practice is implemented. The kinds of documents that may show an assessment team that a CMMI practice may be implemented are:

- **Direct Artifacts**—These represent the primary tangible output of a practice. They are typically listed as work products in the CMMI. One or more direct artifacts will be necessary to verify the implementation of model practices.

- **Indirect Artifacts**—These represent artifacts that are a consequence of performing the practice, but not necessarily a consequence of the purpose for which it is performed. These are typically meeting minutes, review results, or written communication of status.

- **Affirmations**—These are oral or written statements confirming the implementation of a practice. They are typically validated using interviews, questionnaires, and so on.

Documents are reviewed not only for verification but also for the purposes of establishing context and formulating additional areas to be probed. (See also Chapter 8.) Team members take notes as in any other data-gathering session. "Observations" (conclusions about each practice) are generated from these notes. Follow-up actions are recorded first by identifying additional needed information and then by adding notes to the worksheets to remind the team to request additional information.

Regarding the importance of documentation, a major difference in focus exists between a CBA IPI and a SCAMPI assessment. In an effort to reduce the time required to do an assessment, SCAMPI takes a "verification" rather than a "discovery" approach. In a SCAMPI, the responsibility for collecting and presenting relevant documentation to the assessment team is placed with the organization, and the team verifies the documentation's existence. A CBA IPI assessment team reviews the documentation itself to substantiate its relevance to the reference model. When an organization has assessment experience, it does not need much assistance from the Lead Assessor or the assessment team in its collection of documentation. Inexperienced organizations, it should be noted, may have difficulty with the SCAMPI method, which requires an organization to collect and annotate documentation before the Lead Assessor and the team appears. Inexperienced organizations may find this activity extremely time consuming.[8]

At the end of each document review session, the team reviews significant items found and notes any additional information that needs to be collected. Any objective evidence that is not identified in advance of the onsite assessment must be sought during onsite interviews and presentations. After the document review and the questionnaire review, the Lead Assessor may elect to conduct a consolidation session.

Analysis of the initial data set provides critical information for the overall planning of the assessment and helps form the basis for the detailed data collection plan that should be developed before the onsite assessment (data collection) begins. The analysis of initial objective evidence at this stage is focused primarily on the adequacy and completeness of information and the implications for future data collection. The results of this analysis will be the primary basis for determining the extent to which the assessment will be one of verification or discovery.

The assessment team analysis of how much more data it needs to look for may affect the onsite assessment schedule. After the organization gives its initial data set to the Lead Assessor, he or

---

[8.] Experienced organizations find that in a Level 5 assessment, this activity requires a minimum of two person months to collect all necessary practice and PA documentation.

she must decide if there is likely to be insufficient direct artifacts to go ahead with a timely assessment and whether the organization is likely to satisfy the process areas of the assessment. (If documentation does not exist for each practice, the rating of the goals for each PA is affected.) If more than 20% of the objective evidence is missing at the time of team training, the organization might want to rescale or replan the assessment.

It probably goes without saying that in no case should an organization create a misleading document specifically for the purposes of an assessment. This is the equivalent of fudging the data, and it is a complete waste of time and money. Documents will be cross-indexed with interviews and other information, and bogus documents will quickly be revealed.

7.2.4 The Assessment Team Elaborates the Assessment Plan

There is now sufficient information available so that the assessment plan or data collection plan (SCAMPI) may be elaborated in some detail. For every instance of every model practice, the plans specify what objective evidence is available and how, when, and by whom objective evidence will be verified.

This elaboration of the plan prescribes:

- Assignment of PAs to team members
- Summary of initial objective evidence provided by the organization
- Identification of highest priority data needs
- Initial allocation of data needs to data-gathering events
- Identification of instruments (e.g., questionnaires) to be administered
- Identification of participants to be interviewed
- Interview schedule, revised to include more detail
- Identification of a starter set of interview questions
- Identification of documents still needed
- Risks associated with the sufficiency of the data and the adequacy of the schedule

The assessment or data collection plans require gradually adding/eliminating/modifying the team's activities as the inventory of initial objective evidence indicates. The mini-teams may conduct office hour interviews, even during team training, to fill out the inventory of objective evidence prior to the start of the onsite data collection activities.

Practices for which no initial objective evidence has been provided should be identified as high-risk areas for the team to address immediately.

7.2.5 The Assessment Team Begins to Develop Interview Questions

Executing an assessment or data collection plan requires the assessment team to prepare questions that will be involved in or used to guide the coming interviews. Each mini-team or individual team member prepares questions in a particular area and presents them to the entire team for review.

Keep in mind that overemphasizing the early preparation of questions can be counter-productive. There is too little time in an interview for every team member to ask many questions, and it is usually better to maintain some flexibility in interviews to allow follow-up questions. Team members therefore may want to use some of the time set aside to formulate interview questions better to familiarize themselves with the part of the model they have been assigned to cover.

Formulating appropriate interview questions will be considered in more depth in Chapter 9, "Onsite Activities, Part 2: Interviewing."

7.3 Preparing Organization Participants for What Is to Come

Part of the assessment team's job is to brief the members of the organization who will be participating in the coming onsite assessment. This briefing takes place in the opening Assessment presentation (discussed in Chapter 8) and may be supplemented by a pre-onsite assessment participants briefing. (In organizations having previous experience with assessments, the assessments participants briefing may be delivered by organization personnel rather than by members of the assessment team.)

7.3.1 Pre-Onsite Assessment Participants Briefing

In simple terms, an assessment participants briefing (APB) is a one- or two-hour presentation to the staff of the organization who will be participating in the assessment. The briefing explains why an organization has undertaken an assessment, the basic principles behind process improvement, and what will happen before, during, and after an assessment. The briefing should emphasize the kinds of questions each participant will be asked and especially that there are no right or wrong answers. Assessments are about understanding how things work and how they might work better, not about passing or failing. The staff should be told that if they do not understand a question, they should say so, and they should be reminded that not everyone will be able to answer all questions. They should also be informed about the materials that they should bring to an interview. Finally, they should understand that the team will be taking notes but the participants should not, that all interviews are confidential, and that both the assessment team and the people being assessed are under a confidentiality agreement.

The objective of the assessment participants briefing is to set expectations for the assessment. Without the proper setting of expectations, the assessment can fail before the team arrives onsite. The presentation will tell the participants the role of the model and assessments in process improvement, the business value of moving up in maturity level, the objectives and principles of this assessment, the activity flow of the assessment, and specific participant schedules (where each person should be and when). It also will tell them whom they should contact if they have any questions or difficulties.

The assessment participants briefing is interactive, and questions are encouraged.

The organization's site coordinator or a designated briefer from the assessment team gives the details about the scheduled activities. Copies of the master schedule are distributed to each participant in the assessment, and any questions about the schedule are answered. Participants are reminded of the items they should bring with them to the interviews.

A more educational briefing may be needed to talk about model terms in local terminology. In principle, it is the assessment team's job to translate the model terminology for the participants, and participants are not expected to know the model. However, in reality, it helps if the participants have some knowledge of the model being used. Also because the organization has chosen a particular model to follow, it would make sense for the people in the organization to have an understanding of the model.

It is common in assessments for several interviews to take place in which the participants do not understand what is being asked of them. They may also say they do not perform a particular activity even though that might not be the case. Something as simple as the question "Does your manager show you or ask you to review a project plan?' may cause problems (because some organizations do not use the phrase "project plan"). What is important is not the plan's name but rather whether the participants perform a planning function. A CMM or CMMI briefing prior to the assessment allows both the terms and their ambiguities to be discussed, and potential questions can be "translated" into the organization's language.

The sponsor needs to stress the importance of honesty and of laying all the issues on the table. The sponsor's attendance at an assessment participants briefing helps, but the sponsor can also send a strong message via a substitute. It is better for the sponsor to be there, but if he or she can only be at this briefing *or* the opening meeting, priority is given to the opening meeting of the assessment.

Some duplication is necessary between the assessment participants briefing and the opening meeting. These two meetings may be combined if the organization is very familiar with process improvement and has had previous assessments.

The assessment team needs to know who attends these meetings. If a person misses the meeting, he will need to be briefed at the start of his interview, and that will need to be planned into the interview time slot.[9]

There are several key points to consider in selecting the needed orientation level and when to have it provided to the organization:

- **Organizational experience**—If the organization has not had experience with process improvement concepts and has never been exposed to the model, there is a need for orientation in the fundamental concepts. *Explanation and examples about what is meant by the different concepts within the model can prove very beneficial to the organization so that its members can begin to think about how they do things in relation to the model.*

- **Maturity level of the organization**—Although the maturity level of the organization will not always be obvious prior to an assessment, the experience level discussed previously will provide some insight. Organizations that are struggling with concepts at the repeatable level in the CMM or CMMI staged representation will gain more from explanations of those concepts and less from explanation of concepts associated with the managed and defined levels.

[9.] For a SCAMPI assessment, the preparation of participants may be accomplished via video/teleconferencing if necessary. For SCAMPI orientation, the documentation for Process Implementation Indicators (PIIs) and any specific instruments to be used during the assessment are needed. The appropriate people within the organization then can document the initial objective evidence to be used in the assessment.

Because a SCAMPI assessment can be used in several ways, internal process improvement, or supplier selection, different types of orientation may be necessary. For internal process improvement, what has been discussed previously applies. Like the CBA IPI assessment, a strong management sponsorship of the upcoming assessment is needed and should be demonstrated to the participants.

For supplier selection, the SCAMPI assessment team may visit multiple organizations and quite possibly only one organization will be selected for the competition.

For SCAMPI assessments, as with the CBA IPI, preparing assessment participants includes informing them of the need to provide accurate and complete information on instruments. This helps to ensure sufficient coverage of the CMMI model practices and reduces the amount of time necessary for follow-up interviews. The investment in having complete instruments—such as PIIs, questionnaires, or mapping tables—will help not only in the present assessment but also the organization's future assessments.

[Members of the AMIT 01]

- **Organization size**—The number of employees who are impacted by the conduct of an assessment will drive the way orientation should be carried out. For a company of 100 employees, it may indeed be more feasible to gather everyone in an auditorium for an orientation session. For a company of 100,000 employees, this is simply impractical. These considerations also impact the selection of assessment participants.

7.3.2 A Sample Assessment Participants Briefing

The following consists of an outline and selected slides for an assessment participants briefing:

Assessment Participants Briefing

- Title slide
  - Name of assessed organization
  - Assessment dates
- Overview
  - Assessment goals
  - Process improvement review
  - Assessment activities
  - Schedule
  - Questions
- Assessment goals—State the sponsor's business goals that motivate the assessment.
- Assessment sponsors—State the names, positions, and organizations of the assessment sponsor(s).
- Organizational scope—State the portion of the organization that is included in the assessment.
- Assessment team and support
  - Assessment team—Names of team members with organization affiliation.
  - Support—Name of site coordinator(s) and any other support people.

- Process improvement—State definition of process [Figure 7-1].
- Process in perspective—Show triangle of people, process, technology as the major determinants of software cost, schedule, and quality performance [Figure 7-2].

A Definition of Process

The means by which people, procedures, methods, equipment, and tools are integrated to produce a desired end result

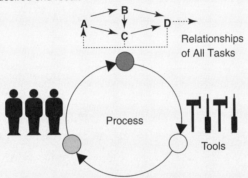

Figure 7-1   *A definition of process.*

Process in Perspective

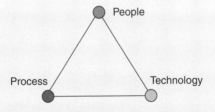

Major determinants of software cost, schedule, and quality performance

Figure 7-2   *Process in perspective.*

- Why focus on process?
  - No magical silver bullet.
  - Fundamental process management premise: "The quality of a software system is governed by the quality of the process used to develop and evolve it." Watts S. Humphrey
- Common points in the quality movement
  - Management must enable and support improvement.
  - Focus on fixing the process, not blaming the people.
  - Improvement must be measured and periodically reinforced.
  - Improvement requires constancy of investments, rewards, and incentives.
  - Improvement is a continuous on-going process.
- Definition of process maturity
  - The extent to which a specific process is explicitly defined, managed, measured, controlled, and effective.
    - Implies a potential for growth in capability.
    - Indicates both the richness of an organization's software process and the consistency with which it is applied.
- Process framework
  - Embodies
    - Process management concepts and principles.
    - Capability maturity model.
  - Provides a basis for orderly exploration.
  - Helps establish priorities of problems.
  - Enables a team to work together on identifying key issues and formulating recommendations.
- Reference model
  - [Figure 7-3 and Figure 7-4]

Level	Focus	Process Areas
5 Optimizing	Continuous Process Improvement	Organizational Innovation and Deployment Causal Analysis and Resolution
4 Quantitatively Managed	Quantitative Management	Organizational Process Performance Quantitative Project Management
3 Defined	Process Standardization	Requirements Development Technical Solution Product Integration Verification Validation Organization Process Focus Organization Process Definition Organizational Training Integrated Project Management for IPPD Risk Management Integrated Teaming Integrated Supplier Management Decision Analysis and Resolution Organizational Environment for Integration
2 Managed	Basic Project Management	Requirements Management Project Planning Project Monitoring and Control Supplier Agreement Management Measurement and Analysis Process and Product Quality Assurance Configuration Management
1 Initial		

Figure 7-3 *Capability Maturity Model Integration (CMMI).*

Level	Focus	Key Process Areas
5 Optimizing	Continuous Process Improvement	Defect Prevention Technology Change Management Process Change Management
4 Managed	Product and Process Quality	Quantitative Process Management Software Quality Management
3 Defined	Engineering Processes and Organizational Support	Organization Process Focus Organization Process Definition Training Program Integrated Software Management Software Product Engineering Integrated Coordination Peer Reviews
2 Repeatable	Project Management Process	Requirements Management Software Project Planning Software Project Tracking & Oversight Software Subcontract Management Software Quality Assurance Software Configuration Management
1 Initial	Competent People and Heroics	

Figure 7-4 *Capability Maturity Model.*

- Model scope—Indicate the process areas to be included in the assessment data collection.
- Assessment objectives
  - Understand the site's current software engineering practices.
  - Identify the site's software process strengths and weaknesses.
  - Identify highest priority issues for process improvement.
  - Determine the satisfaction of the capability maturity models PA/KPAs examined.
  - Facilitate process improvement initiative.
    - Build ownership of results.
    - Provide framework for action.
    - Establish commitment and sponsorship.
- Assessment principles
  - Start with a process maturity model as a standard.
  - Observe strict confidentiality.
  - Involve senior management as assessment sponsor.
  - Approach assessment collaboratively—"Keep an Open Mind and a Level Head" [Humphrey 90].
  - Focus on taking action using assessment results.
- Pre-onsite activities
  - [Figure 7-5]
- Onsite activities
  - [Figure 7-6]
- Reporting results
  - [Figure 7-7]
- Maturity questionnaire
  - A structured set of questions about:
    - Organization-wide processes.
    - Project processes.
    - Organizational support processes.

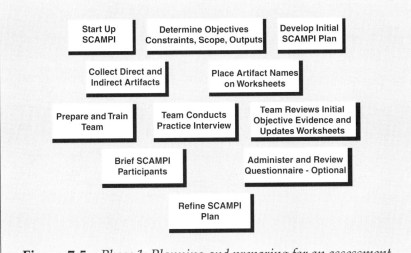

Figure 7-5   *Phase 1: Planning and preparing for an assessment.*

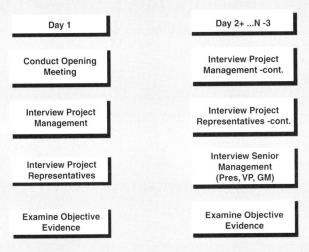

Figure 7-6   *Phase 2: Onsite assessment activities.*

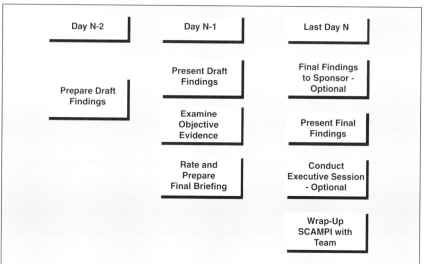

Figure 7-7   *Phase 3, Part 1: Report results.*

- Relation to the Capability Maturity Model
  - Correlation to the PA/KPAs.
  - Questions are asked about each PA/KPA within the assessment scope.
- Role of the questionnaire
  - Framework for subsequent interviews with organization participants.
  - Structure for corroborating data from sources such as documentation.
- Interviews
  - List persons and their organization function to be interviewed:
    - Project leaders
    - Managers
    - Functional area representatives
- Role of interviews
  - Draw on existing expertise and knowledge of resident software professionals.
  - Supplement knowledge gained from responses to questionnaires and from review of supporting documentation.

- Stimulate the thinking process about what is necessary to further improve the organization's capabilities.
- Obtain buy-in of interview participants to assessment outcomes.
- Format of interviews
  - Who will be there?
  - What to bring with you?
  - Kinds of questions that will be asked.
  - Requests for additional documentation.
- Role of findings
  - Highest priority process issues currently facing the organization (model and non-model based).
  - Basis for formulating recommendations.
- Schedule
  - Brief schedule for onsite activities.

Chapter 8

Onsite Activities, Part 1:

The Kick-Off Meeting and Other Presentations. Collecting and Managing Documents Throughout the Assessment. Problems Associated with Immature Organizations.

After all the preparation described in the previous chapters has been completed, the onsite assessment can begin. An assessment sponsor's kick-off meeting starts the assessment. Over the next five to ten days or more, the assessment team attends the organization's presentations, conducts interviews, and consolidates information. At the end of each day of the assessment, the team meets to come to consensus about the data they have gathered and makes preliminary judgments about how the organization has or has not implemented relevant model practices.

During its onsite activities, the assessment team gathers and interprets a mountain of data and copes with unfamiliar categories and conflicting interests under intense pressure. This chapter describes the following:

8.1 The opening kick-off meeting and other presentations in which the organization explains its work

8.2 Mechanisms the assessment team uses to collect and manage documents during the assessment

8.3 Problems typically associated with an immature organization's desire to do well on an assessment

8.1 The Kick-Off Meeting and Other Presentations

8.1.1 The Opening Meeting

At an opening meeting, the assessment sponsor explains to his organization why he has authorized the assessment and what he expects from his people. Depending on the maturity of the organization, the kick-off meeting can last from 30 minutes to one hour. In more mature organizations that have experienced prior assessments, the details of what will happen during the assessment are already known, and the meeting concerns developments since the last assessment and improvement plans for the next year.

The assessment sponsor, the assessment team members, and all assessment participants must attend the opening meeting. Anyone else whom the sponsor wants to invite can also attend the opening meeting. A broad participation of the organization can enhance understanding and buy-in of the assessment results.

The organization site coordinator keeps track of which assessment participants are able to attend the opening meeting and those who can't come. If a person who is to be interviewed misses the assessment participants briefing or the opening meeting, he will need to be specially briefed before his interview.

The logistics for the opening meeting are discussed in advance between the Lead Assessor and the organization site coordinator so that an appropriate room can be scheduled, attendees can be invited, and any other details can be handled, including audio and video equipment.

After the sponsor finishes his portion of the opening meeting, the Lead Assessor should present the members of the assessment team. Each team member introduces himself or herself and makes a short statement about his or her background.

The objectives of the opening meeting are to display senior management sponsorship for the assessment clearly and to supply necessary information. Topics addressed should include the assessment principles (above all, confidentiality—participants must not feel threatened, no matter what they say) and the assessment's objectives. The latter will include a summary of assessment activities conducted to date, an account of activities that are about to occur, the kinds of questions they will be asked, and something about the general conduct of the interviews. The participants are also given an up-to-date schedule of the assessment.

The senior manager must make it *absolutely clear* that he or she is the sponsor of the assessment and that he or she fully supports the assessment and subsequent improvement efforts. He or she should make sure that the assessment is one of the organization's top priorities for the onsite period and should insist that people who are scheduled to be interviewed must be available at the scheduled time. The sponsor must also (publicly and privately) encourage the assessment participants to be open and forthcoming and must explain why this is important. Without such a display of sponsorship at the highest level, the authority of the assessment team can be challenged and undermined.

The sponsor must set the opening meeting as an important event on his or her calendar. Although technically the SEI acknowledges that it might be sufficient "to read a letter of sponsorship from a senior site manager" at the opening meeting, this is recommended only in extreme circumstances. If the senior manager does not take the assessment seriously enough to be present at the opening meeting, why should anyone else take it seriously?

In one assessment, the managing director was unable to attend the opening meeting because he was called to corporate headquarters at the last minute. However, he arranged for two-way videoconferencing equipment both at the assessment site and at the corporate headquarters site. He opened the meeting and listened to the Lead Assessor's presentation and to his organization's responses. It probably was the next best thing to him actually being there. The people in the organization understood the trouble he had gone to and got the message that the assessment was important.

On another occasion, the assessment involved an organization that was used to working by telephone conferencing. A time for the opening meeting was selected, and everyone in the organization was required to telephone in, even if it was the middle of the night. They got the message.

Opening Meeting Features for Organizations with Little Assessment Experience

If the organization has little assessment or process improvement experience, the opening meeting should also review the fundamental concepts of the software improvement model on which the assessment is based. Explaining how much (or how little) interviewees need to know about the practices of the model can be very useful. Organizations that are struggling with concepts at the repeatable level (Maturity Level 2) especially will gain from full explanations, while such explanations don't need to be as thorough for organizations at or near the managed level (Maturity Level 3) and defined level (Maturity Level 4).

8.1.2 Other Presentations

Presentations by the organization to the assessment team can be useful at the beginning of an onsite assessment. Many organizations arrange 30- to 60-minute presentations by project managers about their projects, demonstrations by project teams of what they produce, and briefings by department managers about how they run their departments and how they interact with other departments. Also useful are presentations by directors about organizational strengths and weaknesses or by process improvement managers about future plans.

These kinds of presentations set the stage for the interviews to come, and they also help organization personnel to relax. In addition, they give managers and developers a forum to voice their most important concerns at the beginning of the assessment.

When project managers are later interviewed, they are usually more open about their work because they have already established a connection to the members of the team.

Sometimes it is also useful to arrange short demonstrations or presentations from a few people from the assessed project, even though they are not scheduled to be interviewed. Establishing a connection with as many people as possible in the assessed projects helps the entire organization to "buy in" to the assessment.

8.2 Collecting and Managing Documents Throughout the Assessment

As discussed in Chapter 7, "Planning and Preparing for an Assessment, Part 4: Assessment Team Training and Post-Training Activities," documents[1] both provide real information and establish expectations for interviews and other data collection techniques.

[1.] A document is any lasting representation of information that is available to the people in the organization doing the work (development and management). Documents include paper (or electronic) copies of policies and procedures, code libraries, electronic records, visual media (e.g., slides, poster, and training materials), graphs, charts (e.g., pert charts), working notes, and so on. A document is viewed as external "memory" for the people in the organization. Documents are used as tools for communicating complex issues over time. Documents are *not* restricted to formally published policies and procedures—they include any lasting representation of information that is available to the people doing the development and management [Dunaway 01c].

Documents provide *objective evidence* of the processes used. A fundamental assumption of the CMM/CMMI models is that a process must be documented to be effective: "An effective process can be characterized as practiced, documented, enforced, trained, measured, and able to improve" [Paulk94].

Document reviews during pre-onsite activities help establish contexts and reveal areas that need to be probed. During the assessment, emphasis shifts to data confirmation and answering specific questions.

The level of formality in the documentation reviewed varies with the size and culture of the organization and projects. Documenting your work processes help to ensure that they are consistently followed. However, it should always be remembered that the processes described by documents do not necessarily correspond to practices that are consistently followed. Documents are "necessary" but not "sufficient" to substantiate the existence of working processes [Dunaway 01c].

An assessment team reviews documents to learn the processes that the organization uses and the organization's strengths and weaknesses relative to the reference model. Document review corroborates data from other data sources.

An assessment team examines product-related documents not to ascertain whether documents are well written but rather to check whether documentation exists, is used, and is systematically updated after requirement changes.

Three conceptual "levels" of documentation are reviewed:

- **Organization-level documents** define policies and practices that developers associated with all development activities should know, understand, and use.

- **Project-level documents** describe procedures that implement organizational policies and contain the engineering activities related to a particular development effort.

- **Implementation-level (or track record) documents** have to do with the day-to-day processes associated with a particular engineering activity and are used to measure and track the work performed. They provide evidence of processes being implemented [Dunaway 01c].

Most document review efforts concern implementation-level documents because they correspond most closely to work actually being done.

Team members from the organization can point external team members to specific documentation associated with related topics based on their knowledge of the organization's working environment.

Systematic document searches involve tracing particular "threads" through a related set of documents. Threads often follow the sequential relationship between different work products in the development life cycle. For example, a reviewer might trace a requirements change as it is implemented in the cycle from requirements management to requirements analysis, design, and code and test activities. Alternatively, the reviewer might trace organization-level policies to project plans, operating instructions, and track record documents [Dunaway 01c].

The assessment team checks that the organization's processes are consistent and complete. Gaps and inconsistencies represent activities that are not well defined or controlled by management. These gaps are identified, and they become the subjects of further questions.

When assessing Organization Q, a team member reviewed a project plan and tried to follow the thread for the procedures that the project used to develop size estimates for their products. When these were examined, it turned out that there were at least four different recommended ways to develop the size of the work product. At the organization level, this disparity would not have been inappropriate. But the organization-level document should give guidance as to which method works best for different types of projects. In this particular case, no such guidance existed—the project document did not state which method was used. This was identified as a possible problem and was noted as information needed. When the project manager and software managers were interviewed, they couldn't explain what method was used or why. It turned out that although the process improvement manager had given them copies of the organization template for product size estimating, no project had actually estimated the size of the product. They had only estimated the resources needed and the schedule and could not explain how the size of the product related to resources or the schedule.

Interviewees are asked to provide examples of their "day-to-day" documents and work products. It is preferable for the documents to be given to the organization site coordinator during the pre-onsite activities when there is time to review them. However, a document may be brought to the interview.

When an interviewee is discussing a particular activity, the team will ask questions such as:

How is that activity tracked?

What records are kept?

What measurements are taken?

These questions will often cause the interviewee to refer to a document. If the interviewee has the document with him, it is useful for him to take a few minutes and show the team where the information is located in the document. If the document is not at hand, the team needs to ask the interviewee to bring the document to the organization site coordinator.

The assessment team should establish what needs to be examined as specifically as possible. The team must, however, be sensitive to possible differences in terminology. (The reason the information has not been found may be because the team has been asking for the wrong thing.) Internal team members can usually help clarify such misunderstandings.

8.2.1 Reviewing Organization-Level Documents

Organization-level policies and procedures establish the development environment for all the organization's project activities. These documents define those process guidelines that all projects are expected to know, understand, and use. The richness of the documents demonstrates the degree to which the organization supports the project's development and maintenance of products. The documents define a set of organization standard processes that have been proven to work on past projects. Review of organization-level documents is usually done early in the assessment; however, they can be referred to at any time during the assessment.

Examples of organization-level documents are:[2]

- Organization procedures for estimating size and cost
- Status reporting practices required on all projects
- Metrics required for all projects
- Risk identification and mitigation plans for a project
- Tailoring guidelines and waiver procedures related to organization standards
- Training plans for the organization
- Policies, procedures, and standards for engineering activities such as requirements, design, programming, and testing
- Policies, procedures, and standards for engineering support activities such as configuration management, quality assurance, etc. [Dunaway 01c]

8.2.2 Reviewing Project-Level Documents

The next level of process documents reviewed by the assessment team includes those that define the project development. These documents relate to activities needed to coordinate and integrate a particular development effort.[3]

---

[2] The assessment team looks for the following kinds of information in organization-level documents:

- Planned and required management reports and reviews
- Tailoring guidance
- How exceptions are handled and documented
- Who is assigned responsibility in the document
- Whether the documents have a history of revision
- Sponsorship for the process activities
- Reporting channels for exceptions
- Defined roles for configuration management, quality assurance, and subcontract management
- Organizational training requirements
- Particular development activities that are required (e.g., peer reviews) [Dunaway 01c]

[3] Ideally project-level documents should trace to the organization-level documents. Project-level procedures should be consistent with the organization's standard set of processes. However, in less mature organizations, organization-level documentation may not be available. Therefore, the burden of defining all processes and procedures falls on the individual projects. In these kinds of organizations, the assessment team should look to the project documents for these (engineering and management) procedures and processes.

A project's documents define the detailed processes that are used to manage, coordinate, and integrate all required engineering activities. This level of documentation provides structure to the development by:

- Translating high-level organizational policies and procedures into detailed procedures, plans, and guidelines.
- Defining specific project roles and responsibilities.
- Allocating project personnel and other resources.
- Defining detailed procedures and operating instructions to supplement and enhance organization-level procedures.
- Specifying and planning for required project training.
- Tracking adherence.
- Defining measurements used to manage project activities [Dunaway 01c].

The assessment team reviews project-level documents to establish context, to determine areas to be probed, to confirm interview data, and to answer specific questions about processes in use. Review of project-level documents begins before the onsite visit and continues throughout the assessment.[4]

Project-level documents may include (but are not limited to):

- Systems engineering plan
- Software development plan
- Quality assurance plan
- Configuration management plan
- Schedules

---

[4] The information a team looks for in project-level documents includes the:
- Differences between the processes used in different projects
- Planned/required management reports and reviews
- Tailoring guidance
- How exceptions are to be handled, are handled, and documented
- How changes to the schedule or requirements are handled over the life of the project
- Who is assigned responsibilities by the document
- Defined project-level training requirements
- Resources planned or allocated by the document
- Sufficient detail in the processes to guide actual work practice
- How the tasks described are tracked, measured, and verified
- How exceptions are reported
- How product size is estimated, measured, and revised [Dunaway 01c]

- Detailed procedures and work instructions
- Project notebooks that define how the project collectively understands and integrates the engineering processes

The assessment team will consider how project documents are related to organization documents. The team may also check if and how organization processes are tailored, if required project documents exist as dictated by organizational documents, and if exceptions or waivers are handled and documented in accordance with organization guidance. The assessment team will also look at the relationship between project-level documents and implementation-level documents. For example, they will examine the tracking methods that are defined and used, the measurements that have been defined and are used, and whether standard report formats are defined and used.

8.2.3 Reviewing Implementation-Level Documents

The third type of documents that the assessment team reviews are implementation-level documents, such as status reports, minutes, schedules, and so on. (In SCAMPI, these are known as indirect artifacts.) These documents provide an audit trail or "track record" of all processes used on the implementation.

The purpose, format, and content of implementation-level documents are traceable to organization- and project-level procedures and standards. Implementation-level documents capture information that identifies work activities. They should be easy to use and should capture actual information about work accomplished.

The primary purposes for the assessment team reviewing implementation-level documents are to indicate areas that need to be probed, to confirm interview data, and to provide evidence of actual work being done.[5]

---

5. The information the team looks for in implementation-level documents includes:
- Evidence of actual practices used
- Record of resources used
- Data on process improvement efforts
- Who uses the information in the document and how
- Who reviews the work products
- What measurements are taken and how they are used
- Consistency of work products with project-level plans, procedures, standards, etc.
- How regularly reporting, reviews, and verification activities are conducted
- How deviations from planned work are documented and handled [Dunaway 01c]

Implementation-level documents include:

- Meeting minutes (e.g., from project management meetings, configuration control board meetings, etc.)
- Project status reports and schedules
- Change request forms
- Test records
- Training records
- Software development folders
- Historical data derived from past schedules and status reports
- Analyses of resource trends, cost trends, size trends
- Work products such as requirements specifications, high-level and detailed design documents, etc. [Dunaway 01c]

The assessment team will consider how the implementation-level documents track to the project-level documents.

8.2.4 How the Assessment Team Prioritizes Documents for Review

An assessment does not allocate enough time for the team to examine every pertinent document. However, a large sample should be reviewed to ensure coverage according to the assessment corroboration rules.

The organization can expect the team to spot-check documents and work products mentioned during the interviews and given to the team. For example, there might be a number of problem reports or change reports to choose from. Typically the team will choose a relevant few for review.

The assessment team asks for independent corroboration of data. This may take the form of direct or indirect artifacts as well as interviews. For example, if a project manager says that all programmers use a particular coding standard, the team might ask a programmer to show them the standard he or she uses (along with some code modules produced using the standard). This allows the team independently to confirm the manager's statement and also to examine how well the standard is followed.

8.2.5 Reviewing Documents for General Context

Documents may provide valuable information not related to a particular KPA/PA. The organization will benefit if a team uses this information as a basis to ask further questions. Examples include:

- Creation dates on procedures might indicate that a process is new. This can lead to inquiries about how the information was made available to the people using the procedure and how many people have actually used the new procedure. A new procedure with a very recent creation date could indicate that no one has ever used it and that it was created for the assessment.

- A revision date might indicate that a given process had not been updated for several years. The team would look for signs that the process is still in use and that work is really being done this way.

- The authorization or approval "signature" indicates the level of sponsorship for a process. If, for example, the Software Engineering Process Group (SEPG) manager signs an organization policy, questions would be asked about how important people in the organization regard the policy. Normally you would expect to have an executive sign an organization policy.

- The size and format of a document has a direct bearing on its usability. If a document were extremely large, the team would look to see if people actually knew what the document said and how it was used.

- Cross-references to other documents provide critical links to KPA/PA-related information. (An organization is not expected to keep its process documentation in KPA/PA order, even if it would make assessments easier.)

- For electronic documents, a listing of who is allowed access and what kind of access (create/read/modify) will indicate who controls work product configuration.

- Procedures for version control and archiving indicate the stability of information [Dunaway 01c].

When assessing Organization M, the assessment team noticed that all of its policy and procedure documents were dated a week or two prior to the assessment and that there was a consistent list of signatures on the documents. When they examined this further, it turned out that a small committee had been put together in the month before the assessment to produce all of the company's policies. The documents, needless to say, had little to do with actual practices. Instead they provided strong evidence that creating policies had meant little to the organization.

8.2.6 Library Management

As discussed in Chapter 7, documents for the assessment are maintained in a "library." The organization may supply documents in a hard copy or electronic copy. The organization does not need to make copies of the documents but can loan them to the team. The organization may use them any time the assessment team is not using them, but the documents still remain in the team workspace until after the assessment is completed. When documents are reviewed, the team members flag critical sections for future reference. Documents are usually managed with reference to the KPA/PA worksheets. The team may also maintain separate document reference sheets.

The organization should provide the assessment team efficient, controlled access to all documents while onsite. The assessment team's library management procedures must be user-friendly[6]—if access to documents takes too much time, it will interfere with critical onsite activities.

[6.] The major library management tasks are described in the following. All tasks except for the first and last are repeated throughout the assessment.
1. The librarian verifies the initial document inventory by:
   a. Checking that the documents requested prior to the site visit have been provided
   b. Verifying or preparing the initial data sheets
2. For an assessment team member to request a document during an interview, the team member may ask for it. If the document is immediately available, the document will be added to the inventory. If the document is not available, the librarian will note the request and follow up with the appropriate person to get the document.

The team can request documents during interviews, when the team is reviewing other documents, or during team consolidation periods. In SCAMPI, the document collection plan is updated daily. A data collection report should be available to the team at the start of each day. The librarian (or Lead Assessor) needs to coordinate requests with the organization site coordinator.

Company confidential or proprietary information may require additional care. In general, all team members who are not from the assessed organization need to complete non-disclosure agreements prior to the assessment. There must be at least one person on the team who is able to review the classified information.

8.3 Problems Associated with an Immature Organization's Desire to "Do Well" on an Assessment

More frequently than not, an organization being assessed is under considerable explicit or implicit pressure to do well. (A contract may be riding on the rating, or people may fear that the jobs of relevant managers are on the line.) Such circumstances make it tempting to "game" the assessment to get a higher rating than what the organization's real capability warrants. A company's long-term interests, though, are best served by facing whatever problems exist. (If no problems existed, there would be no reason for an assessment.) The company's real, long-term interests can only be satisfied by honesty and openness in the assessment process. Achieving a culture of openness is in fact the first big step in improving the

---

3. Outside of interviews, the team member will note the document title, session, source, and the team member's name, and ask the librarian to get the document.
4. The librarian or Lead Assessor:
   a. Coordinates the requests with the organization site coordinator
   b. Adds the document to the inventory by assigning a number and entering the number on the data sheets next to the title
   c. Arranges for the organization site coordinator to return all of the documents to the owners at the end of the assessment, or during the assessment if requested by site personnel [Dunaway 01c]

organization's future possibilities. By contrast, a culture of secrecy and "gaming" forecloses the possibility of real improvement and can turn an assessment into a counter-productive waste of money.

Despite these facts, immature organizations (which by definition cannot see beyond short-term issues) will try to manage an assessment so that it produces a positive outcome, so it is crucial for everyone who has the organization's survival at heart to anticipate the kinds of interference that can be exerted. For example:

- Preparing interviewees in mock interviews to talk about what should happen rather than what does happen.
- Grilling interviewees after their interviews to discover what they said so that damaging statements can be explained away.
- Trying to intimidate the assessment team by suggesting there is something lacking in the assessment process or by insisting that the organization is doing more than is being reported in the interviews.
- Encouraging the organization's representatives on the assessment team to discount negative comments made during interviews.
- Defending the organization's maturity in spite of the evidence.

No one likes to admit thinking about such things—much less doing them—but such maneuvers are nearly universal in immature organizations. It is important to anticipate them and understand why they are counter-productive.

8.3.1 The Abuse of Mock Interviews

Especially during a first assessment, immature organizations attempt to spin things positively by staging mock interviews during which "the right answers" are rehearsed. This, however, undermines the way assessments motivate improvement—by providing a forum for the free discussion of how people are doing their jobs, a process that can and should lead to an understanding by all concerned of the overall strengths and weaknesses of the work process.

A good assessment team will get interviewees to think about how they do their jobs and sometimes provoke people to understand why they do what they do for the first time. The point of interviews is not to rehearse the company's written processes and procedures but rather to give people in an organization a good idea of which procedures are really used and how well actual practices work or don't work. Being honest sometimes can mean a lower rating in the short term, but it provides the only sure basis to maintain long-term improvement, often by pointing out potentially useful processes that people are not using—because they mistrust them, because the processes need to be improved, or because the personnel need to be trained or retrained in the processes.

Assessment teams themselves can make things worse by rigidly adhering to a set of scripted questions, which can to an immature organization seem like an invitation to prepare a set of scripted answers. Team members should regard interview scripts only as jumping-off points for actual interviews. The best interviews are those that become a conversation between the assessment team and the people being interviewed.

During the first assessment of Organization X, a relatively inexperienced assessment team asked entirely scripted questions during the first three days of interviewing and seemed to get a promising picture of the organization. However, senior team members came to sense the absence of concrete examples of how the organization really worked. The team therefore decided not to follow the announced script during the next day's interviews. It quickly emerged that earlier responses had described practices that the projects had never really implemented. Later the team learned that each person interviewed had spent at least 50 hours practicing with a consultant the organization had hired. (There were at least 50 people interviewed.) The organization was trying to achieve a Level 2 rating without actually implementing Level 2 practices. But the attempt at "gaming" the assessment was itself a sure indicator of an immature organization. The organization could have better spent the 2,500 wasted consultation hours in almost any other way. Its real desire was not to improve but rather—desperately—not to change.

8.3.2 Violating Confidentiality

An organization's intentional or unintentional interference can go beyond preparing interviewees. In immature organizations, participants are sometimes instructed to answer questions in a narrow way and not to volunteer information. Managers in such organizations may even call in participants after an interview and ask them what transpired. Individuals are put in an impossible position if they know the boss is going to ask them what they said, and from that point on, all openness ceases, and the assessment becomes a waste of time. Process improvement activities are designed to fix the system—not to blame the people. This is why the SEI made confidentiality and non-attribution one of the most important rules of an assessment.

8.3.3 Intimidation

Organizations also interfere in more obvious ways, including trying to intimidate the assessment team.

For instance, Company Y's managing director (who questioned his employees after every interview) asked to see the Lead Assessor halfway through the assessment. He told the Lead Assessor that people were complaining about not getting a fair interview. He had been told, he said, of employees who had wanted to give the team more information but were cut off. The Lead Assessor responded that he would check into it but that there was no immediate need to worry because interviews were often truncated if the territory had been covered at other sessions. However, the manager hardly listened, and he grumbled that the assessment was being improperly conducted. It turned out that the managing director knew the organization was weak in crucial areas and that his questions were aimed at preparing the ground to argue that failure to be assessed at Level 2 was the assessment team's fault and not the company's.

8.3.4 Deliberate Obstruction

Organizations can also try to interfere through their representatives on the assessment team. The organization's team members may consistently discount any problems raised in interviews or may violently disagree with the rest of the team during the consolidation period. Even in less extreme cases, it is natural for internal assessment team members to become protective. Sometimes a team member will not realize what he is doing until the team leader points it out to him, and only then will he adjust his behavior. If the situation does not improve, the team leader must ask the team member to withdraw from the assessment. Although this can be painful at the time (especially if it is a small team), retaining a recalcitrant team member is good neither for the team nor for the long-term prospects of the organization.

A team member from Organization Q was concerned that if the organization did not achieve a certain maturity level, both the managing director and the SEPG manager would lose their jobs. The team member agreed with each finding during the course of the assessment, but on the day that the team was to consolidate its findings, he realized that the organization was not going to achieve its desired maturity level. He told the team that under no circumstances would he give a maturity level less than what the organization expected. The Lead Assessor had to go to the managing director, who was forced to remind the team member that his obligation was to be objective.

Such cases smack in ordinary language of "cheating," but organizations that permit them only care about the maturity rating they will receive. Such interference clearly indicates that the organization's personnel are convinced they have no need to improve.

Assessments are designed to provide the kind of shock that requires a company to look at itself honestly. After that shock, it becomes much easier to change a technical culture—to keep what works and improve what doesn't.

8.3.5 How an Experienced Lead Assessor Should Handle Sensitive Situations

To have any possibility of resolving the problems just described, the Lead Assessor must be perceived as someone who will respect all parties, listen carefully, tell the truth, and uphold the assessment's ground rules. This requires time and leads to the development of working relationships. Lead Assessors can demonstrate trustworthy behavior first and foremost by keeping confidences even on trivial issues. He or she should practice reflective listening: rephrasing what was said in the listener's own words, sharing one's own experience with similar concerns, and offering observations about the situation that demonstrate interest and compassion.

During assessment team training, if some team members obviously have a hidden agenda that will result in inaccurate assessment results, the Lead Assessor may have to speak with the sponsor and have the team member replaced with another person who can be more objective.

Chapter 9

Onsite Activities, Part 2:
Interviewing

Interviewing constitutes probably the most significant part of an assessment, both because it is the assessment's most important data collection mechanism and because the assessment's power to shock, change, solidify, or educate an organization largely works through personal interactions. Ideally interviews develop a sense of a shared mission between the organization and the team. Together they begin using the model's common vocabulary to understand and improve the organization's processes, efficiency, and success.

This chapter, after an overview of assessment interviewing (Section 9.1), will focus on the following:

9.2 Interviewing dynamics

9.3 Assessment team roles during the interview

9.4 The stages of an interview

9.5 Note taking

9.6 Different interview questions for different jobholders

9.1 Interviewing: An Overview

Interviews are essential analytic tools. They probe the extent to which people in the organization understand and use the processes the organization has developed. (A fundamental assumption is that people do not use a process they do not understand.) In addition, interviews can educate people in the organization and help them "buy into" new processes.

The assessment team conducts interviews throughout the onsite visit, except for the last day. Data collection is guided by the requirements of the CMM/CMMI, but the assessment team's task also includes probing for non-model issues that might affect an organization's product development.

Because interview questions are so important, they must be carefully crafted (see Section 9.4). However, the team should not feel "married" to a set of prepared questions. The first obligation of a team member is not to ask the questions he or she has prepared but rather to discern how an organization has implemented its practices. Real understanding often comes from follow-up questions, and team interviews therefore should allow for and encourage follow-up.

That said, the person leading the interview must stay focused on the information that the team is looking for and should prevent the interview from going off on tangents. This flexibility requires a knowledgeable and experienced Lead Assessor.

The duties of a good Lead Assessor during interviews include treating all parties with respect, permitting no interruptions or disparaging remarks, and approaching data with an open mind. He or she should be skilled in diffusing tensions as quickly as possible, without causing embarrassment to any of the concerned parties.

A number of techniques can help make interviews more successful and more pleasant for all concerned. For example, the Lead Assessor should ensure that the interviews are informal so that organization personnel feel free to discuss the real issues in their everyday work lives. Also, he or she must continually stress the primary principles of the interviews (and of process improvement). At the opening of each interview, it should be stated that the interview will focus on the organization's processes, not on the success or failure of individuals. Also, confidentiality—the non-attribution of information—is essential. The Lead Assessor should encourage participants to tell the team anything and everything—both technical and cultural—about the organization. (When the assessment team members take notes, however, they must be experienced enough to distinguish between what is important and what is not.)

Everyone involved in the interview should feel that an interesting and useful discussion is taking place. Participants should feel when they go away from the interview that they have learned something new and useful. In the interview, they should feel free to express their own views and to offer suggestions both to the team and to each other. Bad interviews are ones in which individuals feel they are being tested—or worse, that they are being forced to disclose secrets. (For its part, the organization should never pressure participants with directives like: "Answer only those questions you are asked and under no conditions offer any information you have not been asked for.")

One of the assessment rules is that *no* manager may participate in an interview with his subordinates because the subordinates, no matter how comfortable they are with the manager, will always feel constrained. For the same reason, no manager whose subordinates could be interviewed should serve as an assessment team member.

Although SCAMPI assessments may seem to emphasize documentation over interviews, interviews remain crucial to the SCAMPI method. In every SCAMPI, for example, a minimum of 50% of all practices must be substantiated by interviews [Members of the AMIT 01]. In addition, where documentation is inadequate, a SCAMPI team will emphasize interviews even more, and the assessment process will resemble a CBA IPI.

Both CBA IPI and SCAMPI assessments permit the occasional use of video/teleconference technology, but the practice is discouraged because it does not lend itself to the openness of a personal interview.

9.2 Interviewing Dynamics

During interviews, the assessment team is trying to put together an accurate picture of complex real-world activities. Though both the team and the people it interviews must keep in mind the categories of the CMM/CMMI model for process improvement that give structure to the assessment as a whole, it is natural for different individuals to have different ideas concerning not only what is most important to talk about during the interview but also about how the organization works. These different ideas act as filters and make interviewing a difficult and complex business.

The assessment team is responsible for establishing a rapport with the people being interviewed. Generally, the initial moments of the interview are critical. The person being interviewed needs to know why he is being interviewed, and he needs to understand the interview process. The team members must make the person being interviewed feel comfortable. They should act as though they are invited guests in a home. This is especially difficult to do, though, because most people being interviewed are nervous and unsure of what is going to happen.

After a rapport is established, the assessment team members should really listen to the person they are interviewing and should watch for non-verbal clues about his or her attitude. An angry and distracted expression may mean that the person does not agree with something that has been said or that he or she doesn't understand a question. An effective assessment team member notes body language and follows up with appropriate questions, always with the aim of helping the person being interviewed to speak more freely.

A major factor in producing "buy-in" in the assessment results is the professionalism that the team demonstrates during the interviewing process. Interviews that start late, go off on tangents, or don't allow each participant a chance to express his or her views will detract from the organization's confidence in the assessment and its findings.

Some participants are bound to feel after their interview that they didn't have enough time to say what they wanted. This feeling is natural, but it is usually unfounded. Assessments involve interviewing many people, always asking for similar information. When this information is collected and assembled, an accurate picture of the whole organization usually emerges. This should be explained to the people being interviewed to make them less anxious about what they might not have had time to say. If a person still feels strongly that he wants more time to explain something, though, arranging a "follow-up" interview might be in order.

9.3 Assessment Team Roles During the Interview

The members of the assessment team act as a unit but may perform specialized roles during the interview sessions. These roles are facilitator, timekeeper, and librarian. Most teams are also divided into mini-teams with specific responsibility for asking about areas of the assessment model (see Chapter 7, "Planning and Preparing for an Assessment, Part 4: Assessment Team Training and Post-Training Activities").

The interview facilitator (often the Lead Assessor) is designated to run the interview. He or she must ensure that the interview stays on track and that appropriate questions are asked and answered.

The timekeeper is responsible for informing the facilitator when each section of the interview is due to end and when it is time for the interview as a whole to finish. The librarian is responsible for keeping track of documentation and requesting additional documentation during the interview.

Mini-teams usually consist of groups of two or more people. The mini-teams ask questions about and are responsible for filling out post-interview worksheets on particular KPAs/PAs.

Before an interview, the assessment team should agree on who will be the interview facilitator, who will act as timekeeper, what questions will be asked in what order, and how much time will be allocated to particular questions.

The Lead Assessor is ultimately responsible for ensuring that all necessary questions are asked. This includes specific KPA/PA questions as well as more general ones.

Roles and Responsibilities

Lead Assessor or Lead Facilitator Role

- May be Lead Assessor or team member; facilitator role may rotate

- Conduct interview from pre-scripted questions

- Don't worry about taking notes; trust the team members

- Stay to your pre-planned agenda; schedule time for opening, closing, and questions from facilitator and team members

- Start and stop the interview on schedule

- Maintain control; don't let interviewees or team members take control of the interview

Assessment Team Members' Roles

- Must be able to see and hear interviewees

- Take notes on everything said

- Be ready to ask questions for additional info needed on mini-team PAs

- Stay sufficiently in the background so that note taking is not distracting

Organization Site Coordinator Responsibilities

- Remind interviewees of time and place of interview

- See that all interviewees come to the interview

- Monitor interview room door; close when interview starts

- Provide refreshments for interviewees and team

Librarian Role

- Make notes on any documents offered/requested

- Give interviewee a list of documents to be provided to the team

- Follow up with interviewee to get document(s)

- Return document(s) to interviewee

Timekeeper Role

- Follow facilitator's agenda

- Maintain time schedule; prompt facilitator to stay on schedule

Participants' Roles

- Do not take notes; if notes are taken, leave in interview room

- Any documents promised should be noted by librarian

- No preparation needed; just be forthright and answer questions

9.4 The Stages of an Interview

9.4.1 Opening the Interview

An interview facilitator (usually the Lead Assessor) begins the interview and makes introductions and opening remarks. He or she briefly explains the purpose of the assessment and explains that confidentiality rules and non-attribution policies apply.

Each person interviewed is asked to give his name and say what he does. This practice has proven useful for several reasons. It puts people at ease by allowing them to talk about what they do, how long they have been doing it, and so on. It also alerts the team members about the kind of information they should expect from the interviewee. Some team members might not perform the specific activity that the interview has been scheduled to investigate, and it is useful for the team to know this as soon as possible and to elicit why the organization has asked him or her to participate. (An interview is almost never a waste of time, even if the people being interviewed at first seem inappropriate.)

9.4.2 Phases of the Interview

The interview facilitator usually begins by asking questions from a set of questions previously prepared by assessment team members. Time should be set aside, however, for additional questions as well.

After "open-ended" questions about the interviewee's job(s) and the processes he or she uses, the interviewers then probe for known problems and strengths within the organization or the process. General questions are asked about the organization's environment. Individual team members ask questions related to their assigned areas (KPAs/PAs).

The interview session typically concludes with open-ended questions about the areas within the organization—both model-related and non-model-related—that the interviewees believe could be improved. An example of a concluding question might be: "Is there anything you would like us to look at during the assessment?"

During the interview, any team members can conduct a "spot request" for necessary documents.

A typical interview session spends more time on guided, KPA/PA-specific questions than on open-ended dialogue. However, the time spent on each depends on the comfort level of the people being interviewed and on the maturity level of the organization. In an initial assessment, interviewees usually need more open-ended dialogue.

It is important to remind people being interviewed to tell the assessment team if they do not understand a question or if they cannot answer it. Sometimes people being interviewed do not understand the model terminology or feel defensive because they do not know the answer to a question that is out of their field. It is in fact very useful to hear that "I'm not the one you should talk to about that—you need to ask Mr. Y." No one is expected to know everything. (In fact, if everyone interviewed seems to know all the answers, the team should start to be suspicious.)

9.4.3 Typical Sequences of Questions in an Interview

The interview facilitator usually starts with general questions and then asks more specific ones. At the end of the interview, the facilitator returns to more general questions to provide closure for the interview. Moving from general to specific helps the team achieve required coverage of the reference model and also improves the accuracy of the information collected.

An interview usually starts with context-free, open-ended questions in order to encourage the people being interviewed to explain things from their own perspective and in their own words. These questions provide a wealth of information about the organization, the jobs of the people being interviewed, and any problems in the organization.

Direct questions are then used to ensure coverage of the areas of the model and to probe more deeply into any problem areas that have been identified. Direct questions are used to fill in specifics after the open-ended questions have provided sufficient context to ensure that the questions are relevant.

A sample sequence of questions might include:

- "Will you please tell us about your job and the development activities you participate in?"
- "What are the major risks associated with software/system development on your project?"
- "How are system requirements allocated to software/hardware?"
- "How are changes to requirements handled?"
- "What mechanism is used to review the changes?"
- "Where is that procedure documented?"
- "May we see examples of a few requirement changes?"
- "How would you like to see this process improved?"

In this example, the first two questions are organization-focused. The next questions focus specifically on the Requirements Management KPA/PA in more detail. This set of questions would most likely be used in a group interview, and everyone in the group would be expected to answer all the questions because each individual might be representing a different project.

Everyone being interviewed must be encouraged to be as specific as possible during the interview. Although the team at times may ask open-ended questions, they must ultimately elicit specific answers: examples of how, when, where, and how often a given activity occurs.

People who have had previous experience with assessments, health checks, or gap analyses know the questions they will be asked because they have been through similar interviews before. They may regard the questions as self-evident and become bored, requiring the team members to remind them that (for example) new KPAs/PAs are being investigated.

9.4.4 Typical Time Allotments for Interview Questions

The following charts illustrate time allotments for 60-minute interviews, 90-minute interviews, and 2-hour group interviews.

Typical Time Allotments—Interview Schedule 60 Minutes

5 min.	Introductions
5 min.	Opening remarks
10 min.	Free-form discussion among interviewees (optional)
25 min.	Management questions (facilitator and team members)
10 min.	Closing questions to interviewees
5 min.	Closing remarks (facilitator)
60 min.	**Total**

Typical Time Allotments—Interview Schedule 90 Minutes

5 min.	Introductions
5 min.	Opening remarks
10 min.	Free-form discussion among interviewees (optional)
55 min.	Process area questions (Lead Assessor and team members)
10 min.	Closing questions to interviewees
5 min.	Closing remarks (facilitator)
90 min.	**Total**

Typical Time Allotments—Interview Schedule Two Hours for Group Interviews

5 min.	Introductions
5 min.	Opening remarks
10 min.	Free-form discussion among interviewees (optional)
85 min.	Process area questions (Lead Assessor and team members)
10 min.	Closing questions to interviewees
5 min.	Closing remarks (facilitator)
120 min.	**Total**

Example of How 85 Minutes for Process Area Questions Are Allocated for Requirements

20 minutes: Requirements management
25 minutes: Requirements development
10 minutes: Project planning, project monitoring, and control
15 minutes: Configuration management
15 minutes: Process and product quality assurance
85 Minutes Total

The PAs that are discussed and the amount of time spent on each depend on the group of people who are being interviewed.

9.4.5 Looking for Specific Information: Kinds of Interview Questions

People being interviewed should expect to be asked about three different areas: process, product, and culture:

- **Process-related questions**—Engineering and management processes are at the core of what the assessment (and the models it is based on) are about. These will be tied to one part or another of the CMM or CMMI.

- **Product-related questions**—Understanding what products the organization makes and what their components are is critical to understanding the engineering processes used to build them.

- **Questions about the organization's culture**—These allow the team to probe issues that affect the development efforts or to identify environmental constraints that may inhibit the development process.

Follow-up questions are essential. The following are useful examples:

- "Are there any other questions we should ask you about this activity?"

- "Is there anyone else we should ask about this?"

Follow-up questions allow people being interviewed to speak from their personal perspective, and their answers may influence the rest of their interview and future interviews as well.

9.4.6 Direct or Open-Ended Questions in an Interview

Another way of thinking about the kinds of typical questions asked during interviews is to divide them into "direct" and "open-ended" questions.

A direct question asks for specific information and often results in a one-word answer. These frequently have to do with team members trying to verify information they have already received or attempting to clarify points that are still unclear.

Open-ended questions usually ask "how" or "what." The person being interviewed is free to interpret an open-ended question and provide the details in any way he or she likes.

Examples of open-ended questions are:

- "How did you plan the software development in your project?"
- "How are product size estimates developed?"
- "How are the product size estimates used?"

Open-ended questions are preferred during an interview because they reflect the perspective of the people being interviewed. They also make the people being interviewed feel like they are part of the interview process.

Open-ended questions can concern processes, products, or organizational cultures and obviously can follow up more specific inquiries. They can be either context-free or guided. A context-free question applies to any development activity or organization. For example, a context-free question about the environment may ask, "If you could fix any problem in this organization, what would it be?" A guided question on the other hand might ask, "Can you explain how you establish X?"

Open-ended questions can also be specifically related to the CMM/CMMI models. For example, activity X in the question "How is activity X planned?" could refer to configuration management, requirements management, or any other area where the CMM/CMMI calls for planning. The question is open-ended because the details of the planning process are not assumed—those being interviewed are free to answer in any way they wish.

Although open-ended questions are preferred during the beginning of interviews, interviewers need to ask direct questions as well. Direct questions are used to get specific information, but there is a high risk that they will not be answered unless open-ended questions are asked first and the proper context for the questions has been established.

For example, the question "Have your software development folders ever been configuration audited?" could provide useful information about the software configuration management process, but only if it has been established that the organization has software development folders and that the people being interviewed know what a configuration audit is. Without a context, the terminology involved in direct questions may render the questions unanswerable. The team must carefully adapt questions to the language of the organization in order to be understood by the interviewees [Dunaway 01c].

9.4.7 Additional Sample Questions

Examples of exploratory questions for specific technical groups (all related to some level of the CMM/CMMI) are provided in the following charts.

It is important to ask appropriate questions to the people who are most familiar with the topic and who are therefore most likely to provide the assessment team with valuable information. Here, for example, are some typical questions the team might ask different jobholders about specific process areas.

Requirements Management and Requirements Development Process Areas

---

To Requirements Managers and Staff:

- How were you trained to do your job?

- How do you work with the customer or user to develop requirements?

- How do you keep track of requirements?

To Project Managers:

- How do you receive your project requirements?

- What is the project's process for understanding requirements?

- Who on the project helps develop the requirements?

- Who on the project reviews the requirements?

- How do you handle changes to requirements?

- What happens when developers find that the requirements they are trying to implement do not make sense?

To Implementers:

- What do you do to analyze the requirements for your project?

- If the customer asks you to change something during a demo, what do you do?

- How do you know how the users and/or customer will use the system?

Project Planning Process Area

To Project Managers:

- After the project gets funded, how much freedom do you have to alter what was done by the proposal team?

- How does the project estimate:

  - Product size

  - Resources (person hours and/or cost)

  - Schedule

- How do you decide which project measurements should be collected?

- How do you decide what project data (monthly reports, WBS, minute meetings, etc.) will be under configuration management?

(continued)

Project Planning Process Area (continued)

To Implementers:

- What is your role in estimating the size of the product?

- How do you determine whether your part of the implemented software satisfies the plan?

- How do you estimate how long and how much effort your particular piece of the job will take? Can you walk us through a recent example?

To Configuration Management Practitioners:

- How do you plan your part (configuration management) of the project?

To Quality Assurance Practitioners:

- How do you plan what you will do on the projects?

- Can you explain what happens if a project team says it has too little money to perform quality assurance?

Organizational Process Definition (ML 3) and Integrated Project Management (ML3) Process Areas

To Project Managers:

- What role did you play in helping to develop the organization's management and engineering handbooks?

- How do you refine the processes (both management and engineering) for your project?

To Implementers:

- What role did you have in developing the engineering processes for the organization (i.e., the engineering handbook)?

To Members of the Process Improvement Group:

- How were the organization's management and engineering processes developed?

- How do project teams know what processes they must follow on their project?

- What criteria did you use to select the best documents, templates, and so on from projects?

- How does the organization collect measurements from the projects?

To the CM Staff:

- Where do you find the configuration management processes you use on projects?

To the QA Staff:

- Where do you find the quality assurance processes you use on projects?

Quantitative Project Management (ML 4) Process Area

To Project Managers:

- How did you select the critical processes to be quantitatively managed (or put under statistical process control) on your project?

- How often do you review control charts? What information are you getting from them that you didn't get before?

To Implementers:

- What role do you play in analyzing the control charts?

- How often do you review the charts?

To Configuration Management Practitioners:

- What role do you play in analyzing the control charts used on projects?

To Quality Assurance Practitioners:

- Do quality assurance people use statistical process control (e.g., control charts, Pareto diagrams) to understand how they can improve their performance?

Middle and senior managers are not ordinarily asked PA-specific questions, but it might be useful to ask them general questions, such as the following:

To Middle and Senior Managers:

• What project measurement data do you regularly require from project managers?

• Can you tell us what particular measures give you an early warning that a project is heading for trouble? Specifically, can you name some leading indicators instead of lagging indicators, such as cost? Can you give us a recent example?

• What is your role in process improvement?

• What areas would you like to improve in the next year? Why?

• Have you benefited, if at all, from the statistical process control charts and predictive models now used on the projects?

9.4.8 More Details: Sample Technical Questions Concerning the Area of Software Project Planning (Similar Questions Must Be Formulated for Every Technical Area)

Software project planning involves developing estimates for the work to be performed, establishing the necessary commitments, and defining the plan to perform the work. The software planning begins with a statement of the work to be performed and other constraints and goals that define and bound the software project (those established by the practices of the Requirements Management key process area). The software planning process includes steps to estimate the size of the software work products and the resources needed, produce a schedule, identify and assess software risks, and negotiate commitments.

KPA-Level Questions

Would you please describe how you plan for software development on your project?
Listen Fors:
• Estimates for size, cost, and schedule are derived from allocated requirements and are consistent with each other.
• A software development plan is documented, approved, and controlled.
• Affected groups commit to documented schedules and milestones.
Follow-Up Questions:
• How do allocated requirements play a role in your software planning activities?
• Could you describe how your software planning activities better prepare you for tracking progress of the work?
Goal Satisfaction:
• How realistic are the software plans for developing your project's software?

Goal-Level Questions

Goal 1: Would you please describe how you derive your software project's estimates?
Listen Fors:
• Size, effort, cost, schedule, and critical computer resource estimates are documented, reviewed, agreed to, and controlled.
• Estimates are based on historical information where available.
• Estimates and their assumptions are recorded for tracking purposes.

(continued)

Goal-Level Questions (continued)

Goal 1: Would you please describe how you derive your software project's estimates?
Look Fors: • Documented procedures for deriving estimates.
Follow-Up Questions: • What does your project do to ensure the software engineers that develop estimates are adequately trained?
Goal Satisfaction: • Do the practices you just described ensure that you have realistic and usable estimates with which to plan and track your project's software activities?
Goal 2: Would you please describe how you plan software activities for your project?
Listen Fors: • The project is managed using a software life-cycle model with manageably sized stages. • The software development plan is documented, reviewed, and agreed to by all affected groups and is controlled. • The software development plan is based on customer standards, allocated requirements, approved SOW, and project standards. • Software technical, cost, resource, and schedule risks are identified, assessed, and documented for tracking purposes.
Look Fors: • Software development plan. • Documented procedure for developing the project's software development plan.

Follow-Up Questions:

- What is SQA's involvement in your project's planning activities?

- How does your project deal with late requirements?

Goal Satisfaction:

- Do these activities ensure that your project has a development plan that is suitable/feasible for the software work that is to be accomplished?

Goal 3: Would you please describe how you obtain agreements with planned commitments on your project?

Listen Fors:

- Project groups participate in planning activities for which they are responsible.

- Project groups may negotiate their commitments before they are agreed to.

- Commitments are formally documented for tracking purposes.

- Software technical, cost, resource, and schedule risks are identified, assessed, and documented for tracking purposes.

Look Fors:

- Sample documented agreements between project groups.

- Documented procedure for senior management's review of external commitments.

Follow-Up Questions:

- What is SQA's involvement in your project's commitment process?

- Can you please describe an example of when you have had to assist in negotiating a commitment?

(continued)

Goal-Level Questions (continued)

Goal Satisfaction:

- Do these activities ensure that your project has commitments that are mutually agreed to by all affected groups and individuals?

[Dunaway 01c]

9.4.9 Judgmental Statements Are to Be Avoided

Interviewers should avoid judgmental words such as "right," "wrong," "good," "bad," "should," "ought," "must," and so on. Interviewees should feel free to make such judgmental statements, but the assessment team should always follow up by asking why the interviewee has made those judgments. For example, if the person being interviewed says, "The managers here don't care about programmers," an assessment team member might ask, "What actions have you seen that make you feel this way?" People being interviewed need to express themselves and vent frustration. The team, however, always needs evidence to either substantiate or refute such statements. Follow-up questions of this kind will usually turn up data about practices that have had a negative impact on productivity [Dunaway 01c].

All information must be corroborated. That is, the team must confirm all data with a second independent source. Follow-up questions provide a good way to corroborate and clarify issues without imposing outside interpretations. Assessment team members are ultimately required to make judgments when they come to the rating process (see Chapter 11, "The Final Stages of an Onsite Assessment"), but those judgments are always based on objective data supplied by the organization. (They also must always be the result of a consensus of the entire assessment team.)

9.4.10 Closing the Interview

The facilitator often concludes the interview by asking an open-ended question, such as: "Do you think the team understands enough about your job and the strengths and weaknesses of your organization?"

In closing interview segments, each person being interviewed must be given time to answer one or more of the following closing questions:

- "If you could change anything in this organization to improve quality, what would it be?"
- "If you could change anything about the organization, what would you change?"
- "What do you believe are the greatest strengths of this organization?"

If there is time at the end of the interview, the facilitator may ask:

- "Is there anything you feel was inadequately discussed?"
- "Was there anything you feel the team did not understand?"

People who are interviewed finally need to be reminded about the documents that they should submit after the interview is over. They are also reminded that the confidentiality rule must be respected and that the assessment team will respect it in their turn. The interviewers should specifically request that nothing said during the interview be repeated and that under no conditions should statements be attributed to an individual participant. They are also reminded to come to the Draft Findings Briefing.

9.5 Note Taking

During an assessment, only the assessment team (not the participants) takes notes.

All relevant team or mini-team members are required to take initial notes on questionnaire responses, document reviews, formal presentations, and interviews. These notes may be recorded either on ordinary note sheets or on specially prepared sheets that bear pre-scripted questions. Very experienced assessors sometimes take notes on the data worksheets (see Section 10.3, "Transforming Notes into Observations") themselves.

All members of the team should take notes about the entire interview, but mini-teams should be especially careful to cover their special areas of interest. (Of course, it is difficult to take notes when it is a team member's turn to ask questions, but it is expected that other team members—especially their mini-team partners—will take up the slack.)

Careful note taking is tedious and difficult but crucial for the assessment process. Not only will most of the team's judgments be based on its interview notes, but also the fact that it is perceived to be gathering and reporting information accurately gives the team real credibility, which is critical to the organization "buying in" to the assessment results.

If the team does not gather accurate and usable notes, agreeing on the significance of what the team has discovered becomes extremely difficult.

Notes should record verbatim the statements of the participants being interviewed as much as possible. Because of the necessity for confidentiality, however, individuals are not named, though they may be indicated by a code or number. Also because of confidentiality, notes are not transmitted with other assessment materials to the assessment sponsor and are destroyed at the end of an assessment.

Team members should supplement the verbatim statements that comprise the bulk of their notes with reminders of the flow of the interview they observed. Both verbal and non-verbal information is recorded in interview notes. (Non-verbal information helps to remind the team, for example, that a participant appeared uncomfortable and may not have been entirely open in his answers. In such a case, it may be useful to schedule a follow-up interview.)

The notes should record the date, time, and subject of the session.

Above all, information should be tagged as it is being recorded to identify data that relates to a particular practice or KPA/PA. Notes, after all, are taken not only to jog the memory but as the first step toward discerning and sorting the very particular analytical grid of information on which the results of an assessment depend.

It is certainly useful for team members to have a mental picture in mind of the process area implementation indicator (PII) worksheets that will later need to be filled out when they begin to take notes. This will focus their attention. Experienced note takers may even want to use draft pages of the worksheets as the primary medium for their notes.

Notes may be taken by hand or with the aid of a computer. Interviews should not be tape-recorded, however, because recordings make people nervous and because they do not filter information in the same way that taking and organizing notes do.

As soon as an interview ends, notes should be reread and revised for clarity, adding things that might not have been recorded and clarifying sections that are confusing.

9.6 Different Interviews for Different Jobholders

Different jobholders are interviewed in different ways. Project managers and the assessment sponsor are interviewed individually. Most others (requirements developers, design developers, system engineers, middle managers, and executive managers) are interviewed in small groups of two to ten people. (The optimum number may be four to six.)

The rule of every interview should be that everyone being interviewed gets a chance to answer all questions.

9.6.1 Project Manager Interviews

Most project manager interviews come early in the assessment schedule. Other project manager interviews are interspersed with the group interviews so that coverage of the practices of the reference model can be obtained.

Before being interviewed, project managers are encouraged to gather examples of their "day-to-day" project management activities and give them to the organization site coordinator.

Each project manager interview typically lasts one to one and a half hours. If the organization runs a large number of projects, after the key project manager interviews are concluded, an additional group interview of the remaining project managers may be conducted.

In most assessments, the Lead Assessor will facilitate the project manager interviews. The team physically arranges the room to make the project manager comfortable. Eye contact with team members should be maintained.

The Lead Assessor opens the interview. Open-ended questions are asked about the organization and its processes, with mini-teams asking questions about their particular KPAs/PAs. The project manager being interviewed should be encouraged to bring data that will help him explain his job, how he plans his project, and how he monitors his project.

After the Lead Assessor completes the first set of questions, he or she will ask the team: "What other information do you need to know?" The Lead Assessor reviews the documents requested during the session with the project manager and adds them to the document list. The librarian makes note of any documents requested during the interview and gives a copy of the notes to the interviewee at the end of the interview.

After the project manager leaves, each team member updates his notes immediately. The team also identifies any significant information that still needs to be gathered and prepares for the next interview.

9.6.1.1 Unexpected and/or Sensitive Situations

The following disconcerting situations illustrate problems to watch out for:

> Organization F selected four project managers for individual interviews without consulting with the Lead Assessor. When the team interviewed the first "project manager," it turned out that he had responsibility only for requirements on a particular product. The second project manager was responsible for the design of the same product. The organization, it turned out, used the title of "project manager" for development specialists. Discovering this only at the end of the first day, the Lead Assessor needed to adjust and prolong the assessment schedule, causing no

small inconvenience. Moral: A project manager in one organization may not be a project manager in another.

A similar example: In Company A, two project managers were scheduled to be interviewed for the same project. The organization explained that each product development had two project managers, one responsible for requirements collection and management and a second with equal responsibility for development and testing. Together, the organization sponsor suggested, the two would be able to give a complete picture of the most important project in the company. At some point, however, it became clear that the person ultimately responsible for delivering a quality product on time and within budget was someone else entirely with the title of VP. When the Lead Assessor asked to set up an interview, however, the VP said he would prefer to be interviewed with his two subordinate project managers. He had just been promoted to his position, he explained, and he did not feel comfortable speaking about the project alone. On intuition and against assessment guidelines, the Lead Assessor made an on-the-spot decision to agree. In this case, it was the right one. By participating with his subordinates, the VP had a chance to learn not only about how the project had been run but also about how other companies ran similar projects. He made comments during the interview such as, "That is a really good question. I am going to go back and ask my team that question." After the interview, he immediately set up meetings with his staff and discussed a number of the items raised in the interview session. These meetings continued throughout the week of the assessment. It was true that the two subordinate project managers were made uncomfortable during the interview. Therefore the team set up follow-up interviews with them. But the benefit to this VP and the company was substantial. (The VP several years later became managing director of the company.) The story illustrates the positive impact assessments can have on an organization, above and beyond ratings.

Sometimes the assessment team becomes frustrated and begins to treat interviewees harshly. This has serious consequences and should be anticipated and resisted.

In Company X, which was matrix-organized, project managers were responsible for the entire product, hardware and software. During one project manager interview, the assessment team asked standard project planning, monitoring, and control questions. This particular project manager, however, despite initially being very amiable, knew nothing about the planning and tracking of his product. The team did not pick this up and continued to ask for the same information in a variety of different ways. By the end of the interview, both team members and the project manager were frustrated. The project manager went away from the interview feeling defensive and embarrassed. It took over a year for him to feel positive about process improvement again.

This kind of situation frequently occurs in immature organizations. Assessment teams should anticipate this and react accordingly. In these cases, it is useful to end the interview gracefully and then set up an additional interview with the software manager. (As an organization becomes more mature, the likelihood of such situations decreases.)

9.6.1.2 *Project Manager Seating Arrangement: A Sample Configuration*

The next chart, Figure 9-1, shows a typical seating arrangement for an individual interview.

9.6.2 Group Interviews

The protocol for a group interview is similar to that for the individual interview, except that the team has the added burden of collecting data from four to six (or more) individuals in one session. Usually the groups consist of people selected from the assessed projects all doing a similar job. A typical group might

consist of people responsible for system and software requirements, or for design, or for coding and unit test, or for integration and system test, or for quality assurance, or for
configuration management, or for engineering process group
(software/systems), management processes, among other
fields. (In the software engineering process group or engineering process group sessions, it is common to have up to eight
people in a session.)

Each group interview typically takes one and a half to two
hours.

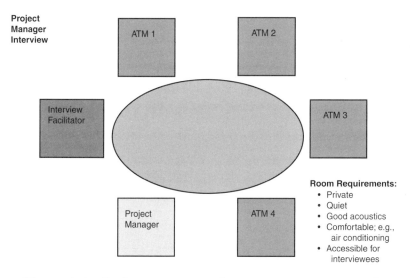

Figure 9-1   *Project manager seating arrangement: an example.*

9.6.2.1 Sensitive Situations in Group Interviews

Typical problems in group interviews include the following:

One person may dominate the answers for the group, keeping
the team from gathering sufficient data. Practitioners do not
always have experience with interviews and may allow (or
even want) one person to dominate a session. The team should
try to prevent this from happening. It is best to make it clear
that the questions will rotate through the group and that all the
people in the interview session will answer some questions.

In less mature companies, not every project performs the same
activity in the same way. This also needs to be anticipated.

When assessing Company R, a group of design engineers was asked how they performed peer reviews. One person from the group answered the question. His project did Fagan Inspections. But the assessment team never asked the other design engineers if they did peer reviews the same way and assumed that if one project did a complete job, the others would have done it as well. It turned out that only one project performed peer reviews, a fact that emerged later and then had to be confirmed with some difficulty.

Sometimes no matter what the team does, some people say very little. Though disappointing, this should not be regarded as a failure. These individuals at least will have learned about how other projects do the same job.

In Company E, one developer said very little even when questions were directed to him. He would either grunt, give the shortest possible answer, or say he agreed with another person being interviewed. However, this person had been listening carefully during his interview and had considered whether the CMM/CMMI method might make his product better. The result was that after the assessment, he volunteered for improvement activities and ultimately became a Lead Assessor.

9.6.2.2 Two Variations of a Group Interview Seating Configuration

Participants can feel more like they are part of the process if their seats are interspersed with that of the assessment team (see Figure 9-2). The downside is that this arrangement can seem disruptive because of note taking, shifting focus, and so on. The Lead Assessor should experiment with both configurations. (The second configuration, featured in Figure 9-3, in which the participants sit on the same side of the table, makes the interview easier to conduct and solidifies the participants as a group but can make them feel as if they are an opposing team.)

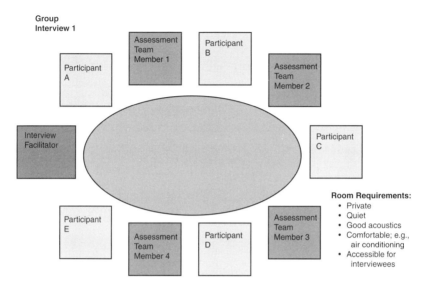

Figure 9-2   *Group interview: one example of a seating arrangement.*

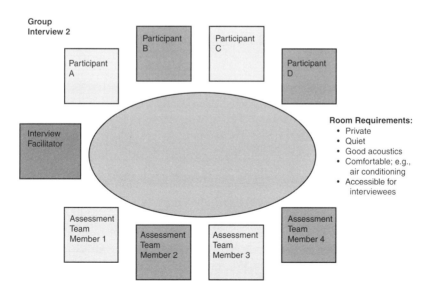

Figure 9-3   *Group interview: a second example of a seating arrangement.*

9.6.3 Middle Manager Interviews

Middle manager interviews are best placed in the schedule after the project manager and developers have been interviewed. Managers are at least one step removed from the day-to-day operations of a project, but they frequently are aware of the functioning of the whole organization and of differences between projects in a way that project managers are not.

Topics appropriate to ask middle managers about include, for example, review processes, verification processes, inter-group coordination, and training.

Middle managers should also be asked something about middle management's role in process improvement at the project level, but it should be understood that they might not know many specifics. Still it is useful to suggest to them that it is their job to become aware of project-level problems early. Therefore, they probably should be asked such questions as, "Do you understand the processes in use at the project level?" "Can you identify differences in use by various projects?" "Do middle managers understand the problems on the project as seen by the developers?" "Have they addressed these problems?" "If so, how?" "Did it help?" "If not, why not?" (In a majority of cases, middle managers are aware of problems and have tried to do something, although they may not have realized that what they have tried to do has not worked, or they may not yet have had time to put a plan in place.)

The normal flow of a group middle manager interview is to begin with a free-form question that asks them to discuss their jobs. Then the assessment team can proceed to "open-ended" process-related questions. The objective is to gently probe for their responses to problems within the organization that have been turned up by other interviews. The interview session concludes with a return to open-ended questions relating to organizational areas that the middle managers believe can be improved.

Although middle managers are interviewed as a group, it is probably best not to assemble too large a group. Typically middle managers try to "one up" each other, and the results are not always productive.

Executives who are not comfortable being asked direct questions may wish to make presentations to the team. However, someone should point out to them that their perspective is important to the assessment in that it can provide a clear picture from the top of the organization.

During an assessment of Company Y, four directors were interviewed. One had just shifted from marketing to become the head of a troubled project. When the interview began and the four were asked about their jobs, this director launched into a marketing performance. Because this interview took place toward the end of the assessment, though, the team was already aware that the project had real problems, in configuration management above all. After the director finished his performance, the Lead Assessor asked him about configuration management, at which point the director sobered up and began more seriously to address the problems on the project. He provided invaluable information that would have been unavailable had it not been for the persistence and tact of the Lead Assessor.

9.6.4 Senior Management Interviews

Interviewing senior managers is not officially part of the CMM or CMMI assessment methods. However, senior manager interviews can supply otherwise unobtainable parts of the puzzle. For example, only senior managers may be able to explain executive directives that may be impeding work in the divisions. (Sometimes the latter include constraints put upon a managing director by a larger company of which the organization is a part.)

Senior managers are ultimately responsible for ensuring that process improvement takes place. They also have a unique role in understanding what needs to be changed and how to prioritize those changes. It is therefore very useful to talk to them, especially at a point after all the other interviews have taken place.

The assessment sponsor is encouraged to explain what plans he has for the organization (strategically and tactically) and what problems he sees from his perspective. Any clear trends (or issues) that have emerged from other interviews should be brought up with him, and he should be encouraged to discuss them from his perspective. He may also be able to give the team the names of other people who can also provide a global understanding of the trends that have emerged from the assessment.

> When assessed, Organization N was clearly performing at a very high maturity level. However, when questions about project cost estimates came up, not much information seemed to be available. Only the senior executive understood what the team was asking for, and he directed them to a small group of managers, some of whom had already been interviewed but had not touched on the issue. It turned out that the managers had not been communicative about cost estimating because the information was company-confidential. Had it not been for the senior executive, though, the assessment team would have come to a wrong conclusion about the maturity of the organization.

Executives from different organization areas, such as finance, contracts, manufacturing, human resources, and so on, are also important to include in interviews (especially the financial officer). Investing in process improvement can save a great deal of money in the long run, and when the financial officer understands this, he or she may become a valuable advocate for process improvement.

In some companies, manufacturing divisions will have been performing process-improvement activities for quite some time. (Many process-improvement principles were first developed to improve manufacturing.)

Process improvement impacts all areas of a company. The more areas that are included in an assessment, the more effective the assessment will be for the whole organization.

During an assessment of Company Y, all the executive vice presidents (personnel, contracts, manufacturing, engineering, finance, and legal services) were interviewed as a group. Each was asked what he thought about process improvement. The only executive to clearly articulate an answer was the executive vice president of manufacturing. Manufacturing had worked on process improvement for the previous five years. They had set up a Six-Sigma program and had substantially improved their performance and the company's profit. The other executives had vaguely known this was occurring, but they now listened attentively to the details of the division's success. The interview session provided significant support for the software process-improvement effort.

9.6.5 SCAMPI Interviews

As in CBA IPI assessments, SCAMPI interviews are held with managers and practitioners responsible for the work being performed. The team uses interviews to understand how the processes are implemented and to probe areas where additional coverage of model practices is needed.

As in a CBA IPI assessment, project and/or program management people are typically interviewed individually, but in SCAMPI, they can also be interviewed as a group according to project.

The configuration of SCAMPI interviews is similar to CBA IPI interviews, except that in theory, SCAMPI teams are seeking not to elicit data but rather to verify data that has already been ascertained during the document review. (In practice, this difference looks less clear-cut. When documentation is not available to confirm whether an organization has implemented a certain practice, SCAMPI interviews are used as a discovery mechanism as in CBA IPI.)

Another difference concerns SEI rules that in certain circumstances allow SCAMPI interviewing to be conducted by less than a full team, allowing parallel interviewing by mini-teams and providing some additional flexibility.[1] (On-call and office hour interviews are also permitted.) When interviews are handled by mini-teams, team-wide review and consensus meetings are still necessary.

All SCAMPI interviews, including mini-team interviews, must include at least two members of the assessment team.

---

[1] There are three basic forms of interviews used in SCAMPI:

Standard Interviews

The most structured approach, these interviews are scheduled in advance and employ a series of scripted questions. Each interview typically involves interviewees with similar responsibilities in the organization (QA, system engineers, etc.). This is identical to CMM assessments. The schedule and location of each interview session is told to the interviewees in advance. The team prepares questions and follows the interview process. The entire team is present for these interviews. Tracking the coverage of individual PAs is assigned to team members. A single questioner may lead the interview, with the rest of the team listening and taking notes, or questioning may be distributed among team members. The number of interviews planned is defined during assessment planning. In a SCAMPI, if the team has collected enough data, the team may decide to cancel one or more interviews (this is rarely if ever done in a CMM assessment) [Members of the AMIT 01].

On-Call Interviews

On-call interviews are a more flexible approach to scheduling interviews. Prospective interviewees are identified and notified in advance, just as described with standard interviews. However, the interviews are only held if team members decide that there is a need and that the time will be well spent. The prospective interviewees are asked to block a period of time for such a contingency and are informed the day before the scheduled time if they will be needed. These interviews need not include the entire assessment team. Parallel interviews may then take place. However, at least two members of the assessment team must participate [Members of the AMIT 01].

This is a different approach than in a CMM assessment. There, all assessment team members are present for first-time interviews. Only in follow-up interviews can the team separate, and at least two members of the team conduct the follow-up interview.

Office Hours Interviews

Office hours interviews represent an agreement for availability that permits pairs of team members to visit interviewees at their desks, cubicles, or offices. As with the on-call interviews, the prospective interviewees are tentatively scheduled. Most prospective interviewees are able to continue with their daily work and accommodate an interruption if the team needs to speak with them. Here again, only if specific data needs are identified will the interview occur. The interviewees should be informed that they might receive only limited advanced notice for this interview—usually a day in advance [Members of the AMIT 01].

Chapter 10

Onsite Activities, Part 3:

The Day-to-Day Consolidation of Data

Daily consolidation activities have three primary objectives:

- To summarize the information obtained during data-gathering sessions in a relevant and useful way.
- To determine from the summarized data whether practices necessary to satisfy categories in the CMM or CMMI are being adequately implemented. This step assembles the pieces of ratings decisions to be made by the team in the last phase of the assessment process.
- To determine whether more data must be collected to facilitate necessary judgments. After it has been determined that obtaining additional information is necessary, additions to the assessment (and consequently last-minute changes to the assessment plan) need to be scheduled.

Figure 10-1 demonstrates how the consolidation process fits into the overall assessment process.

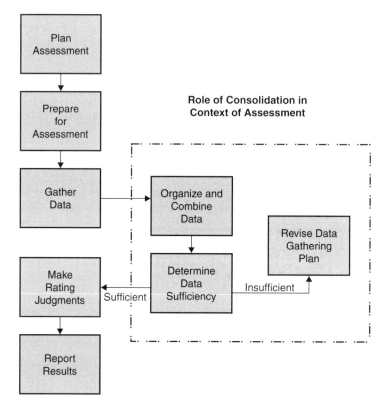

Figure 10-1   *The consolidation process.*

After an initial overview (Section 10.1), this chapter will focus on the following topics:

10.2 Taking notes on questionnaires, documentation reviews, presentations, and interviews

10.3 Transforming notes into observations

10.4 How consolidation leads to day-to-day alterations in the assessment plan

10.5 Consolidation is a consensus process

10.6 Warning: consolidation consensus must not be deferred until the final stages of an assessment

10.7 A lurking disaster to consensus: misunderstanding the model

10.8 The special requirements of the SCAMPI consolidation approach

10.1 Consolidating Data: An Overview

When consolidating collected data, the assessment team members synthesize and summarize the information already obtained during data-gathering sessions and eventually construct "observations" that relate organizational practices to the reference model.

The information involved in consolidation comes not only from interviews but also from presentations and document reviews, some of which will have been conducted early in the onsite phase of the assessment or even before.

It is essential that all determinations during consolidation be made on the basis of information obtained from multiple independent sources.

The team *must* come to consensus on the accuracy and validity of all "observations." Consensus, although sometimes difficult to achieve, ensures that the assessment team assumes ownership of the assessment results. One disgruntled team member who later claims that he or she did not agree about an issue can compromise the assessment results.

The process of reaching consensus takes place during every phase of an onsite assessment. Though it sounds like something that belongs to the end of an assessment, consolidation is a daily activity that an assessment team must perform immediately following every documentation review and presentation and at the end of each day's interviewing. (Consolidation discussions even go on between interviews.) After each occasion and especially at the end of a day of interviewing, it is crucial that the team records on its data worksheets all pertinent data and makes sense of its relevance to the assessment. Otherwise, even with good note taking, information quickly blurs.

For every hour of interviewing, the team should plan 45 minutes to one hour to consolidate the interview notes onto data worksheets. The required time depends on the team members' experience, their knowledge of the model, and how easily they come to consensus.

The Lead Assessor has the responsibility of monitoring the focus, quality, and progress of the team's consolidation activities, both for individual team members and for mini-teams, and he or she should be actively involved in ensuring that sufficient data is being collected to satisfy all areas being investigated. The Lead Assessor provides guidance and individual feedback to team members as appropriate.

The Lead Assessor must review consolidation materials to ensure that:

- Team members are taking adequate notes.
- Notes are annotated properly.
- Observations are based on facts documented in the notes.
- Observations are properly recorded.
- Both strengths and weaknesses are identified.
- Mini-teams are properly merging observation statements and checking for coverage.

If at the end of the data-gathering process, the appropriate data has not been obtained to determine the status of an area of investigation, the Lead Assessor and the organization site coordinator must arrange to obtain the needed information. If the needed information cannot be obtained, no rating can be provided for the given KPA/PA.

Partly because it takes place each day after interviewing, and partly because it requires the team to put pieces of a large puzzle together, the consolidation segments of an assessment tend to be both challenging and contentious. The team correlates practices in the organization with the components of the model. Documentation and interviews have provided the team with an overall sense of the organization's practices, how they are performed, and how many projects are performing the practices, but translating this overall view into specific judgments is not a quick, easy, or conflict-free task.

10.2 Team Members Take Notes and Prepare to Construct "Observations" About Questionnaires, Documentation Reviews, Presentations, and Interviews

All team members are required to take initial notes on question-naire responses, document reviews, formal presentations, and interviews.

Before and during consolidation, all notes are reviewed and incorporated into a manageable summary of information first by each team member and then by mini-teams and the team as a whole.

Assessment team members review their notes immediately following interview sessions, annotate them, highlight significant information, and cross-reference them with the primary KPA/PAs to which each note applies. Even at this early stage, members should continuously try to discern what "strengths" are relevant to satisfying KPA/PA goals and what "weaknesses" are serious enough to probe further. Retaining mountains of "strength" and "weakness" statements will only prolong and confuse the consolidation process.

Ultimately, the team's summaries produce a set of "observations" (see Section 10.3), which are specifically keyed to practices within a KPA/PA. Observations are usually generated by mini-team members and are eventually combined into one set for each KPA/PA plus a catch-all set of non-model–related observations. For all KPAs/PAs within the scope of the assessment, the team will create observations for all practices of the KPA/PA. Observations draw attention to an organization's practice's strength (S) or weakness (W), or they record the provision of an acceptable alternative (A) to the practices defined by a CMM/CMMI KPA/PA goal. Observations must be annotated to identify the session(s) in which the data was gathered, to clarify whether the observation pertains to strengths or weaknesses, and to specify related CMM/CMMI practices.

10.3 Transforming Notes into Observations

10.3.1 General Rules

The process of transforming notes into observations is a complicated one, about which teams may need guidance. Ultimately, the team's observations are systematized into observations that are specifically keyed to practices within a KPA/PA. The following explains how notes should be transformed. Helpful rules for creating observations include (1) use simple complete sentences, (2) make observations as relevant to the categories of the assessment (or "finding-like") as possible to avoid rework later, and (3) avoid attributing statements to any individuals.

Observations are usually statements created by mini-teams that categorize information either heard or seen in data-gathering sessions. When an observation is presented to the team, discussions usually occur to make any modifications needed to satisfy the team members. Accuracy of each observation needs to be agreed to by the entire assessment team.

Each observation should be discussed in regard to its **accuracy**—whether it is based on information provided, whether it is relevant to a component of the model or otherwise has a significant impact to the organization's process capability, and whether it has some significance in relation to a strength or weakness of the organization or to a practice of the model.

After an observation is deemed accurate, it is the team's responsibility to verify that the observation is **valid**—that is, that the accurate observation is corroborated by at least two independent sources and is consistent with other observations.

In addition, for each practice in the model being investigated, the team must agree that the data collected sufficiently cover the practice to (1) understand the extent of implementation of the practice, (2) represent the organizational scope of the assessment, and (3) represent the life-cycle phases in use within the assessment scope.

Sufficiency of coverage relates to a particular practice or component of the model and may be satisfied by a composite made up of multiple observations relating to the practice.

The overriding concern during consolidation is obtaining sufficient objective information to cover all the practices of every KPA/PA included in the assessment. Sufficient data must be collected for each practice within the assessment scope to cover the organization being assessed and the development life cycles used by the organization.

Observations should be accurate, valid, and sufficiently thorough to provide for final rating decisions (see Chapter 11). Until sufficient coverage is obtained for each practice within the assessment scope, data collection activities must continue.

For each KPA/PA, the individual mini-teams will:

- Review their notes for the assigned KPAs/PAs.
- Write accurate observations and transfer them onto the individual KPA/PA worksheets.
- Update existing observation(s) to include additional sources, improve accuracy, or eliminate redundancies and inconsistencies.
- Update the needed information section.

For each KPA/PA, the team as a whole:

- Reviews notes relative to given KPAs/PAs. (Generally KPA/PA mini-teams present new or updated observations.)

- Ensures that observations are accurate.[1] If not, they must be discussed and either updated or removed.

- Ensures that observations are valid[2] (i.e., accurate, corroborated by multiple sources, and consistent). If an observation is not accepted as valid, the team may rewrite the observation and/or decide that more information must be collected.

---

[1] **Accuracy** is required for each observation according to the following criteria:
- **Worded appropriately**—Clear, no absolutes, expressed in terms of the organization being assessed, and phrased without attribution to a particular source. Observations must be worded clearly and phrased in organization terms that can be understood by both the assessment team members and the organization. Use of absolute statements should be avoided because the sampling that is performed during the assessment is never complete enough to substantiate such statements. Also, observations should also be phrased so that the source of the observation is not recognizable and confidentiality commitments are not compromised.
- **Based on specific information**—Based on information that has been heard or seen by the assessment team. The absence of information is itself a piece of data but must be validated by other observations.
- **Relevant**—Can be categorized in terms of the CMM/CMMI or has significant impact on the organization's process capability. Observations must be relevant. If an observation cannot be associated with a particular practice, it cannot be recorded as an observation relative to a KPA/PA. Such an observation can, however, be recorded as a non-model observation if the assessment team believes it has a significant impact on the organization's process capability. When some of the practices performed in a KPA/PA are confirmed, but others are not, the observation must include more detailed information.
- **Significant**—Can be classified as evidence of strength, weakness, or acceptable alternative practice. This can apply to both model-related observations and non-model-related observations.
- **Not redundant**—An accumulated record should not contain redundant observations. When KPA/PA mini-teams organize observations into a single set for each KPA/PA, redundancy is eliminated by combining similar observations, rewriting overlapping observations, and deleting duplications. All of the sources upon which the new observation is based must be identified [Dunaway 01c].

[2] **Validity of observations**—The assessment team must judge each observation to be **valid** by consensus as each mini-team presents the observations, one at a time for each KPA/PA in the scope of the assessment. Each observation will be determined to be **valid** according to the following criteria:
- **Accurate** using criteria discussed in the preceding sections
- **Corroborated**
- **Consistent** with other validated observations

Corroboration—An observation is considered to be fully corroborated if the minimum **rules of corroboration** are satisfied:
- The observation is based on data from at least two independent sources, e.g., two separate people or a person and a document.

- Ensures that there is sufficiency[3] of data for each CMM/CMMI practice within the assessment scope. If there is not sufficient data, the team decides what additional information is needed and which interview or document review should be arranged to obtain the information.

- The observation is based on data obtained during at least two different data-gathering sessions.
- At least one of the two data sources indicates work actually being done; e.g., a person performing the work or an implementation-level document [for a CBA IPI].

The intent of requiring corroboration that "work actually being done" is to ensure that a practice is really in place and not just documented. Examples of work being done would be meeting minutes, status reports, action item tracking reports, or someone saying that they enact a practice [Dunaway 01c].

Although questionnaire responses are considered valid data sources, a questionnaire response is the weakest source of data due to possible ambiguity or misunderstanding of the respondent. Interviews must be adequately incorporated into the data collection process. A questionnaire response cannot corroborate a document without getting the information from an interviewee to ensure that the questionnaire response was understood [Dunaway 01c].

Consistent—A set of validated observations is consistent if it has the following characteristics:

- It does not include weaknesses for CMM/CMMI-related practices that directly conflict with evidence of acceptable alternatives.
- It does not include weaknesses that directly conflict with evidence of strengths.

A direct conflict between two observations requires that they both address the same aspect of a practice or set of practices and apply to the same part of the organization. It is possible for some aspect of a practice of be strong while another is weak. In such cases, two observations should be made: one observation indicating that some projects are weak in a particular area, and one observation indicating that some are strong in the same area [Dunaway 01c].

[3.] **Sufficiency of data**—Sufficient data must be collected for each practice during an assessment to cover:

- The organization being assessed.
- The development life cycle(s) in use in the assessed organization.
- The model components within the assessment scope.

Coverage of the organization is sought by choosing representative projects and participants who are interviewed during the assessment. Coverage of the development life cycle is sought by the cross-section within the organization of projects and groups of people representing the project activities. The data-gathering techniques employed in the CBA IPI method are intended to ensure that the same topics are covered with representatives of the different projects selected. Coverage of the organization and development life cycle must be considered during the consolidation of information to ensure that this coverage has been achieved [Dunaway 01c].

10.3.2 Two Common Problems: Under- and Over-Emphasizing the Relevance of Information

Experienced assessors understand that "strength" and "weakness" statements recorded in initial notes do not always translate into judgments that a given KPA has been satisfied, and they recognize that retaining a great many irrelevant statements of "strength" or "weakness" will only prolong and confuse ratings decisions later on. The problem is actually more common with statements of "strength." Inexperienced team members do not always understand what data is relevant to a judgment about whether a practice is being performed. They are also naturally eager to give the organization the benefit of the doubt. However, if too many insignificant "strength" statements are recorded and retained during the assessment, it is possible to misread them at the end of the assessment as proof that the organization is actually performing a practice when in fact it is only performing a portion (sometimes a tiny portion) of it. It is therefore essential from the beginning of consolidation to try to winnow and summarize information according to the relevant categories of final judgment, rather than including and retaining every little positive (or negative) detail.

On the other hand, it is also possible for inexperienced assessors to place too much emphasis during the early stages of consolidation on the full extent to which the organization has implemented a practice. Such assessors want to make fine distinctions and quantify success, but they misunderstand how process maturity models work. The models ask only whether the organization has implemented process improvement goals, not how well individual practices have been implemented. Because a practice has not been implemented well does not necessarily mean the organization will not satisfy that KPA/PA because satisfaction depends on goals, not practices—ends, not means—and there may be other practices the organization is performing well that will satisfy the same goal. It is one of the prevailing rules of process improvement models to encourage organizations to find their own way to satisfy goals, not mindlessly to tie them down to the letter of the law. Many inexperienced assessors have not realized this, however, and want to hold organizations accountable to the way they think a practice should be performed (often the way it has been performed in their own organizations).

A related problem arises when inexperienced assessors see that the organization has shown no evidence of performing a particular activity. Especially if the assessors come from inside the organization, they begin to worry that the goal will not be satisfied, even though the practices needed to satisfy goals can involve a variety of activities. It is very useful for a team to understand exactly what it means for a practice to be performed. Noting that no evidence seems to exist for a certain activity can actually have a positive effect. At this point, the Lead Assessor can go to the organization site coordinator and ask him or her to assemble other people or documentation for review. It often turns out that the organization is actually satisfying the model's practices and goals via activities that no one remembered while being interviewed. Only after all the data has been collected can the team decide whether a practice is being performed that will satisfy the overall intent of the KPA/PA goal.

10.3.3 Transferring Notes into Observations: Examples

10.3.3.1 An Example of Different Kinds of Note Taking

The following example illustrates notes taken by two team members and shows how they are transformed into observations. Frequently notes contain information that affects more than one practice in one PA. As is usual, note-taking ability differs from one team member to the next. (In this particular example, this difference will not affect the outcome of the observations.)

Notes Taken by Team Member 1:

From Interview 1: Marketing works with the customer. They call in human factors specialists to help understand how the customer will use the system. The system engineers create system requirements, and the software engineers create software requirements.

From Interview 2: Although marketing works with the customer on our project, the system engineers also work with the customers and users. Prototypes are built, and the users are brought in to see if they can use them.

From Interview 3: On project 1, the system and software engineers review the customer requirements to create the system and software requirements and determine how the system will be used. On project 2, the software engineers deal directly with the customer and users. We have them review the way we think the system will be used. Project 3: The system engineer works with marketing to develop the system requirements. Marketing signs off on all system requirements and is involved in the detailed requirements Fagan inspections.

From the Project 1 Systems Requirements Document: Traceability matrix found to customer requirements, sign off includes customer and marketing.

Notes Taken by Team Member 2:

From Interview 1: Marketing works with the customer.

From Interview 2: System engineer creates requirements.

From Interview 3: Software engineer creates requirements.

10.3.3.2 Observation Statements Based on Notes

The following illustrates how mini-teams and assessment teams transform notes about strengths and weaknesses into observations keyed to practices in specific process areas. The examples involve two specific practices in the requirements management (Level 2) and requirements development (Level 3) process areas of the CMMI. Once completed, observations are placed on a PII worksheet.

1.0 Sample Observation Statements

For Requirements Development Process Area, Specific Practice (SP) 3.1 (Establish and maintain operational concepts and scenarios):

Observation RD 1: Marketing, systems engineering, and sometimes software engineering are responsible for defining how the systems will be used. On some projects, prototypes are created and human factors specialists are used. (Sources: Interviews 1, 2, and 4)

Observation RD 2: How systems will be used is found in system description or in requirements. (Sources: Project 1 System Description Doc., Projects 2 and 3 Requirements Doc. Section 4-9)

For Requirements Management Process Area, Specific Practice (SP) 1.1 (Develop an understanding with the requirements providers on the meaning of the requirements):

Observation RM 1: Marketing works with the customers. On some projects, marketing, system engineers, and software engineers work with the customers and users. (Sources: Interviews 1, 2, and 3)

Observation RM 2: Customer requirements are found in marketing specs (Sources: Projects 1, 2, and 3 and marketing spec)

2.0 Examples of Accurate and Inaccurate Observations Based on Notes

Accurate Observation RD1: Marketing, systems engineering, and sometimes software engineering are responsible for defining how the systems will be used and the operational scenarios. On some projects, prototypes are created.

Inaccurate Observation: Projects create prototypes to determine operational scenarios. Projects have traceability matrices. (Notes only indicate traceability matrix found for one project. The above statement is inaccurate because it implies a wider use of traceability matrices than what had been found in interviews and document review.)

3.0 Examples of Valid and Invalid Observations Based on the Same Notes

Valid Observation: The previous statement observation RD 1 was valid because all team members agreed that the previous statement was corroborated in three interviews.

Invalid Observation: The statement would not be valid if several team members didn't have this information in their notes and had not remembered or heard what was said, or if interviews or documents did not corroborate that operational scenarios had been created.

4.0 Examples of Sufficient and Insufficient Observations Based on the Same Notes

Sufficient Observation: The observation RD 1 sufficiently covers the practices because it was heard from a broad representation of the organization.

Insufficient Observation: If only one interview and only one document had stated the preceding, the observation could have been found to be valid, but the practice would not be sufficiently covered because a broad focus of the organization is required.

10.3.4 Observations: Suitable Recording Media

Observations may be recorded in one of several ways. They can be written on sticky notes attached to a KPA/PA wall chart or, more efficiently, written as additions to electronic KPA/PA worksheets. Electronic worksheets for managing the observations are generated from team members' notes; Excel spreadsheets or Word tables are very effective (see Table 10-1). Electronic KPA/PA worksheets are recommended because of their flexibility (they also provide a complete record of the data). Team members' work is made visible to each other when a projector is used in conjunction with the electronic worksheets, and information is displayed on a screen. This offers a time advantage when seeking team consensus. However, laptop computers are needed at least for each mini-team. For some organizations, this is not possible, so the manual method of wall charts is used. The Lead Assessor and the team members will choose the system that will be used (based on what is most appropriate for the organization) and will practice using the system during team training.

Table 10-1 *Worksheet Example for Project Planning*

Goal	ID	Goal/Practice	PIID Strengths	PIID Source/ Type A, B, C	PIID Weaknesses	Model Practices FI, LI, PI, NI	Information Needed
SG1		**Establish estimates. Estimates of project-planning parameters are established and maintained.**					
	SP 1.1	Estimate the scope of the project. Establish and maintain a top-level work breakdown structure (WBS) to estimate the scope of the project.					
	SP 1.2	Establish and maintain estimates of the attributes of the work products and tasks.					
	SP 1.3	Define the project life-cycle phases upon which to scope the planning effort.					
	SP 1.4	Estimate the project effort and cost for the attributes of the work products and tasks based on estimation rationale.					

(continued)

Table 10-1 *Worksheet Example for Project Planning (continued)*

Goal	ID	Goal/Practice	PIID Strengths	PIID Source/ Type A, B, C	PIID Weaknesses	Model Practices FI, LI, PI, NI	Information Needed
SG 2		**Develop a project plan. A project plan is established and maintained as the basis for managing the project.**					
	SP 2.1	Establish and maintain the project's budget and schedule.					
	SP 2.2	Identify and analyze project risks.					
	SP 2.3	Plan for the management of project data.					
	SP 2.4	Plan for necessary resources to perform the project.					
	SP 2.5	Plan for knowledge and skills needed to perform the project.					
	SP 2.6	Plan the involvement with identified stakeholders.					
	SP 2.7	Establish and maintain the overall project plan content.					

Goal	ID	Goal/Practice	PIID Strengths	PIID Source/ Type A, B, C	PIID Weaknesses	Model Practices FI, LI, PI, NI	Information Needed
SG 3		**Obtain commitment to the plan. Commitments to the project plan are established and maintained.**					
	SP 3.1	Review all plans that affect the project to understand project commitments.					
	SP 3.2	Reconcile the project plan to reflect available and estimated resources.					
	SP 3.3	Obtain commitment from relevant stakeholders responsible for performing and supporting plan execution.					
GG 2		**Institutionalize a managed process. The process is institutionalized as a managed process.**					
	GP 2.1	Establish and maintain an organizational policy for planning and performing the project-planning process.					

(continued)

Table 10-1 *Worksheet Example for Project Planning (continued)*

Goal	ID	Goal/Practice	PIID Strengths	PIID Source/ Type A, B, C	PIID Weaknesses	Model Practices FI, LL, PI, NI	Information Needed
	GP 2.2	Establish and maintain the plan for performing the project-planning process.					
	GP 2.3	Provide adequate resources for performing the project-planning process, developing the work products, and providing the services of the process.					
	GP 2.4	Assign responsibility and authority for performing the process, developing the work products, and providing the services of the project-planning process.					
	GP 2.5	Train the people performing or supporting the project-planning process as needed.					
	GP 2.6	Place designated work products of the project-planning process under appropriate levels of configuration management.					

Goal	ID	Goal/Practice	PIID Strengths	PIID Source/ Type A, B, C	PIID Weaknesses	Model Practices FI, LI, PI, NI	Information Needed
	GP 2.7	Identify and involve the relevant stakeholders of the project-planning process as planned.					
	GP 2.8	Monitor and control the project-planning process against the plan for performing the process and take appropriate corrective action.					
	GP 2.9	Objectively evaluate adherence of the project-planning process against its process description, standards, and procedures, and address noncompliance.					
	GP 2.10	Review the activities, status, and results of the project-planning process with higher-level management and resolve issues.					

10.4 How Consolidation Produces Day-to-Day Alterations in the Assessment Plan

Consolidation is an iterative process that continues throughout the assessment.

It is to be recalled that in the early stages of an assessment not much data relevant to the components of the model will be collected. However, relevant data continues to accumulate as the assessment progresses. The focus of the document review changes over the course of the assessment. The initial document review is focused on establishing organizational context and identifying possible areas to probe. As the assessment progresses, the emphasis shifts to confirming interview data and answering specific questions. In a SCAMPI assessment, document review takes on a more fundamental role early in the process. The team reviews the documentation prior to the start of the assessment to verify that all practices for each PA have a document associated with the practice. The focus of interviews also shifts over the assessment period. As the assessment progresses, the focus of interviews narrows until the team is primarily looking for very specific data items.

Consolidation affects the way the assessment team prepares for subsequent interviews as well as the manner in which extra interviews and reviews are scheduled. Both of these kinds of decisions are based on the information that is still needed, which depends on the further needs that consolidation has identified. The team continues to review information needed to ascertain the status of each KPA/PA and revises its assessment data-gathering plan as appropriate by scheduling follow-up document reviews, interviews, or demonstration sessions.

When at the end of a day's consolidation activity the team reviews the information it has transcribed onto its data worksheets, it also plans questions for the following day and decides whether additional interviews and demonstrations need to be scheduled and/or additional documents need to be reviewed. To determine whether to schedule an additional interview or to add a participant to an interview session that has already been scheduled, the assessment team needs to decide whether topics associated with the required additional information are going to be covered in the remaining interview sessions (and whether the participants scheduled for those sessions are the appropriate persons to address those topics). If not, the team schedules extra follow-up interview sessions and/or demonstrations. Evolving changes to the plan must be coordinated with the organization site coordinator. Plans for follow-up interviews and demonstrations may grow out of any consolidation sessions.

10.5 Consolidation Is a Consensus Process

Consolidation *must* be the product of team consensus. Consensus first allows team members to feel genuine ownership of recommended solution and then gives their recommendations a real authority when they are considered by the organization at large.[4]

In general, to achieve consensus, it is important that team members:

*   Share viewpoints and actively participate in discussion.
*   Listen carefully; then identify and rank issues.
*   Focus the discussion on data.

When teams have difficulty coming to consensus, it is usually the result of one of a few recurring circumstances—insufficient information may have been collected, team members may have misunderstood the categories of judgment prescribed by the process maturity model, team members may have preconceived notions about the strengths and weaknesses of the organization (which may be their own), or team members may be acting under the pressure of interests governed by their place in the organization (or a connected organization).

Consensus is facilitated by goal-oriented, objective, informed, relevant communication. If team members disagree at any point in this decision-making process, the team should

---

[4.] The general characteristics of consensus are:
*   Common basis of understanding.
*   General agreement on a clear alternative to which most team members subscribe.
*   No strong minority dissension.
*   Team members understand the decision clearly and are prepared to support it.
*   Retention of group integrity and mission focus [Dunaway 01c].

immediately identify the data required to resolve the disagreement and attempt to obtain that data. Additional data is obtained, the issue is revisited, and, if consensus is reached, no more data is required. If consensus is not reached, the process of obtaining additional data continues. If the Lead Assessor sees that team members are uninformed or confused about the categories prescribed by the process maturity model, he or she should take strong and immediate steps to discuss the disagreements and give a tutorial about the letter and spirit of the relevant requirements.

If, on the other hand, it seems that the team's lack of consensus is due to preconceived notions or interested judgments about the organization, it is the Lead Assessor's duty first to allow team members to express their views fully and then to alert team members (either during discussions or in private conversations) that the difficulty seems to have grown out of a lack of objectivity. If the situation descends to such discussions, the problem is serious and will require great tact and resolve on the part of the team and especially of the Lead Assessor.

A common problem involving team members from organizations associated with the one being assessed derives from their intramural sense of competition. Such members commonly contend that that their own organization "does it better," and if these team members feel that their own organizations have been unfairly criticized for the way they perform an activity, the process of judging the assessed organization becomes a perfect place to vent. The Lead Assessor must be constantly on guard for such situations and must be prepared to diffuse them by bringing the assessment back to the facts and the objective criteria of the model.

Example: For a Level 4 assessment of Organization T, two team members had been chosen from another division in the same company, which had not succeeded in a previous Level 4 assessment. These team members did not believe that their own assessment had been fair, and over two weeks they consistently overemphasized whatever problems they found. The internal team members of course felt aggrieved but understood that they were in no position to argue—it would look too defensive. Noting this pattern, the Lead Assessor during consensus sessions ensured that the two team members were always given time to discuss their concerns and was careful to schedule extra reviews to gather as much information as possible. After each review, the issues these two team members had raised seemed to be resolved, but at the end of each day, they voiced a variation of the same concerns all over again. Still more interviews were arranged. Finally, when the team agreed that no more interviews or documents needed to be reviewed, the rest of the team concurred that the organization was operating at Level 4, but the two skeptical team members still dissented.

Recognizing that the team was never going to come to consensus about the rating, the Lead Assessor attempted to resolve the situation by bringing the discussions back to the data and the expectations of the model. First he asked the two skeptics to make a presentation the next day and explain exactly what areas they felt did not satisfy the Level 4 requirements and why. The Lead Assessor then asked the three internal team members to explain why they felt the organization did satisfy the Level 4 requirements. Before the presentations, the Lead Assessor explained the background and meaning of the relevant Level 4 requirements to the team. After he was through, the team realized that the two groups were not so far apart. Although there were some questions about how the organization was approaching a problem on one current project, the team agreed that the organization in the past had demonstrated a viable approach to similar problems. The team also agreed that the organization was approaching the current problem practically and within the scope of the means outlined in the model.

The Lead Assessor had convinced the team that achieving Level 4 did not necessarily mean that all the organization's issues had been resolved but rather that the organization was approaching its problems as the model suggested by using statistical process control. At that point, the team felt confident enough to rate the organization at Level 4.

10.6 Warning: Consensus Must Not Be Deferred Until the Final Stages of an Assessment

During the middle stages of an assessment, it is easy for an assessment team to regard the process of consolidation as a mechanical exercise that can be put off until later. If it is already late in the day, the team may wonder why consolidation has to be done now. But too little early discussion almost always leads to major disagreements later on.

The same difficulties arise when, during daily consolidation meetings, the team as a whole defers to mini-team members instead of engaging with the adequacy of the evidence being presented to them.

If a Lead Assessor allows this pattern to continue, at the end of the assessment when ratings must be assigned, the shallowness of early moments of consensus will become apparent, and the team may be left with real disagreements about important issues. Problems circumvented by earlier shortcuts have a way of reappearing. Without real participation and discussion in the daily consolidation sessions, ratings meetings can disintegrate into drag-out quarrels.

Organization F asked the seven members of its assessment team to look at all Level 2 and Level 3 PAs. The organization had been involved in process improvement for at least five years and was confident not only that they would be rated at Level 2 but also that they were well on the way to reaching Level 3. The Lead Assessor divided the team into two mini-teams. One team was responsible for project planning, project tracking and oversight, and integrated software management. The other team was responsible for software quality assurance, software product assurance, and peer reviews. Each team asked detailed questions and at the end of the interviewing period conscientiously filled out the PA sheets. For the first several nights of team consensus meetings, one of these mini-team members led discussions about whether PAs had been satisfied. The part of the team not involved in that area was glad to nod in agreement on each point because they did not want to contest their colleagues' authority and because they wanted to get home as soon as possible. However, as the assessment went on, it became evident that the organization was not performing some Level 2 activities and that many team members had not really thought about any PAs other than the ones for which their own mini-teams were responsible. When the team as a whole was required to come to consensus about a rating based on the full range of PAs, a very acrimonious disagreement ensued, and the team encountered many more (and more unpleasant) late hours than they had avoided.

One obvious way to avoid this kind of assessment-busting situation is not to use mini-teams. If the whole team works on all KPAs/PAs, one cause for late disagreements can be entirely eliminated. But this solution only works with small teams of four or five people.

Another common but avoidable problem: In the early stages of an assessment when filling out the data sheets for each KPA/PA, many team members will note strengths but not weaknesses. They assume that whatever weaknesses they have noticed can be traced to information they have not yet encountered, rather than real holes in the organization's processes. Thus they do not flag the holes in the information, even after they have been instructed to note all potential weaknesses. Among other things, this habit means that follow-up activities must be piled up at a very late stage of the assessment. Even more seriously, it allows acrimonious debates about satisfying KPAs/PAs to take place by displacing some information and giving a temporary advantage in consensus discussions to team members who want to make the data look more positive than it is.

10.7 A Lurking Disaster to Consensus: Misunderstanding the Model

The two recurring problems just discussed are part of a longer list that experienced Lead Assessors should anticipate during consolidation sessions. The Lead Assessor's strategies for resolving them will play a large part in defining whether the assessment is successful.

A group of very serious problems of this sort will be discussed in regard to ratings decisions in the next chapter.

One problem that deserves to be considered in the context of daily consolidation and consensus, however, grows out of the common situation in which team members have misunderstood the nature or purpose of part of the model and as a result have begun to disagree vociferously over what has been said during interviews. Such arguments have caused many assessments to fall apart, and so the team should be prepared for them, and the Lead Assessor must handle them with great care.

Teams cannot come to consensus about whether the information they have collected corresponds to the implementation of a particular practice when they do not all agree about what the practice entails.

Example: Company P had postponed an assessment several times. The organization was competing for a multi-million dollar contract and was required to be rated at Maturity Level 3. About five years before, one project in the organization had been assessed at Maturity Level 3. Since then, however, the organization had been reorganized several times. The assessment team consisted of seven members, two of whom were internal. The two internal members moreover did not fully participate during the early stages of the assessment, a situation that interfered with full discussions and real consensus. One had difficulties remaining with the team because of family problems and ended up missing several hours of each evening consolidation session. The other had never performed an assessment before and was shy about participating, either in the interviews or in the consolidation discussions. The Lead Assessor, who had been careful to get agreement from each team member about individual observations, found himself at the end of the assessment in a difficult situation.

When the team started to characterize trends, it became clear that based on the observations, the organization would not satisfy one or two of the Level 2 KPAs. The team member who had missed a number of evening meetings spoke up and said he could not agree, even after follow-up interviews were scheduled. This part of the problem vividly illustrates the need to keep the team together from the beginning and to continuously facilitate daily consensus. Had the internal team member been available throughout the consolidation process, his disagreements would have been resolved one way or another before the assessment reached its critical point.

A more fundamental problem, though, had to do with the team's understanding of the model. Concerning the satisfaction of one PA, the present but silent internal team member now declared that he had always disagreed with the team's interpretation of the model and therefore now refused to concede that his organization was not performing the activity. No amount of team discussion would change his mind. Yet further interviews were scheduled, and in one of them, the organization's process improvement manager stated in so many words that he knew the organization was not performing the relevant activity. He added that it had been his hope that the shock of the assessment would wake the organization up.

Even then, however, the internal team member refused to agree with the rest of the team.

Had the team been together and open, the Lead Assessor would have had an opportunity to discover the internal team member's misunderstanding of the model and might have been able to present an ad hoc tutorial to the entire team, making it much more difficult for one member to hold out. By the time the problem emerged, however, it was too late. The assessment fell apart and could be concluded only by turning it into an informal health check. The lack of a formal rating, though, ended the organization's chances for winning its contract, and its software improvement effort sputtered to a halt.

10.8 The Special Requirements of the SCAMPI Consolidation Approach

SCAMPI places a heavy emphasis on methodically planning and tracking data collected during the assessment. The extensive pre-onsite document review allows the team members (if they choose) to narrow the onsite search for new information. This front-loaded work (refer to Section 7.2.3, "The Assessment Team Begins to Review Documents") helps the team develop an understanding of the information that is needed and how that information will be used. As with a CBA IPI assessment, of course, the assessment team looks for information to confirm that the practices implied by the documentation have in fact been implemented.

The assessment team continually manages the data collected and identifies new data collection activities to fill known information needs. Instruments such as questionnaires tend to be used early in the assessment, providing leads to other data collection activities. Presentations are sometimes used to provide a flexible forum where members of the organization can explain important information about the organization's practices. A document review provides the most explicit representation of the existence of CMMI practices. Finally, interviews are conducted.

For each of the information-gathering activities, the team:

- Determines if the information is acceptable as objective evidence of CMMI practices.

- Relates the evidence of the organization's procedures to corresponding practices in the model.
- Ties procedures to where they belong in the organization.

When the team has finished its data collection, the gaps found are confirmed with the organization.

10.8.1 Verify Objective Evidence

The organization provides a set of objective evidence of practices that fulfill the CMMI objectives at the beginning of the assessment, and the team verifies whether those practices have been implemented. For project-level practices, the team must confirm that each selected project is implementing these practices. For practices at the organizational level, the team must observe implementation at the organization level as well as implementation of the same activities at the project level.

The team must confirm:

- The validity of direct artifacts (e.g., documents).
- The validity of indirect artifacts (e.g., meeting minutes).
- The validity of affirmations (e.g., assertions).
- That direct artifacts (corroborated by indirect artifacts or affirmations) verify the implementation of each necessary CMMI practice. (This differs from CMM assessments, where a direct artifact is not required to substantiate every practice.)
- Obtain face-to-face affirmations that:
  - Each model practice within the scope of the assessment can be demonstrated.
  - At least 50% of the organization's practices implement the CMMI's specific and generic goals.
- Generate statements describing gaps in the organization's implemented practices.

For practices implemented at the project level, direct and indirect evidence must be obtained for every project in the assessment. For practices implemented at the organization level, direct and indirect evidence is examined for the assessed organization but not necessarily for each project sampled.

One or more direct artifacts are needed to verify implementation of each model practice[5] [Members of the AMIT 01].

The work products listed in CMMI provide examples of artifacts that are used as indicators of the organization implementing a practice. (The CMM does not distinguish between direct and indirect artifacts, and these are only examples. Alternatives can be used for both direct and indirect artifacts.)

The team must have a clear understanding of the implemented practices to be able to compare them to the model. Where implemented practices differ from intended practices, the team's worksheets are annotated to accurately reflect this. These annotations constitute statements describing a gap or weakness.

If organizations do not provide adequate documentation in advance, the assessment team has to discover the documentation on-site. After the documentation has been reviewed, the assessment team indicates an observation in their worksheets. For each practice in the model included in the assessment, and for each instance of expected use, the team will document a characterization (observation) of the extent to which the practice has been implemented. The team also determines whether project-level practices represent the general practices of the organization [Members of the AMIT 01].

Table 10-2 summarizes rules for characterizing the implementation of practices. Keep in mind that "Consensus of at least a subset of appraisal team members (e.g., mini-team members) is necessary for instantiation-level characterizations" [Members of the AMIT 01].

Table 10-3 summarizes rules for deriving organizational characterizations. Consensus of the entire assessment team is necessary for organizational characterizations.

---

[5] Direct artifacts are the primary tangible output of a practice, while indirect artifacts are typically meeting minutes, etc. (refer to Section 7.2.3).

Table 10-2 *SCAMPI Rules for Characterizing the Implementation of Practices*

Label	Meaning
Fully Implemented (FI)	• The direct artifact is present and judged to be appropriate.
	• At least one indirect artifact and/or affirmation exists to confirm the implementation.
	• No substantial weakness was noted.
Largely Implemented (LI)	• The direct artifact is present and judged to be appropriate.
	• At least one indirect artifact and/or affirmation exists to confirm the implementation.
	• One or more weaknesses were noted.
Partially Implemented (PI)	• The direct artifact is absent or judged to be inadequate.
	• Artifacts or affirmations suggest that some aspects of the practice are implemented.
	• Weaknesses have been documented.
Not Implemented (NI)	• Any situation not covered above.

REF: [Members of the AMIT 01]

Table 10-3 *SCAMPI Rules for Aggregating Project Characterizations to Derive Organizational Characterizations*

Condition: Practice Implementation Characterizations for the Assessed Projects	Outcome: Aggregated Characterization for the Organization	Remarks
All X (all one label; e.g., FI, LI, PI, or NI)	X	All have the same characterization.
All labels, either LI or FI	LI	All are characterized as LI or higher.
Any PI but no NI	LI or PI	Team judgment must choose LI or PI.
Any NI	NI, PI, or LI	Team must choose NI, PI, or LI.

REF: [Members of the AMIT 01]

Chapter 11

The Final Stages of an Onsite Assessment:

Summing Up and Presenting Results

At the end of an assessment, after interviewing is finished, the assessment team must (1) consolidate its provisional observations and (2) present them to an assembly of the organization in a draft (or preliminary) findings meeting, which asks the organization to verify the accuracy of the findings; the team must then (3) consolidate the confirmed information into a series of KPA/PA ratings and determine a global maturity level rating for the organization being assessed and (4) organize a final findings meeting that presents the verified conclusions and their associated ratings within the larger picture of the organization's working processes.

The draft findings meeting (or meetings) are crucial. They test whether the team has understood how the organization works.

After responses recorded in the draft findings meetings are considered and followed up, the preparation of ratings immediately follows.

Ratings are constructed out of the accumulated information of many previous stages of agreed upon consolidation and ought to be only the last step in a long process of objective and consensus-driven determinations. Often, though, the preparation of ratings presents a moment of conflict. After the assessment team assigns a final rating, it is too late to reverse the consequences. At this stage, especially in immature organizations that may have been required to undertake an assessment against management wishes, short-sighted managers may try to influence the internal team members or in other ways prevent the team from assigning a lower-than-expected maturity rating. Some assessments reach a crisis at this stage, and a few come off the rails. Interference may come in the form of a quarrelsome draft findings meeting, sudden disagreement with established statements of weaknesses during the team's own final ratings meeting, or last-ditch complaints at or just before the final findings meeting.

To any reasonable senior manager, it will be clear that forcing an assessment team to produce an artificially favorable rating can only harm the organization in the long run. Assessments should produce a shock that forces an organization to look into the assessment "mirror" and recognize the state of its current procedures before it can improve. This shock is the start of making the organization stronger, not weaker.

At the final findings meeting, held on the last day of the assessment, the team makes a full presentation to the assessment sponsor—the president or managing director—of the organization being assessed—who from this point on must play a pivotal role in motivating the organization to implement a post-assessment improvement plan. It is paramount that the tenor of this meeting encourages rather than discourages improvement.

At the end of the final findings meeting, the assessment sponsor "owns" the final assessment results and assumes responsibility for organizing follow-up improvement activities.

This chapter discusses:

11.1 Consolidating Draft Findings

Draft findings are a provisional description of all the strengths and weaknesses of the organization's assessed processes, and they constitute the end product of the assessment team's data-gathering and consolidation activities.

The team should especially highlight those weaknesses that represent a real risk to the organization. A vital goal of any assessment is to help an organization identify its most important weaknesses.

In its consolidation of draft findings, the assessment team refines its accumulated observations by:

- Rewording "weakness" observation statements to maximize their validity by clarifying them, eliminating judgmental terms, using the organization's language as much as possible, and eliminating attributions. Most of this has usually been done during day-to-day consolidation.

- Consolidating multiple findings classified as strengths and weaknesses into a categorical statement relevant to each KPA/PA and its goals.

- Stepping back, thinking about the main intent of a given KPA/PA and its goals, and then deciding which weakness statements have genuine relevance to these goals.

- Communicating to the organization the activities that must be improved if the organization is to succeed.

- Listing strengths and weaknesses for each KPA/PA and for non-model findings. Especially where there is a possibility that a KPA/PA might not be satisfied, there must be a separate item to say so and to identify what weaknesses are involved.

- Extracting and summarizing valid observations classified as strengths and weaknesses from the individual KPA/PA worksheets. It is necessary at this point to reword and/or combine observations to achieve an appropriate degree of general relevance.

  - Note: If the statements are too stuffed with nonessential details, senior management will never get the message.

- Conducting a review to see if there is still any information needed. (This is possible but unlikely at this point in an assessment.)

- Compiling a list of information still needed for KPA/PA and for non-model findings.

- Extracting and summarizing valid observations associated with non-model findings and incorporating them into a separate list.

  - Non-model observations and suggestions sometimes turn out to be the most important things that come out of an assessment. They include comments on the underlying culture of the organization and should in no case be downplayed.

Usually, only the strengths and weaknesses that the team has agreed on as valid in the last consolidation session are retained.

11.1.1 Draft Findings Presentation—A Sample Template

The following is a sample of items typically covered in a draft findings presentation. Each assessment team will create draft findings in the format appropriate to the organization.

Draft Findings Presentation—A Sample Template

- Title of slide:
  - Name of assessed organization.
  - Assessment dates.
- Model scope:
  - Indicate the process areas included in the assessment data collection. Each process area investigated during the assessment is included in the presentation. The process areas are grouped by Maturity Levels.
- For each process area, include:
  - The description of process area.
  - Strengths observed.
  - Weaknesses observed.
- Multiple slides may be created for each process area.
- Non-model findings:
  - Indicate issues identified that impact the organization that might not be related to the model.
- Questions and comments are encouraged from participants. Facilitator accepts comments; team members record comments. No apologies or promises to change the finds are made. Comments are considered when the team concludes all draft findings presentations, and the team reconvenes.

11.2 Draft Findings Meetings: An Overview

Provisional final consolidation observations are presented back to the participants who have provided the information on which they are based at a draft findings meeting, which usually takes place the day before the last day of an assessment.

Draft findings presentations are provided for all those who have been interviewed during the assessment. The purpose is to provide the interviewees an opportunity to validate that the assessment team has heard them correctly. The participants are encouraged to comment on the findings and to correct any misinterpretation of the data the team may have made. They are also encouraged to identify any remaining information that should be reviewed. Participants can significantly help the team to clarify and sharpen its statements. Comments almost always help. Not everyone is always happy or satisfied with all the words a draft findings report uses, but nearly everyone feels better to have been given a chance to comment on the report before it becomes final.

In short, draft findings meetings are a way for the team to say to the organization: "This is the way things look to us, based on what you have told and shown us. Have we got it right?"

Drafts findings meetings also make it easier for the findings to gain a level of acceptance from the organization participants. After the participants tell the team, "This looks right to us," they effectively become owners of the team's report.

Draft findings presentations do not include ratings. They are meant to provoke feedback, and the feedback provided by the organization in the draft findings review will impact the rating. Hence rating at this point is premature and counterproductive (the discussion should not be contaminated by defensiveness about ratings).

Based on feedback from the draft findings presentation and any subsequent data collection, the assessment team rates the organization's processes, updates draft findings, and produces a final findings presentation.

At a draft findings meeting, the Lead Assessor usually begins with an update of the team's activities and explains the objectives of the meeting. He or she explains that the team will report the observations that have been made about each individual KPA/PA. The Lead Assessor explains that these findings are a consolidation of a number of interviews and document reviews and that they do not represent what any *one* person has said. He or she also ensures that everyone understands the issues involved and agrees that the findings are accurate. Significantly, the Lead Assessor at each point inquires whether anyone has any more information to provide.

Draft findings meetings should take place in a relaxed atmosphere, and participants should feel free to comment on the findings at any point.

Individual members of the assessment team usually then present the draft findings for each KPA/PA, one at a time. Assessment team members who are not presenting should be seated among the participants and should record comments, disagreements, and body language. The assessment team should not argue with participants. (Sometimes it is difficult for the team not to sound as if they are defending "their statements" rather than the participants' views. This attitude, though natural, should be resisted.)

If a participant disagrees with a finding, a team member should record his comment and if necessary arrange another interview.

Consolidating information gathered at draft findings presentations means rephrasing and summarizing what participants have told the team or what the team has seen in documents. When presenting comments about draft findings, the team needs to take care to record what has been said accurately. This sometimes is difficult because the team is frequently tired at this point in an assessment, and little time is left to craft further statements. However, this data should be handled with at least as much rigor as previous data. (If participants can recognize the words they have used during draft findings meetings in the final findings report, it reinforces the fact that the report is a statement of their collective voice.)

The assessment team does not agree to any changes during the draft findings sessions but will take suggested changes under careful consideration and come to consensus later about whether to include the changes.

11.2.1 There Can Be Multiple Draft Findings Meetings

The SCAMPI procedure requires at least one draft findings session. However, it is best if there are two or more draft findings sessions. One session should be for practitioners, and the second should be for project, middle, and senior managers (but not the assessment sponsor). If there is concern that project managers cannot be entirely open around senior managers, this second session may be divided into two—one for the project managers and another for senior managers.

11.2.2 Practitioner Draft Findings Meetings

The suggestions of technical participants are usually helpful, and they range from word changes to clarification of concepts. In general, practitioners have a great deal to gain if the team can convey to upper management what is really working and what isn't working in their organization. Technical participants, therefore, usually try hard to work with the assessment team.

11.2.3 Management Draft Findings Meetings

Although nothing is presented at a draft findings meeting that has not already been offered (at least twice) by members of the organization, the big picture can often come as a surprise to the organization, provoking vociferous opposition, especially from middle-level managers. In these cases, the draft finding meeting may turn into a free-for-all.

Managers sometimes have to confront weaknesses at draft findings meetings they hoped they wouldn't have to address or thought they had already fixed. Middle managers can also be afraid that executives or corporate management will use these weaknesses against them. These managers also may fear that if the organization does not achieve an expected maturity level, their jobs could be on the line. In an organization that continues to sustain a culture of blame, these fears can have more than a kernel of truth.

Before its first assessment, the managers of Organization J thought that the organization should be rated at least Level 4, if not Level 5. However, during the draft findings meeting, management realized that the assessment team had discovered a number of unanticipated weaknesses and that the organization would probably be rated at Level 1. One of the senior managers rose up to defend his company. He said that the organization made state-of-the-art, one-of-a-kind products and that, no matter what the assessment showed, the company could not do so unless it was first-rate. The senior manager said that the assessment was clearly flawed and that its results could not be trusted. The assessment ended in frustration, and the organization did not improve. Ten years later, it still displayed Level 1 weaknesses, and several of its one-of-a-kind systems had dramatically failed.

There are ways to forestall or quiet such situations, however, and a heated but productive discussion may improve the accuracy of the assessment.

One way to head off furor at a managerial draft finding meeting is to arrange smaller feedback sessions with appropriate people through the earlier stages of the assessment. If the team has not found data to show that important practices have been implemented, it is useful to meet either with the sponsor or the organization site coordinator and explain this. The Lead Assessor at that point should ask who else might be interviewed and what other documents could be reviewed to provide evidence about a particular practice. When key individuals such as the sponsor or organizational site coordinator are kept in the loop, draft findings come as less of a surprise and produce less heat.

Also, in general it is best to conduct technical draft finding meetings before the managerial ones. Technical staff will usually discuss the accuracy of findings dispassionately, which then makes it easier to convince managers that found weaknesses are real.

In no case should assessment team members argue at the participant meetings. Instead they should explain that the findings do not represent the team's opinions but rather evidence that has come from the people who are doing the work. The team should also eagerly elicit new evidence that might upgrade the findings, in the form of the names of additional people to interview or additional documents to review.

Because public resistance only makes it harder for the organization to make post-assessment adjustments, responsible managers should also be prepared to argue for the objectivity of the assessment process and then help their colleagues to work through whatever ratings are assigned. They may be helped to do so by remembering that although final ratings often come as a surprise, everything they are based on has been documented at least twice.

Organization X hoped to be rated Level 3 and was convinced that it would not get an upcoming contract unless it did. An assessment, however, showed significant shortfalls. Three internal members on the team consistently agreed that the organization needed to work on significant areas before it could achieve Level 3 and that it was presently not performing the practices expected in a Level 3 organization. The practitioners did not have a problem with the stated strengths and weaknesses, and the practitioner draft findings meeting went smoothly. At the management draft findings session, however, when all Level 2 PAs were reviewed slide-by-slide, heated discussion arose about what the model required. At the beginning of the Organization Process Definition PA review (associated with Level 3), it became clear that the organization had significant weaknesses, and the entire room exploded. Software managers violently disagreed with the statements their subordinates had made. Systems and project managers disagreed with each other. Everyone started talking (actually shouting). The assessment team member who was presenting the slides happened to be a manager from the organization. He tried to explain that he had taken part in all the interviews and that the draft findings statement in fact accurately reflected what the developers told the team. Remaining PA reviews produced similar shouting, and a similar defense became necessary in each case. Finally, one of the senior VPs took the floor and said, "Look, we all know that what the slides show is true. Our products still have problems. Let's stop arguing and think about how we can make the situation better." The room calmed down, and the meeting became more constructive. The managers were asked to help with the wording of the recommendations for the final presentation to the president. Several executives, project managers, department managers, and software managers volunteered to work with the team in putting the final presentation together, making them feel a part of the assessment team. That year the organization was rated at Level 2. Two years later, it achieved Level 3, and two years after that, it achieved Level 5.

No maturity level is determined before or during a draft findings presentation, nor is one given.

Draft findings meetings end by informing participants of the time scheduled for the final findings presentation to the sponsor and reminding them that they all are invited to attend. The report at that point represents a communication from everyone who has participated in the assessment to the sponsor. The assessment participants should also be reminded not to divulge any of the draft findings prematurely, as they are still preliminary and may change by the time of the final presentation.

11.3 The Team's Final Consolidation: Ratings, Including the Maturity Level Rating

Assessments culminate with the rating of individual KPA/PAs and the establishment of a global maturity level rating for the organization, which is the end of a long process. This book has concentrated throughout on staged process improvement models, which result in a single maturity level rating for the organization, and that emphasis is maintained here. However, in what follows, an additional section has been provided to explain how the process of establishing a capability level rating works using the CMMI continuous representation model.

11.3.1 Final Consolidation

After the draft findings meeting and any needed additional interviews, it is time for the assessment's final consolidation. This is usually done the day (or the night) before the last day of the assessment and the final findings presentation.

During final consolidation, the assessment team completes the KPA/PA worksheets for the last time and, before any rating takes place, determines once again if there is sufficient data to clearly describe all the processes of the organization within the assessment scope. If there is still not enough coverage for a KPA/PA, that KPA/PA will be clearly marked "Not Rated." This, however, will impact the maturity level rating because all applicable KPAs/PAs need to be rated for any maturity level to be achieved.

11.3.2 Rating: The Process

As with the previous stages of consolidation, consensus is required for all rating decisions.

Goals and KPAs/PAs in the CMM/CMMI are characterized as satisfied or unsatisfied based on the implementation of the model practices by the organization.

Rating is slightly different from the preparation of draft findings because it involves the rigorous translation of the organization's strengths and weaknesses into the analytical categories of the model. For this reason, the Lead Assessor, who will be more familiar with the model than the rest of the team, may have to play a more prominent role in this stage of consolidation than in previous ones.

Rating judgments made by the assessment team depend on (1) the quality of the data available to them, (2) their ability to reliably judge the implementation and institutionalization of practices in the organization, and (3) their ability to correlate these practices with the model (CMM/CMMI).

Rating is performed for each goal for each KPA/PA within the scope of the assessment. Supplying an organizational maturity level rating is optional in both a CBA IPI and SCAMPI. The organization's sponsor must determine prior to onsite activities if he or she wants a maturity level to be recorded. Ratings are reported to the organization during the final findings presentation.

Judgments made concerning ratings at each level within the CMM/CMMI structure build on judgments made at finer levels of detail within the structure:

- The rating of a goal for a particular KPA/PA is based on examination of each relevant practice and the extent of its implementation and institutionalization, after sufficiency of coverage has been achieved.
- The rating of a KPA/PA is determined when each of the KPA's/PA's goals have been rated.
- A maturity level rating can be determined when all KPAs/PAs within that level and each level below have been rated.

11.3.2.1 Prerequisites for Rating

Most of the groundwork for ratings usually has been accomplished during previous phases of the consolidation process. In particular:

- The team should already have a good understanding of how the organization has implemented each relevant practice within the assessment scope because data has been gathered for each practice since the beginning of the assessment and has been consolidated on the team's worksheets.
- From the beginning of consolidation, when a weakness has been identified with regard to model-related activities, the team will have explored whether the organization has managed to mitigate this weakness with an acceptable alternative practice.

The assessment team reconfirms (see Section 10.3.1) that the observations used as the basis for ratings are:

- Accurate
- Valid

- Consistent
- Thorough (i.e., they fully cover the area being investigated)

The assertion that observations are "consistent" implies that none of the observations conflict with other observations and that no identified weakness has been mitigated by any acceptable alternative practices.

The fact that the observations meet the "coverage" criteria for the area of investigation means that they address each of the practices of the model in enough depth to determine the extent of their implementation.

If no weaknesses are found in a set of KPA/PA practices that are based on accurate, valid, consistent, and thorough criteria, then the team determines that that KPA/PA has been satisfied.

11.3.2.2 Final Rating Process

After all the data consolidation activities are finalized, the final rating process begins:

- All KPAs/PAs that are outside of the organization's scope of work are designated "not applicable."
- All KPAs/PAs that are outside of the assessment scope or for which insufficient data was collected are designated "not rated."
- For the remaining KPAs/PAs, each goal is examined for each KPA/PA and rated as "satisfied" or "unsatisfied."
- For a KPA/PA to be satisfied, each of its goals must be satisfied. Otherwise, the KPA/PA is rated "unsatisfied."
- If all KPAs/PAs within and below the maturity levels under consideration are rated, the maturity level can be determined.

11.3.2.3 Rating Goals

An organization's process relative to a particular goal associated with a KPA/PA must have one of the following two ratings:

- **Satisfied**—Each of the organization's practices associated with the goal is implemented and institutionalized either as suggested by the model or with acceptable alternative practices. The aggregate of the weaknesses, if any, does not have significant negative impact on the goal being achieved.

For SCAMPI, the definition of a goal rated **satisfied** is more precise:

- All associated practices are rated either largely implemented (LI) or fully implemented (FI).
- The aggregation of the weaknesses does not have a significant impact on achieving the goal [Members of the AMIT 01].

- **Unsatisfied**—One or more of the practices associated with the goal are not adequately implemented or institutionalized either as suggested by the model or with adequate alternative practices, and the aggregate of the weaknesses associated with the goal has a significant negative impact on the goal being satisfied [Dunaway 01c].

All goals are considered to be applicable if the KPA/PA is applicable. If a KPA/PA is designated "not applicable," then none of the goals are deemed applicable. If a KPA/PA has been designated as "not rated," none of its goals are rated.

The following rules are followed when rating a particular KPA/PA goal.

The goal **must be satisfied if the findings**:

- Indicate that the organization effectively implements all model practices related to the goal.

or

- Indicate that the organization implements alternatives to the model practices, which satisfy the goal.
- Identify related weaknesses that when considered in aggregate do not have a significant negative impact on the associated KPA/PA goal.

The goal **cannot be satisfied unless the findings**:

- Identify valid strengths in the organization's implemented practices.
- Indicate that the process is institutionalized and has been in place for a satisfactory period of time relative to the development life cycle in use. (The rule of thumb sometimes used is a minimum of six months; however, a satisfactory length of time depends on the specific process and its duration.)

The goal **must be unsatisfied** if the findings identify related weaknesses in the organization's implemented and institutionalized practices that when considered in aggregate have a significant negative impact on the goal.

The goal **cannot be rated** if the organization is unable to perform the practices or if the practices have only been performed outside of the assessed organization and therefore outside of the assessed organization's control.

The goal **cannot be rated** unless the related data are sufficient to determine the extent to which the associated model practices are implemented and institutionalized.

In other words, the assessment team assumes that a particular KPA/PA goal is satisfied unless associated weaknesses, considered in aggregate, have a significant negative impact on the related KPA/PA goal. In the latter case, a rating of unsatisfied is given [Dunaway 01c] [Members of the AMIT 01].

11.3.2.4 Rating of Process Areas/Key Process Areas

When all goals for a KPA/PA have been rated either "satisfied" or "unsatisfied," the KPA/PA can be rated as follows:

*   A KPA/PA is rated "satisfied" if and only if each of the goals is rated "satisfied."
*   A KPA/PA is rated " unsatisfied" if one or more of its goals are rated "unsatisfied."
*   A rating of "partially satisfied" can be indicated for a KPA/PA that has at least one of its goals "satisfied." However, this counts the same as "unsatisfied" when considering maturity level rating.

If a KPA/PA is outside the organization's scope of work, the KPA/PA is designated "not applicable"—a designation that will not impact the maturity level rating. If a KPA/PA is outside the assessment scope, or if sufficient data were not available to determine goal satisfaction, the KPA/PA is designated "not rated," and the KPA/PA must be considered "unsatisfied" for the maturity level rating.

11.3.2.5 Maturity Level Ratings

An organizational or global maturity level rating is not required for an official CBA IPI or SCAMPI. Some organizations using the CMM/CMMI only want to focus on certain KPAs/PAs and do not want to assess all KPAs/PAs within a maturity level. The results of this kind of an assessment can be just as useful in furthering an organization's process improvement program as the results of maturity level assessment.

For organizations that choose to have the assessment team provide an official maturity level rating, the scope of the assessment must include all the KPAs/PAs necessary for the maximum maturity level included in the investigation.

The highest level that is examined will determine the organization's highest possible rated maturity level. For example, the fact that not all Level 4 PAs/KPAs have been rated forces the highest possible rating to be Level 3, even if some Level 4 PAs/KPAs have been rated as satisfied.

Ratings for each goal for each KPA/PA are recorded on a KPA/PA profile worksheet that shows the composite KPA/PA ratings that are to be presented at the final findings presentation.

In addition, if the organization desires to receive individual KPA/PA profiles for each maturity level, the team prepares those as well, alongside the composite KPA/PA profile that shows all maturity levels.

Results of two assessments cannot be combined to produce a maturity level rating. Although it may be useful for an organization to conduct a partial assessment to monitor progress, combining results from assessments performed at different times has a high risk of being misleading [Dunaway 01c].

Figure 11-1 shows an example of a process area profile (staged).

Source: SEI SCAMPI Team Training Materials 2003

Figure 11-1 *Process area profile (staged).*

11.3.2.6 An Example of How Initial Questions Lead to Rating Determinations as Traced from a Technical Interview Through Final Findings

Tracing from Initial Questions to Final Findings

1.0 Interview Stage: Questions Asked and Answers Noted

Project Managers Questions

Question 1: Can you explain how you estimate the size of the product?

PM 1: My software manager does that, and all I see is the manpower figure.

PM 2: Sure, we calculate how many people we need for the job based on how many we needed for the last job.

PM 3: I depend on my software manager.

Question 2: Are you aware of anyone calculating for example if the product would be larger or smaller, or more complex or less complex than the last product?

PM 2: I am not sure what you mean. There was no change to the hardware.

Question 3: Are you aware of any formula (guideline, or even a template) that is written down that would help calculate the size of the product?

PM 1, PM 2, PM 3: No.

Software Managers Questions

Question 1: Can you explain how you estimate the size of the product?

S/W Mgr 1: Since this was a new project with a new methodology, I looked at every requirement and quickly estimated how many lines of code it would take to implement that requirement. We did try to look at function points, but we didn't find it to be as useful.

S/W Mgr 2: I started with the lines of code from the last version of the product. I then estimated how many new and changed lines of code were needed for every new requirement.

S/W Mgr 3: Since this was an object-oriented project, we first calculated the number of objects we were planning to develop. We also came up with an estimate for lines of code. We are trying to see if one way of estimating is better than another.

Question 2: Are you aware of any formula (guideline, or even a template) that is written down that would help calculate the size of the product?

S/W Mgr 1: This is contained, along with our calculations, in the software management plan.

S/W Mgr 2: In the software management plan.

S/W Mgr 3: In the software management plan.

Question 3: Do you discuss how you calculate the size of the product with the project manager or senior manager?

S/W Mgr 1: Not specifically. The PM has never asked for it; he only asks for the number of people that we will need on the project. Executives have never asked me about how the size of the product was estimated or what it actually is.

S/W Mgr 2: No. It is best not to tell the project manager too much.

S/W Mgr 3: We have a new project manager, and these calculations were done before he arrived. He never asked to see the history. I did show the estimates to the old project manager, and I am not sure whether or not he showed them to the executives.

Project Team Leaders Questions

Question 1: Can you explain how you estimate the size of the product?

Team Leader 1: The software manager asks to me to give him lines of code estimate for my subsystem. I look at the requirements assigned to my subsystem and estimate how many lines of code it will take to do the job based on my experience.

Team Leader 2: I ask each of my team members to tell me how many new or changed lines of code it will take to do the changes they need to do for their job. I review it and then give a total figure to the software manager.

Team Leader 3: I work with the software manager to calculate the number of objects that I will be responsible for. For lines of code I give him my estimate.

Question 2: Are you aware of any formula (guideline, or even a template) that is written down that would help calculate the size of the product?

Team Leader 1: My software manager told me how to calculate the lines of code. It may be in the software plan. But to be honest, I never looked.

Team Leader 2: I have been doing this for 10 years. I just know how to do it.

Team Leader 3: I went to a class with the team, and in the class, we were taught how and what to calculate when using object-oriented design. Our notes certainly had the methodology we were supposed to use. Lines of code calculations I have been doing forever. I helped write Standard Operating Procedure 1-220 that describes how to do this.

2.0 Transferring Notes to Observations Using a Data Worksheet

Based on information noted previously:

Goal	ID	Goal/Practice	PIID Strengths	PIID Source/Type A, B, C	PIID Opportunities for Improvement	Model Practices FI, LI, PI, NI, NY, NA	Information Needed
SG 1		**Establish estimates. Estimates of project planning parameters are established and maintained.**					
	SP 1.2	Establish and maintain estimates of the attributes of the work products and tasks.	Lines of code were estimated. Requirements were reviewed and estimated based on requirements.	(C) S/W manager 1, 2, 3 TL 1, 2, 3		Largely implemented	
			Objects were estimated.	(C) S/W manager 3 TL 3			
			Software management plan describes how it was done.	(A) S/W plan 1, 2, 3 (C) S/W manager 1, 2, 3 (A) Procedure SOP 1-220			

Figure 11-2   Observations recorded.

Goal	ID	Goal/Practice	PIID Strengths	PIID Source/Type A, B, C	PIID Opportunities for Improvement	Model Practices FI, LI, PI, NI, NY, NA	Information Needed
			Although some could not say if estimates were documented, they explained how to calculate size as written down in procedures.	(C) TL 1, 2, 3			
				(C) PM 1, 2, 3	Some project people were not aware of how the size of product was calculated or how used.		
				(C) S/W mgr 1, 2 , 3	In most cases, size of product was not reviewed with PMs or executives.		

Figure 11-2 (continued)

Project Planning

3.0 Draft Findings: Project Planning

Strengths:

Size of product is calculated (lines of code and objects).

Weaknesses:

Not everyone reviews the estimates for the size of the product and how product size is to be used to calculate resources and schedule.

4.0 Response from Draft Findings Meeting

Participants suggested that the team be more explicit about which groups were not reviewing the size of the product. (In this case, the problem was that senior and project managers were not meeting their reviewing responsibilities.)

5.0 Final Findings: Project Planning

Strengths:

Size of product is calculated (lines of code and objects).

Weaknesses:

In most cases, senior management and project management do not review how the size is estimated for a product and how that estimate is used to calculate resources and schedule.

6.0 Rating for the Practice

The team agreed that the Project Planning PA specific practice 1.2 was largely implemented, and this result was noted in the determination of the rating for Specific Goal 1.

7.0 Recommendations in the Final Findings Report

In senior management project reviews, project managers should be required to report on the size estimates and explain how they impact resources and schedule estimates.

11.3.3 Ratings: The Process Is Not Always Smooth

Assessment teams use the same decision-making process for ratings as they did in previous consolidations—they do it by consensus. However, although the final consensus should represent an easy and logical last deduction from the numerous moments of consensus that have preceded it, occasionally this is not the case, for reasons that are infrequently discussed but nevertheless important to remember.

11.3.3.1 Coming to Consensus About Rating KPAs/PAs

One of the most difficult moments in an assessment is when the assessment team must come to consensus about whether the organization has satisfied the goals of assessed KPAs/PAs. The "satisfied/not satisfied" rating of each KPA/PA directly impacts the maturity level rating of the organization. If a goal is found to be unsatisfied, the corresponding KPA/PA also must be judged not satisfied and therefore also the maturity level on which the KPA/PA resides. (If the organization chooses to use the continuous model, individual PA capability level ratings are compiled, but an organizational maturity level rating is not assigned.)

Even if the assessment team agrees about the requirements of the model and has previously come to consensus about observation statements indicating weaknesses, a great deal of heat can be generated when rating begins.

In general, if the organization's practices for each KPA/PA are either all strong or all weak, there isn't much room for controversy. However, when there is a mix of strong and weak evidence for a number of practices, the team's task becomes truly vexing. Finding a weakness does not automatically mean that a given goal is "unsatisfied." The team must use judgment as to whether the weakness is significant—that is, whether it impacts the implementation of the goal.

One kind of problem at this stage of an assessment involves the fact that both CMM/CMMI models may seem ambiguous in their description of some required practices to team members who are not really familiar with the logic of the CMM/CMMI. During the rating session, these apparent ambiguities can provoke heated arguments. Teams often quarrel, to give only three examples, about what is meant by (1) "objective" SQA of the process and product, (2) product size, and (3) the need in large organizations to involve not only software managers but also project managers in the assessment process and in the improvement program.

Arguments have also traditionally arisen concerning a more general ambiguity about how completely practices must be implemented to satisfy a goal. (Sometimes even if a practice was not implemented at all, it was still possible to satisfy the goal if the team thought the gap was not significant.) The SCAMPI method has attempted to address this larger problem by requiring that the team come to consensus in its day-to-day consolidation on whether a practice is fully, largely, partially, or not implemented. If a practice is partially or not implemented, the corresponding goal must be rated not satisfied.

On an assessment of Organization V, after each day's interviewing, one internal team member argued with the team about every weakness the team reviewed. These daily consolidation meetings lasted well into the evenings. The other team members and the Lead Assessor would repeatedly remind the skeptic that determination of weakness was always based on what had been said in the interviews. The internal team member was asked if his memory of the interviews was different from the others, and he would say no, but he would add that he didn't agree with the team's characterization of what the interviewees said. He was asked if there were additional people he thought the team should interview or if some people should be interviewed again. Every night after long battles the team would finally come to consensus.

The skeptic was of course afraid that any weakness the team recorded would result in a lower rating for his organization. When it came time for the final ratings, however, the situation curiously reversed itself. The internal team member argued that the weaknesses that had been agreed upon meant that the organization could not satisfy the pertinent KPAs. The other team members, however, now equivocated. All the issues were argued out again. The organization achieved Maturity Level 3, but only after universal exhaustion.

One of the happier endings to a ratings quarrel involved Organization F. In the middle of an assessment, the management of Organization F thought it was performing many Level 3 activities and was certainly a solid Level 2 organization. However, as the assessment progressed, it became clear that many of its Level 2 processes exhibited serious weaknesses. The team dutifully rated the full set of Level 3 KPAs, but all proved to be unsatisfied. Tempers flared when the team started to look at Level 2 KPAs, and the Lead Assessor suggested that the team break for the day and reconvene the next morning. After a night's sleep, the organization's SQA team member acknowledged that the organization was not performing the Level 2 activities described in the model and acknowledged that it was important for the organization's senior management to understand this so that they could encourage real improvement. Because of his remarks, the team took another hard look at the evidence and was finally able to reach consensus. Because the team undertook its task with a new sense of seriousness, the remaining Level 2 KPAs were assessed dispassionately, and the organization was rated "Level 1." All this took place two hours before the final briefing. The assessment was completed, and the organization did improve afterwards, but the team came very close to not reaching consensus.

11.3.3.2 How Lead Assessors Can Negotiate Instances of Intransigence as Ratings Are Consolidated and Assigned

At the crunch time of any assessment, there is almost always a tendency for team members from the organization to resist ratings of weakness and for the team as a whole to feel sympathy for an organization that is about to fall short. However, the Lead Assessor, who is charged with keeping in mind the long-term benefit of the organization, has a duty to counter these reactions.

An experienced Lead Assessor should negotiate problems of ambiguity by patiently pointing to places in the models that clarify these issues.

When ratings based on a clear pattern of evidence are resisted, it is best first to go back to the facts that have been collected and ask if more data needs to be collected, and if any observation that had been agreed to should be changed (and why). This will focus the ratings discussions on the evidence that has been consolidated since the beginning of the assessment.

In cases where negative consequences to the organization resulting from an honest assessment are present, it may be useful to talk about those consequences and if possible try to mitigate them. (If an internal team member is worried about losing his job, the Lead Assessor can go and speak to the president or managing director about the situation. In most cases these fears are unfounded.) In cases where fears exist that the whole organization would suffer, it is sometimes possible to turn the assessment into a "health check" and schedule another assessment in the future when the organization's deficiencies have been corrected.

John, the process improvement manager and a VP in Company D, scheduled an assessment in the last quarter of the year. The year before, a health check had been conducted, which showed significant weaknesses at Levels 2 and 3. Although not much process improvement work had been conducted, John felt it was important for his organization to have an official assessment rating, even though a poor rating would negatively affect his company's bid for an important contract. The assessment was begun, and eventually it became clear that the organization would be rated at Level 1. Because the rating could have prevented the organization from winning its contract (a contract that corporate headquarters had spent a substantial amount of money bidding on), the Lead Assessor checked with both the president of the organization and the president of the corporation. They were both grateful for the consultation, and both agreed that the assessment should be turned into a health check. The bid for the contract remained unaffected, and the corporation's commitment to process improvement was sustained.

Sometimes teams try to argue that if an organization is given the benefit of the doubt, it will respond to this encouragement by an eagerness to improve. However, the reverse is often the case, and the Lead Assessor should communicate this to the team. Telling an organization that it is better than it really is can make it complacent, causing it to postpone or cancel improvement activities and risk future decline. (The organization may even take the team's "generosity" as a sign that process improvement is subjective and without rigor—just another empty program that will fade away like all the others.)

This rule holds even when the rating only concerns one KPA.

Organization E had followed a course of process improvement for over three years and had nearly finished its first assessment. As in many immature companies, however, some of its managers felt that they only needed to improve in a few areas, and so they had not taken the program seriously. During the ratings stage of the assessment, the assessment team agreed that the organization had only satisfied one Level 2 PA (requirements management) and had failed to satisfy the others. Then on the last day of interviewing, it became clear that there were real problems even in requirements management. When it came time to finalize the maturity ratings, some team members felt that the organization would be demoralized if they did not at least satisfy one PA. One team member identified strongly with the organization and suggested how bad any of them would feel if their organization was judged deficient in every area. After many hours of discussion, though, the team stuck to the facts and finally agreed that no Level 2 PA had been satisfied. No one felt good about the decision, but about two months later, the Lead Assessor had the chance to speak to some of the organization's developers, who told him that their management requirements procedures were even worse than they looked, and that they would have considered the assessment discredited if the requirements management PA had been marked "satisfied." An honest rating in this case was the beginning not of discouragement but rather of heightened morale in the organization.

11.4 CMMI Continuous Model

Although this book is not primarily concerned with assessments based on the CMMI continuous representation, it may be useful to review the differences that exist between this kind of SCAMPI and the ones discussed previously.

11.4.1 Rating

When using the CMMI continuous representation model (rather than the CMMI staged representation model), the team is not rating the organization as a whole, only that part of the organization defined by the scope of the assessment. Assigning a capability rating then becomes an optional activity, at the discretion of the assessment sponsor.

Rating capability levels on the Capability Level Rating Table (see Table 11-1) for each PA depends on the highest level and all levels below for which its specific goals and the generic goals are satisfied.

Table 11-1   *Capability Level Ratings*

Capability Level (CL)	Engineering Process Areas	Other Process Areas
0	Default Rating	Default Rating
1	Generic goal for CL 1 is rated Satisfied. All specific goals are rated Satisfied—including base practices only.	Generic goal for CL 1 is rated Satisfied. All specific goals are rated Satisfied.
2	Generic goals for CLs 1 and 2 are rated Satisfied. All specific goals are rated Satisfied—including specific practices at CLs 1 and 2.	Generic goals for CLs 1 and 2 are rated Satisfied. All specific goals are rated Satisfied.

Capability Level (CL)	Engineering Process Areas	Other Process Areas
3	Generic goals for CLs 1, 2, and 3 are rated Satisfied. All specific goals are rated Satisfied—including specific practices at CLs 1, 2, and 3.	Generic goals for CLs 1, 2, and 3 are rated Satisfied. All specific goals are rated Satisfied.
4	Generic goals for CLs 1, 2, 3, and 4 are rated Satisfied. All specific goals are rated Satisfied—including specific practices at CLs 1, 2, and 3.	Generic goals for CLs 1, 2, 3, and 4 are rated Satisfied. All specific goals are rated Satisfied.
5	Generic goals for CLs 1, 2, 3, 4, and 5 are rated Satisfied. All specific goals are rated Satisfied—including specific practices at CLs 1, 2, and 3.	Generic goals for CLs 1, 2, 3, 4, and 5 are rated Satisfied. All specific goals are rated Satisfied.

[CMMI Product Team 01b] and [Members of the AMIT 01]

The rating of PA capability levels is carried out from top to bottom or from bottom to top.

The bottom-up approach:

- Judges whether or not the PA is at Capability Level 1 based on the specific and generic goals being satisfied. In this case, only the base practices are considered in rating the goals.
- Judges whether or not the PA is at Capability Level 2, based on the specific and generic goals being satisfied. The advanced practice for Capability Level 2 must be considered in rating the goals for the engineering PAs.
- Proceeds incrementally until the team cannot rate the goals as being satisfied.

The top-down approach:

- Begins at the highest desired capability level (which was determined during assessment planning) and judges whether or not the organization is operating at that PA capability level.
- If the PA is not at the highest desired capability level, considers whether or not it can be judged to be operating at the next lower level.

- Proceeds incrementally until the team reaches a point at which all of the relevant goals are rated as satisfied, or until ratings lead to Capability Level 0 [Members of the AMIT 01].

The rating of goal satisfaction works the same as it does in the staged model. It is a judgment based on the implementation of practices that map to the goal. In rating specific goals for the engineering PAs, the set of specific practices that relate to the goals differs for Capability Levels 0, 1, 2, and 3 through 5. Depending on the capability level at which the rating is performed, there are up to four unique sets of specific practices associated with the specific goals that are considered.

The Lead Assessor is responsible for choosing one of the two optional rating approaches.

Determining if the PA is satisfied is performed the same way as it is in the staged model. (See Section 11.3.2.4, "Rating of Process Areas/Key Process Areas.")

11.4.2 Determining the Capability Profile

When using the CMMI continuous model, the team determines a Capability Profile that graphically depicts the capability level rating assigned to each PA with the scope of the assessment. The Capability Profile is optional and is at the discretion of the assessment sponsor.

A simple bar chart is used to display the capability level for each PA. The horizontal axis represents the PA, and the vertical axis represents the Capability Level dimensions 0, 1, 2, 3, 4, and 5 [Members of the AMIT 01].

Figure 11-3 is an example of a process area profile (continuous).

11.5 The Preparation of Final Findings

Final findings presentations include information such as the number and type of interviews held, the number of questionnaire participants, an account of the assessment process, a list of projects investigated in depth, strengths and weaknesses of KPAs/PAs investigated, and the KPA/PA profile.

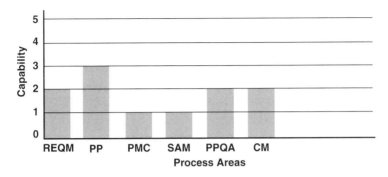

Source: SEI SCAMPI Team Materials 2003

Figure 11-3 *Process area profile (continuous).*

After rating is completed, the team revises (beginning with the first KPA/PA) all the draft findings charts for use in the final findings presentation. Needed changes are made, including adding or deleting strengths or weaknesses. The team uses this opportunity to carefully describe weaknesses that were discussed during final consolidation. Any recommendations that the team has noted for improving existing processes are also noted at this time. This is done for every KPA/PA within the scope of the assessment.

A summary KPA/PA profile is completed that lists all the KPAs/PAs and KPA/PA ratings satisfied, not satisfied, not rated, or not applicable. This chart also displays the maturity level rating for the organization.

The team must clearly address the organization's overall strengths and weaknesses (those things that cut across the organization or that have to do with the organization culture).

A set of recommendations is usually appended (though this is not mandatory). Such recommendations make it easier for the organization to begin to think about how those areas in most need of improvement can be tackled.

As throughout the assessment, the team must come to consensus on each and every statement and slide.

Preparing the final presentation also involves deciding on the order of the slides and the person or people who will present them. In most cases the presentation should consist of an introduction (on the assessment process, how many people were interviewed, which projects, etc.), an account of the strengths and weaknesses of each KPA/PA, an overview of the organization's strengths and weaknesses, and finally a summary display of the KPAs/PAs and the maturity level rating. Recommendations are one of the last items. The presentation must conclude with an indication of how the organization is going to follow up on the assessment results, such as action planning, training, and so on.

The Lead Assessor may decide to change the sequence of the presentation, depending on the involvement of the sponsor. If a president or managing director seems not to be focused on each and every KPA/PA but is interested in what is said about the organization's culture and how it could be improved, placing the presentation of overall strengths and weaknesses and the section with recommendations before the KPA summary might be preferred. If the sponsor becomes interested in the overall organizational comments, he or she may then be more amenable to listening to the detailed KPA/PA analysis.

Another decision that needs to be considered is when to announce the ratings. Most teams think it is best to leave this to the end of the presentation so that the audience remains attentive. However, it may be that participants neglect most of the data in their anxiety to hear the ratings. Various presidents and managing directors whom we have interviewed have told us they much prefer getting the rating out of the way so that they can concentrate on the meat of the presentation. Clearly it is useful to discuss this decision with the leaders of the assessed organization beforehand.

Although the sponsor doesn't have to be told the results of the assessment before the final presentation, it is usually appreciated. Most senior managers do not like to be surprised. When pre-briefed, they can play a significant and useful part in the final presentation and a more involved part in the post-assessment improvement program (see Section 11.6, "Presenting Final Findings Informally to Senior Management [Optional]").

Choosing who presents the results is important. A particular presenter can either help an organization accept the results or provoke hostility. This choice is particularly important if the results are not what the organization had expected.

The Lead Assessor may of course give the entire final findings presentation himself. Some organizations will accept the data more easily if an outside authority presents it.

On the other hand, if respected internal assessment team members present some of the technical findings in their own words, the organization may accept the information more easily.

11.5.1 Final Findings Presentation—A Sample Template

The following represent typical items found in a final findings presentation. Each assessment develops a presentation appropriate to the organization.

Final Findings Presentation—A Sample Template

> **(Final findings presentation is to provide the sponsor with the results of the assessment. Typically, there is a broad audience from the assessed organization.)**

- Title slide:
  - Name of assessed organization.
  - Assessment dates.
- Findings presentation includes agenda:
  - Scope of assessment.
  - Overview of assessment.
  - Reference model.
  - Findings.
  - Rating process.
  - Next steps.
- Business goals—insert sponsor's business goals that motivate the assessment (optional).

(continued)

Final Findings Presentation—A Sample Template (continued)

- Organizational scope—state the portion of the organization included in the assessment.

- Assessment team and support:

  - Names of assessment team members listed in alphabetical order with organizational affiliation specified.

  - Support staff—name(s) of site coordinator(s) and other support staff.

- Overview of assessment:

  - Quantify number of interviewees, e.g., project managers, management representatives, software practitioners.

  - Number of questionnaires completed.

  - Number of observations recorded.

  - Number of final findings recorded.

- Onsite activities—include chart showing onsite activities.

- Reference model—include chart showing process areas of reference model.

- CMM/CMMI scope:

  - Indicate the process areas included in the assessment data collection.

- Include 1-3 slides for each process area within the model scope of the assessment indicating strengths and weaknesses.

- General strengths.

- General weaknesses.

  - Indicate issues identified that impact the development processes that might not be related to the reference model.

- KPA/PA profile—use a chart that indicates all of the process areas of the reference model, showing which process areas are satisfied, not satisfied, not applicable, and not rated. The maturity level may also be shown on the profile.

- Recommendations.

- Next steps—indicate by dates when the final report is to be delivered (optional), when action-planning activities are scheduled, and when a re-assessment is anticipated.

11.5.2 Examples from Final Findings Presentations

*1.0 An Example of a Final Findings PA Strengths
        and Weaknesses Statement
        (Level 3 PA = Organizational Process Focus)*

Description:

The purpose of the Organizational Process Focus PA is to plan and implement organizational process improvement based on a thorough understanding of the current strengths and weaknesses of the organization's processes and process assets.

Strengths:

A number of people are involved in process improvement:

SEPG.

CMMI project.

Various new tools and component development initiatives.

The managing director oversees all major activities.

Most people know that they can provide improvement suggestions to the SEPG.

Weaknesses:

Process improvement activities are not always well coordinated:

> For example, SEPG and CMMI Project are not aware of all process improvement activities.
>
> Plans are not clearly coordinated between all activities.
>
> There are different steering committees for each activity (although some members overlap).
>
> Responsibility between process improvement activities is not always clearly defined.

Most people do not submit improvement ideas to the SEPG, and if they do, they do not receive a timely response from the SEPG:

> This has caused some people not to continue to submit ideas.

Most of the technical people doing process improvement do not see a need to coordinate with the SEPG.

There are no clear criteria for prioritizing candidates for process improvement (both large and small activities).

When improvement projects are done, there are few measurements, few lessons learned, and not enough information fed back to the SEPG:

> This may prevent the organization from learning and improving.

2.0 Examples of Final Findings Strengths and Weaknesses Statements Having to Do with the Process Improvement Activities of the Entire Organization Rather than with a Particular Process Area

Strengths:

There is an overall sense that process improvement activities undertaken over the last two years have benefited the organization.

Quality has improved.

Production errors have been reduced.

Quality reviews have been positively received.

Peer reviews have helped to improve quality of the products.

Customer relationship is good.

In general, the procedures have made life easier.

Project Management procedures are a big strength, and people use it.

It is easier to participate in projects across different sites.

It is seen as a benefit that all people must follow the same procedures and must document what they have done (new people not totally lost, and reuse is easier).

Fewer people work late hours.

People in the organization have all said:

They have a sense of belonging and pride in working here.

There are many skilled people willing and able to go the extra mile.

People in the organization have a lot of knowledge about the business.

Weaknesses:

The message from management is perceived as:

Process improvement (CMMI) is not as important as project work.

The company has a tradition of being a "not invented here" organization.

Not many take action to improve the processes they use.

The concept of identifying defects before test is not engrained in the organization.

Some view "more processes" as only more bureaucracy.

It seems some people think that creating a firm structure kills innovation.

Need to understand mature organizational behaviors.

No culture of blaming people (picking scapegoats).

Being self-critical—"I can do this better."

Realizing that looking for defects in all phases is the key to better productivity, predictability, and quality improvements.

Other Key Weaknesses:

Most people do not know the number of defects found before test, during test, and in production.

The different process improvement initiatives are not coordinated and controlled centrally.

Development methodologies are not captured at the organizational level, and in some cases, different methodologies are used on the same project.

Senior management does not consistently review summary measurements for the project processes, e.g. configuration management, design, function tests, etc.

3.0 Final Findings Presentation: Sample Recommendations

The Organization Should Implement Inspections

Purpose: To detect, measure, and fix defects before test. This approach will improve quality and ultimately lower the project cost.

Implementation: Inspections are a defined methodology, which the organization should adopt. This means training people in how to conduct inspections and collecting, regularly analyzing, and reporting results. The inspections will replace some of the known peer reviews that are currently being conducted.

Target audience and areas: Developers should conduct inspections for requirements, design, code, test plans, and test procedures.

Number of defects per review are categorized by severity and should be reported into the Measurement and Analysis Tool as a basis for statistical analysis.

The Organization Should Restructure Its Process Improvement Program for Greater Benefits

Purpose: To ensure that all process improvements are collected, evaluated, and implemented consistently throughout the whole organization.

Implementation: New structure should be created and put in place to drive this effort.

Target audience and areas: The whole organization will be involved in this effort.

The Organization Should Provide Support to the Developers

Purpose: Good and reproducible education.

Facilitate and support the learning process.

Facilitate job rotation within the organization and thereby increased possibility for personal development.

Implementation: Developer cookbook with underlying technical methodologies should be created.

A mentoring program should be reestablished for IT specialists and IT professionals.

Target audience and areas: Developers in all application areas and the IT specialist focus group.

Senior Management Needs to Improve Reporting Procedures

Purpose: To provide management with early warning indicators.

Implementation: Monthly project reviews that include data on quality, productivity, and predictability (max 10 key measurements per project in a stoplight chart).

Target audience and areas: Senior manager and executive staff.

11.6 Presenting Final Findings Informally to Senior Management (Optional)

No matter how hard senior managers try to keep the long-term goals of their organization in mind, it is only natural for them to have their heart set on achieving a "good" rating. If they have scheduled a Level 3 assessment, they want to be Level 3. In some cases, they have told their corporate managers that they *are* Level 3. In other cases, bonuses have been tied to the maturity level rating, and in a few cases, their jobs may be at stake. It is not unusual, therefore, that when senior managers do not like what they hear, they may lash out at the team and even make threats.

Here again, an experienced Lead Assessor must remember that the function of an assessment is honestly to reflect an organization's strengths and weaknesses. The assessment process should never be corrupted. However, a Lead Assessor should also be sensitive to senior management constraints and concerns and try to work with them to mitigate real problems. The best way to do this is to meet with senior managers at least once before the assessment begins and several times during the course of the assessment, including one meeting early on and another right before the final findings. Bringing the senior manager in on the findings makes him feel more a part of the assessment and makes it more likely that he will want to implement its recommended solutions. (Lead Assessors be warned, however, that an adamantly hostile senior manager may accuse the Lead Assessor of trying to pre-judge the assessment when informed at an early stage that significant pieces of KPAs/PAs seem to be missing.)

Even when senior managers seem to be intractable, an informal pre-briefing before the final presentation can save what might have been an impossible situation.

On one assessment, after the draft findings and ratings meetings, the Lead Assessor along with several assessment team members scheduled a meeting to communicate the results personally to the president of the organization. The organization had not achieved the maturity level rating (Level 3) he expected. The president looked concerned and asked the Lead Assessor "Would it be possible to consider a smaller portion of the organization? If it were rated at Level 3, would the organization be rated Level 3?" The Lead Assessor explained that things didn't work that way. The president then asked in a menacing way whether there was *any way* at all for the assessment to produce a Level 3 rating. The Lead Assessor again had to say no. The president then said that he could probably find a Lead Assessor who would give the organization a Level 3 rating. Maybe the people in the assessment had been too hard on themselves. The Lead Assessor got through the rest of the meeting as well as he could, but after this attempt to intimidate him he expected the worst from the final findings meeting. He was surprised. The president (who did not have a software background) listened to the substance of the final presentation. Then, having been prepared by the pre-briefing, he announced that although he did not understand everything about the KPAs, he did understand the team's account of the overall organizational strengths and weaknesses, and he agreed with them. Moreover, he added, he had to assume that because they were accurate, the rest of the assessment was also accurate. By this time, he had come to terms with his disappointment and had started to process the results of the assessment as information to be added to his existing knowledge of the organization. He not only had started to think of the results as useful, but he also had decided to play a role in transmitting the results. The pre-briefing had helped transform the assessment from an exercise in futility to a significant (if painful) moment in the organization's attempt to improve itself.

11.7 The Final Findings Presentation

The final findings presentation is a key mechanism for transitioning ownership of the assessment findings back to the organization. This is accomplished partly when the people in the organization recognize that their feedback during the draft findings meeting has been incorporated into the final findings.

The final findings presentation delivers the assessment's results to the sponsor and to anyone else the sponsor wants to include, as well as everyone who participated in the assessment. The presentation should sound as if it were an articulation of what the organization itself had said, and the assessment team should stress that its major contribution has been to gather together information that no one person in the organization could have possibly known, and to analyze this information in light of current state-of-the-art software engineering standards.

The Lead Assessor usually presents the introduction, the summary chart listing the KPA/PA and maturity level ratings, the statement of organizational strengths and weaknesses, and a list of recommendations.

The Lead Assessor must present this material in the most positive manner. No one fails an assessment, and the fact that an organization has chosen to be assessed almost always means that a significant part of its operations is oriented toward improvement. Even if the organization has not attained the maturity level it sought, the Lead Assessor should explain, for example, that the current organizational processes provide an excellent basis for immediate improvements of particular kinds, or that the organization is in fact performing activities *on some projects* at a very high level, and that with work, the whole organization can be brought up to that level. Technical issues should never be described as insurmountable, and the Lead Assessor should explain how organization-wide cultural issues that perpetuate certain problems can be changed and how this in turn can facilitate the institutionalization of many technical improvements in a very short timeframe.

Organization N hoped to be Level 2 but did not quite make it because it had mounted a too-ambitious SQA program that failed to perform certain Level 2 functions. At the final findings meeting, the Lead Assessor pointed out that the

> SQA plans were highly sophisticated and, when refined, would greatly benefit the entire corporation. He also noted that it would not be very long before the SQA program would be up and running, and that when it was, the organization would be well on its way not just toward Level 3 but toward Level 5. Without making specific promises, his optimism transformed the mood of the meeting, and the organization did in fact keep up with process improvement and before too long was reassessed at Level 2.

At the end of the presentation, the president or managing director thanks the team and addresses the organization. His speech is the beginning of the next phase of the improvement process.

In most final findings presentations, questions are permitted, but they are rarely asked. Participants sometimes are requested to offer reactions to the presentation on a questionnaire stating whether they believe that the findings were accurate, if they believe action would be taken based on the assessment results, and so on.

This information can be useful to the organization in moving forward with the process improvement initiative.

11.8 Post-Final Findings Executive Session (Optional)

In some assessments (especially when there has been no executive pre-briefing), the president or managing director and his staff may want to ask the assessment team questions about the substance of the presented final findings after the meeting is over. This request should always be honored, as explanation can only help. A post-presentation executive session helps involve the sponsor in the assessment and the improvement activities that follow it. However, everyone involved should be reminded that confidentiality remains in effect.

11.9 Assessment Wrap-Up

An assessment wrap-up is an informal meeting between the members of the assessment team devoted to discussing lessons learned, completing any required SEI feedback forms, and talking about ways to improve before the next assessment.

Three major goals are associated with an assessment wrap-up:

1. To complete the transmission of assessment results to the assessed organization, prepare a context for assessment follow-on activities, and assign responsibility for writing the final report, if one was required by the sponsor.

2. To ensure that the assessment team members have an accurate understanding of their roles in any post-assessment activities, such as final reports, action planning, and so on.

3. To provide feedback to the SEI. This feedback informs the SEI about the results of the assessment and helps the SEI to improve the assessment method. The achievement level of the organization assessed also enters the SEI's database and provides additional information about the state of the practice in process improvement around the world.[1]

11.9.1 Organization Wrap-Up

Because members of the assessment team are also members of the organization assessed, the wrap-up meeting impacts the way the assessment results are absorbed by the organization. The team should make sure that any issues already raised by the assessment's sponsor about the assessment findings are addressed, and that there is a common understanding of the manner in which any remaining commitments to the organization will be fulfilled. (The latter includes further guidance to the sponsor about completion of the assessment and responsibility for improvement activities.)

A confidence report is communicated to the sponsor in the form of a verbal or written statement that identifies those elements of

---

[1.] At the date of this book's publication, approximately 2,000 assessments had been recorded by the SEI. For an analysis of feedback from over 200 assessments, see the 2001 publication by Donna Dunaway and Michele Baker [Dunaway 01a].

the assessment that the Lead Assessor believes should produce exceptionally high or low confidence in the assessment results.

The Lead Assessor identifies (if necessary) individuals responsible for fulfilling remaining obligations and sets a schedule for work on a final report if the organization so wishes. If a final report is requested, it should be submitted within 60 days of the end of the assessment (refer to Chapter 4, "Planning and Preparing for an Assessment, Part 1: Senior Management Responsibilities"). Often, the final report is forgone in favor of an action plan to be created by members of the assessed organization. This plan serves as a bridge between the assessment and follow-on improvement activities.

Finally, the Lead Assessor hands all detailed assessment data (minus identification of sources) to a responsible member of the organization (usually an organization assessment team member designated by the sponsor). Confidentiality is to be maintained indefinitely. Team notes are shredded. Documents are returned to their sources by the organization site coordinator.

11.9.2 Assessment Data Sent to the SEI Appraisal Database

The Lead Assessor is required to make sure that a statement of the assessment data as recorded in appropriate forms is returned to the SEI within 30 days of the conclusion of the assessment. These statements include:

- A copy of the final findings presentation, including the KPA/PA profile and the maturity rating.
- A PAIS form (Record of Entry to Process Appraisal Information System), which describes the organization to the SEI and registers the assessment data with the SEI.
- For a SCAMPI: An Appraisal Disclosure Statement (ADS) is required. The ADS includes information about the following:

  A description of the organization assessed

  Assessment dates

  Assessment method used

  Reference model used

  Process areas within the assessment scope

Key participants (sponsor, team leader, team members, site coordinator)

Ratings (process areas, maturity level)

Evaluation by the Lead Assessor of whether the assessment was properly conducted and of the accuracy of the results.

The SEI keeps all assessment data confidential. It does not disclose the name of an organization or project that has returned data to the SEI. The SEI uses assessment information to prepare reports on the worldwide state of the practice, and these reports are posted as the Maturity Profile on the SEI web site, `www.sei.cmu.edu`, and updated twice annually [SEMA 03].

11.9.3 Feedback Relating to the Effectiveness of the Assessment Method

The SEI requires several feedback forms be sent to back to them after the completion of the assessment.

1. A Team Member Feedback Form, which addresses questions such as:

   What model (CMM/CMMI) training was provided prior to the assessment?

   How would you rate your model knowledge?

   Did your experience meet the team member selection criteria?

   Did the Lead Assessor provide assessment team training for you? Describe.

   How well did the training provide for your role as a team member?

   Were the interviewees forthcoming with information? Describe.

   How would you rate the performance of the assessment team?

   How would you rate the performance of the Lead Assessor?

   Additional questions are asked regarding the level of difficulty of model understanding, time management, and execution of onsite activities.

   How would you improve the assessment method?

2. A Lead Assessor Feedback Form. This form addresses questions such as:

Do you believe that the assessment findings accurately describe the state of the development process in the assessed organization?

Were the interviewees forthcoming and honest in providing information during the assessment?

Were the assessment team members objective in performing their responsibilities?

How would you rate the performance of the assessment team?

How confident are you that the organization will support the implementation of improvements based on the assessment findings?

Additional questions are asked regarding the model understanding, time management, and execution of onsite activities.

What performance improvements would you like to see in future assessment teams?

3. A Sponsor Feedback Form. This form addresses questions such as:

How important are these issues in your organization; i.e., defects found after release, schedule and planning more effectively, estimate resources more accurately, and satisfy corporate requirements for process improvement?

How important were the objectives of the assessment; e.g., to initiate the process improvement program, achieve a maturity level, and/or monitor process improvement progress? Were these objectives achieved?

Do you think that the assessment findings accurately reflect the state of the software process in the organization?

How well did the Lead Assessor set your expectations for the assessment?

How would you rate the performance of the assessment team for this assessment?

How would you rate the performance of the Lead Assessor for this assessment?

How much involvement did you have in determining the assessment scope, both the organization scope and the reference model scope?

How well do you expect the assessment findings to provide guidance for planning follow-on process improvement activities?

How confident are you that you will be able to actively support the implementation of improvements based on assessment findings?

What improvements to the assessment would you suggest?

4. For a CBA IPI: A Lead Assessor Requirements Checklist. This form can be used early in the assessment by the Lead Assessor as a planning tool. It consists of a checklist to aid the Lead Assessor in ensuring that each of the required activities of a CBA IPI have been satisfactorily conducted [Dunaway 01b].

11.9.4 Confidence Report Template for CBA IPI

For a CBA IPI, the Lead Assessor must (either verbally or in writing) provide a confidence report to the assessment sponsor to report any issues that might affect confidence in the accuracy and completeness of the assessment results. The confidence report is delivered during the assessment so that remedial action may be taken if needed and if possible. The confidence report must address the kind of risks that could produce a low confidence in the accuracy and completeness of the assessment results. Examples of confidence factors that need to be considered are:

- **Composition of the assessment team.**
  - Members' qualifications, e.g., team members need sufficient model and method training. If most team members are inexperienced in assessments, the use of the CMM model, or the organization's products, this may be problematic for the team's effectiveness.

- Size of the team, e.g., a requirement of four team members must be met. A team larger than 10 is problematic and can affect time management and the ability to reach consensus.
- Potential biases of any team members, particularly if they have a vested interest in the assessment results.
- **Organizational scope of the assessment.**
  - Cohesiveness of the appraised entity in terms of its management structure, geographic location, and product lines.
  - The extent to which the participants are forthcoming concerning any shortcomings in the organization processes.
  - The number of projects and the extent to which they are representative of the appraised entity; e.g., a significant project might be omitted due to some process insufficiencies.
  - The number of people and the extent to which they are representative of the appraised entity.
  - The extent to which data collected covers the selected projects and is corroborated by the selected participants.
- **Use of data collection techniques planned and achieved.**
  - Combination of data collection techniques used; i.e., instruments, documents, interviews, and presentations.
  - Extent to which the data collected is corroborated.
- **Validation of findings.**
  - Rules of corroboration used in validating findings.
  - Validation of findings by the appraised entity; e.g., draft finding presentations.
- **Time spent (the amount of time spent per unit appraised; e.g., process area and organizational unit).**
- **Adherence to the assessment plan.**

11.9.5 Assessment Acknowledgement Letter—Template

Lead Assessors are frequently asked by the assessed organization or an associated contracting agency to acknowledge that an organization has performed a CBA IPI or SCAMPI assessment. Because the SEI does not certify or acknowledge received assessment results, a Lead Assessor may choose to send a letter such as the following:

[Date]
[Sponsor Name and Address]

Dear **[Sponsor's Name]**:

Thank you for permitting me to participate in your recent [specify CBA IPI or SCAMPI], which concluded with the Final Findings Briefing on **[last day of onsite period]**. As the Lead Assessor, I want to commend each of the assessment team members for their dedication and for the fine job that they did. **[Name of site coordinator]**, as site coordinator, made our jobs easier with **[his/her]** smooth handling of the assessment planning and logistics. It was a pleasure to work with this intelligent, cooperative group of people.

[Name of assessed organization] has worked hard on the process improvement initiative. Your own strong management support has been a key element in your accomplishments. I share your pride in the assessment team's findings that indicate **[Name of assessed organization]** has achieved a Maturity Level **[X]** by satisfying all of the (key) process areas at Level **[x,y,z]** in the [CMM or CMMI]. The assessment also acknowledges, as indicated in the Final Findings Briefing, that **[additional PAs/KPAs rated]** have also been satisfied.

I look forward to further work with **[Name of assessed organization]** in your continued efforts to achieve process improvement.

Best regards,
[Name of Lead Assessor]

SEI-authorized Lead Assessor

Copies to: **[Assessment Team Members]**

Chapter 12

How to Use the Results of an Assessment Productively

12.1 Introduction: After an Assessment

After an assessment, either euphoria or shock reigns. Both should quickly give way to a disciplined plan to build on the momentum of the assessment and to follow up its findings and recommendations by putting in place an organization to institute necessary changes. If too much time passes, this momentum—and an assessment's power to motivate change—evaporates.

This chapter concerns procedures for establishing a post-assessment action plan and addresses crucial questions related to who drives such planning and how it unfolds:

12.1 What happens after an assessment?

12.2 Where does a disciplined post-assessment plan come from? Who drives it? Who makes it work?

12.3 How ambitious should it be? What should its duration be?

12.4 What does it look like? How must it unfold? In what spirit should it be undertaken?

12.5 After a post-assessment plan has been completed, how do you manage the introduction of improved processes?

The chapter and the book conclude with a prolonged case study (Section 12.6) of one successful company that, following a disconcerting Level 2 assessment, put in motion first a one-year plan to institute the assessment's recommendations and then a multi-year plan of reiterated assessments. They are now Level 5, and the increases in productivity that they have reported (47%) are truly impressive.

This chapter is addressed to senior managers who put follow-up action plans in motion and to the managers and personnel who must carry the plans out.

Organizations need to see both assessments and maturity levels as means to business goals or as toolkits to improve, not as tests to be passed. This is true not only when things go badly but also when they go well. If an organization congratulates itself because it has "made it" to a higher rung on the maturity ladder, it may not have the will to keep on improving and may slip backwards in the near future [Eickelman 03]. If an organization keeps the connection clear between process improvement and substantial payoffs in reliability and profit, it will avoid the pitfalls both of defensiveness and smugness and will resist trying to game the next assessment or resting on its laurels from the last one.

Process improvement takes hold when an organization begins to understand that improvement means not just progressing up an artificial maturity scale but also enhanced profits and efficiency in the business. After an assessment, organizations will resist planning improvements for the sake of their "grade" on the next assessment but will welcome plans that make clear how they will make their products faster, cheaper, and better. When an improvement is suggested after an assessment, therefore, it ideally should become the responsibility of the part of the organization that will be enhanced by the change. This sub-organization should be able to tailor the change to its own requirements and needs to be able to experience first-hand the difference that the change will make. In this way, project managers will eventually come to expect that process improvement and success go hand-in-hand.

This change in attitude should be encouraged at all levels of the organization. Post-assessment improvement work is not something that distracts from "real work"—it's a way to help everyone work better.

12.1.1 What Happens the First Day After an Assessment

After an assessment, either an organization is demoralized because it has been judged worse than it thought it was, or it is euphoric because it has been judged better than it dared hope it could be. Neither emotion leads to change. It is the job of the assessment sponsor to pick up the pieces, convene a meeting of participants and change agents, and systematically analyze the results of the assessment and its recommendations. Then, just as in any other project, the job must be broken down, authority must be delegated, jobs must be assigned, and estimations must be made of what needs doing, what it will cost in effort and money, and how long it will take.

The day after a Level 3 assessment showed serious problems in how most of Organization X's processes were created and followed, the sponsor scheduled a retreat that included the internal assessment team members, the director of software engineering, all the project software engineering managers, and the SEPG manager and his staff, along with other key personnel. They took a half-day for a post-mortem, and then the sponsor drew up the beginnings of a plan that considered the assessment's findings and recommendations that they accepted point-by-point. The SEPG team then wrote up the points, and the list was reviewed, approved, and prioritized by a Management Steering Committee. The assessment sponsor then presented the plan to the company president and his VPs, who reviewed and approved the plan. Between two weeks and a month later, the plan had started to be implemented.

Counter-Example: The day after an assessment showed that Organization Y had satisfied all Level 2 PAs, the organization was paralyzed. The senior manager, enthusiastic but unengaged, talked about hiring a process improvement manager to lead the post-assessment improvement plan. But because he and his subordinates felt good about the state of the assessment, there was nothing urgent about his plans. Two months later, no one had been hired, and only a few people in the organization were still thinking about what the assessment had shown and what should be done next. Because a Level 2 assessment is really about solidifying management practices, it is a transitional exercise. If too much time is allowed to elapse, the provisional processes upon which the improvements must be built start to change. In the case of Organization Y, the danger was real and inevitable. Six months later, it was unclear whether a second assessment would find things as good as they were.

12.2 Who? (Who Drives a Disciplined Post-Assessment Plan? Who Makes It Work?)

Post-assessment process improvements need to be driven by senior management to succeed. There is no substitute for a managing director's or a president's authority, commitment, and resources.

Senior management, however, must be not only committed but also informed. Senior managers need to learn what questions to ask and how to ask better ones as the effort progresses. In addition, a management structure needs to be created that will extend the reach of senior management without diluting its effect.

On the other hand, the plan needs to provide for initiative and modification by the managers and engineers who are responsible for implementing it.

12.2.1 Senior Management: The Push from Above

No improvement effort will get beyond empty words unless senior management commits its authority, effort, and resources. This means more than establishing an SEPG or process improvement group to "do what they can." It involves taking responsibility for leading the effort, vesting real authority in subordinates who are directly responsible to senior management, and learning enough about the logic of the process (and its payoffs) to keep a personal thumb on the pulse of change.

Senior managers must not only lend their authority to the improvement effort—they must lead it. This requires learning about process improvement and asking the kind of questions that elicit useful answers.

Accepting a responsibility for process improvement amounts to increasing senior management's own process discipline in an area, that is, software, in which few managers are expert. As Pat O'Toole has accurately observed, "If all your senior management does is *sponsor* the effort, it's probably doomed anyway! I believe that senior management must lead the charge by exhibiting the same process-disciplined behavior that they expect the troops to adopt…Unless management is willing to align their own behavior with the direction they are trying to establish, it is simply another case of 'do what I say, not what I do.' The commitment of senior management to establish a process-disciplined organization is reflected much more clearly by their own behavior than it is in a policy statement lifted from the pages of the CMM/CMMI" [O'Toole 03].

12.2.2 Two Time-Honored Mistakes

12.2.2.1 Mistake 1: Appointing a Process Improvement Manager Who Has No Real Authority

All too often, senior management begins an improvement effort by appointing a process improvement manager and instructing him that he (or she) is responsible for moving the organization to the next maturity level by a certain date. The process improvement manager enthusiastically takes on the assignment but soon discovers that his decisions are likely to be overruled whenever there is a more "critical" goal to achieve. If the PI manager is not on the senior management staff or has not been given the authority of the senior manager, he cannot hope in an immature organization to be anything but the fall guy when the organization does not reach its desired quality maturity level. Conflicting business decisions always threaten to take priority over an improvement effort, and only senior management can ensure that improvement stays on track.

12.2.2.2 Mistake 2: Hiring a Consultant to Make Everything Better

A second common mistake involves farming out all or part of the improvement effort to a consultant entirely outside the organization. Here the distance between the improvement effort and the ordinary business of the organization is even more pronounced.

At its most basic, process improvement means articulating and refining existing processes. It often seems that these can be produced (for instance, by SEPG groups) without involving developers, but this is not the case. Developers are unlikely to accept them if they are not involved in their creation.

Organizations change only when they agree about which parts of their current procedures work and which do not. This must come from an internal perspective, or else it is seen as alien and either silly or threatening.

Hiring consultants produces shiny new processes that no one is ever likely to take off the shelf. Working out new processes within the projects themselves is more cumbersome, but it leads to a genuine basis for real improvement.

As Stan Rifkin has observed, unless an organization knows "why" it is adopting new processes, it never gets the "how" right [Rikfin 03].

12.3 When Should Post-Assessment Planning Begin? How Ambitious Should It Be?

The organization wants to improve as soon as possible. However, it is important to establish what needs to be done first and in what sequence to do the rest. After an assessment, things can still go seriously wrong.

Going too slow or too fast are equally dangerous. Taking more than a month or two to develop a realistic action plan means allowing everyday events to take over again and putting improvement on the back burner indefinitely. On the other hand, trying to take on too much improvement all at once can paralyze an organization.

Process improvement should be managed like any other project. Plans need to be made and resources allocated. Progress needs to be measured and monitored.

A typical post-assessment plan is described in Section 12.4. It includes a statement of the organization's business goals, a list of processes and projects that have the greatest impact on those goals, and a statement of the real long-term goal of all software process improvement, including a scheme to reduce defects at every stage of the development cycle.

A post-assessment plan cannot change an organization overnight. It should target those projects that are most important for the short- and long-term health of the organization. Some may be prototype projects for the changing direction of the business. Others may be critical projects for the current health of the organization. Still others might be projects that are about to go into the manufacturing phase.

12.3.1 What Should the Duration Be of a Post-Assessment Plan?

Medium Term

A realistic goal for a post-assessment improvement plan is to organize a way to alter individual processes on critical projects so that at a minimum, after one year, half of the relevant criteria for KPAs/PAs at a given maturity level will have been satisfied, and within two years, all of them will have been satisfied. Some organizations have found that if senior management leads the post-assessment improvement, the time needed for significant improvement can be substantially reduced.

Long Term

A one-year improvement plan, however, will not turn a company around. To do that, companies should schedule a regular plan of yearly follow-up assessments to transform the improvement process from a pressurized one-time affair to a gradual, evolving, quantified effort. Yearly assessments measure and encourage gradual improvement and can prevent an all too typical pattern of sudden bursts of effort followed by apathy and half-improved programs that are left to wither on the vine.

12.4 What Does a Post-Assessment Improvement Plan Look Like? How Should It Unfold? In What Spirit Should It Be Undertaken?

12.4.1 The Principles of Building a Post-Assessment Process Improvement Action Plan

After an organization has taken a deep breath and organized itself to follow up the findings and recommendations of an assessment, step one is for the authorities and structures outlined previously to lay out and implement a one-year action plan, with another assessment or "health check" scheduled at the end of the year. (Many organizations believe in alternating between informal "health checks" and official CBA IPI or SCAMPI assessments.)

After reviewing the relevant list of projects and KPAs/PAs that need improvement, and deciding which improvements are appropriate, a detailed plan of what needs to be accomplished should be drawn up for each area. This plan should include information as to when and how. Part of developing a process improvement culture involves yearly reviews of what remains to be improved.

Developing a process improvement plan entails laying out the activities needed to accomplish a specified improvement, determining the expected duration and required resources for each activity, and then developing a schedule that recognizes that some activities may depend on the successful completion of others. Then an evaluation of available resources can be made, and an assessment of the fit between the improvement schedule and other project and/or organization schedules can be undertaken.

Process improvement should then be managed like a project. The plan needs to be monitored and controlled. Measurements should be established and reported regularly to different levels of management. These can include Gantt charts; rate (status of activity completion) charts; and budget, resources, and risk charts.

A number of organizations have found that requiring project personnel to spend half their time on process improvement ensures making improvement real and immediate. Because they implement the improvements on their own projects, the two halves of their work become parts of a whole.

Status reports should be reviewed monthly not only by the process improvement project managers but also by a management steering group and by a senior management steering group (including the president/managing director) [Cheung 03].

12.4.2 The Contents of a Post-Assessment Process Improvement Action Plan: An Overview

A post-assessment process improvement plan should include the following, some of which have already been mentioned:

- Identifying long-term and near-term business strategic goals.
- Tying business goals to assessment recommendations and improvement activities. A process improvement plan in a mature organization will include a description of how the

organization's goals are distributed over individual departments and are related to individual process improvement
activities.

- Describing specific process improvement objectives, activities, and tasks.
- Describing and assigning roles and responsibilities for
  improvement activities.
- Identifying risks and resource constraints.
- Gaining provisional approval of the plan by senior and
  project management.
- Scheduling improvement activities. (This also means recognizing their logical sequence.)
- Conducting serial closed-loop reviews of the plan leading
  to final approval by project managers, personnel, and senior
  managers.

12.4.3 A Template of a Simple Plan to Identify and Track the Execution of Improvement Goals

Project or Team Name	
Team Members	
Date Last Revised	

Desired Results (Identify Goals or Objectives)

Description	Source

Schedule Milestones (Activities and Results or Events and Dates)			
Description	*Original Plan*	*Current Plan*	*Actual - Done*

Issues and Risks

	Description of Issue or Risk	*Actual or Potential Effects*	*Who Is Involved*
1.			
2.			

[Source: Caputo 98]

12.4.4 The Components of a Thorough Process Improvement Plan: A Template Designed for a Mature Organization

The following Software Process Improvement plan template[1] presents a sample organizational software performance improvement program for a given division. It lists organizational goals that have been developed in concert with senior management based on the company's business goals and objectives.

Sample Template

1.0 Yearly Organizational Goals

The executive staff is to develop organizational goals, which will then be elaborated into engineering goals. Subsequently, the engineering goals will be developed into software

---
[1.] Thanks to Pete Howard.

engineering goals. Finally, software engineering activities will be planned to achieve the software engineering goals.

2.0 Processes That Have Greatest Impact on Organizational Goals

A Management Steering Group (MSG) identifies the processes most important for meeting organizational goals (for example, via a prioritization worksheet). This identifies the processes that directly or indirectly will have the greatest impact on achieving the organizational goals. The MSG then determines which of the highest scoring processes in the Prioritization Worksheet has the greatest scope for improvement. The worksheet identifies the following:

- Highest scope for improvement
- High scope for improvement
- Medium scope for improvement

3.0 Table for the Mapping Activities Against Processes

See Table 12-1.

4.0 Table for the Mapping of Goal Measurements

A primary measurement is used to monitor how well the organizational goals are being achieved.

5.0 Creating a Quantitative Management Plan

Quantitative management activities are conducted by the software engineering organization and by projects with software content.

Table 12-2 contains the detailed measurements that will be used by the projects to track their performance in meeting the organizational goals.

Describe who maintains process capabilities for peer reviews and defect profiles based upon the project's performance. Describe who will continue to evaluate peer review and defect data from projects that have implemented quantitative management.

Table 12-1 Mapping of Activities to Priority Processes

Para.	Description	Defect Prevention/ Develop Corrective Action Proposal	Requirements Management	Risk Management	Intergroup Coordination	Peer Review	SW Test	SW Code & Unit Test	SW Design	SW Requirements Analysis	TCM

Table 12-2 *Organizational and Detailed Measurements*

Software Engineering Goal	Primary Measurement for Goal

6.0 Creating a Defect Prevention Plan

Organization's Goals

The software engineering organization's defect prevention activities will be aligned with the software engineering organization's goals.

Defect Prevention Infrastructure

Software defect prevention activities are conducted by [Title] and by projects with software content in accordance with a defect prevention process.

The [Title] manager leads the software engineering organization's defect prevention activities.

The following indicates possible assignments for an organizational causal analysis team:

The organizational defect prevention manager:

- Assigns personnel to develop corrective action proposals for organizational issues.
- Selects tools to support defect prevention activities in accordance with the technology change management process.
- Manages the defect prevention activities in accordance with the defect prevention process.

A defect prevention manager is assigned to lead each project's software defect prevention activities. The defect prevention manager assigns project personnel to causal analysis teams to develop corrective action proposals in accordance with the "develop corrective action proposal" process. He assigns project personnel to implementation teams to implement corrective action proposals in accordance with the defect prevention process.

7.0 Scheduling Organization-Level Defect Prevention Activities (for a Level 4 or Level 5 Organization)

The schedule for the organization-level defect prevention activities is shown in Table 12-3.

Table 12-3 *Organization Defect Prevention Schedule*

Activity	Schedule
Hold organization defect prevention meetings	Monthly
Hold quarterly meeting with defect prevention managers	February, May, August, November
Collect and analyze defect prevention metrics; feedback to software engineering and SQA personnel; status, effectiveness, risks, and issues to senior management	Monthly

As new projects collect a certain number of operational defects or systemic defects, the appropriate project personnel will be trained and will start performing defect prevention.

8.0 Creating a Software Technology Plan

Software technology is implemented in accordance with a technology change management process. Proposals for technology can be categorized in two ways:

- Recommendations from the process improvement planning activities. The recommendations are based upon the software organization's goals and are documented in this plan.

- Recommendations include inputs from the engineers and projects; new technology that is required by a project but not in general use within the organization, recommendations from a Software Technology Insertion Review Board, and so on.

Personnel that are drawn from across engineering staff a Software Technology Insertion Review Board.

Additional staff members are drawn from multiple sources including project, SQA, and software engineering personnel, and from the Software Engineering Process Group (SEPG).

The budget for the year to run the board and conduct Software Performance Improvement Plan improvements and opportunistic investigations is [X$].

9.0 Creating a Rewards and Recognition Program

Each quarter, the Management Steering Group (MSG) evaluates the people in the organization that have made significant contribution to the software process improvement program and recommends them for rewards and recognition. The rewards will be selected by the MSG based upon contributions.

10.0 Approval Authorization for Organization Process Definition (OPD) Updates

The SEPG should be authorized to decide on (i.e., accept or reject) most OPD updates. However, if the updates will take more than a certain number of hours to implement, or if the change may have a large potential impact on product quality or productivity, then the updates will be referred to the MSG for acceptance.

11.0 Tracking Software Process Improvement Measurements

In addition to the measurement and reports called out in the software process improvement process, the following measurements will be made to determine the status of the software process improvement activity each month:

- Actual versus budget for the software performance improvement activities.
- Milestone completion for the software performance improvement activities.

12.0 Assigning Software Performance Improvement Schedule and Budget

The software process improvement budget for [year] is [X$]. There are additional sources of funding related to the software performance improvement activity including funding [X$] for:

- Capital expenditures
- Training
- CMMI support
- Software Technology Review Board
- Project funding
- Dues and fees

13.0 Planning Activities to Address Assessment Weakness

In year 1, an assessment (i.e., SCAMPI or CBA-IPI) was held. Table 12-4 is a listing of opportunities that remain and will be addressed in [year X] as part of the SPI activity.

Table 12-4 *Assessment Opportunities for Improvement*

Finding #	KPA/PA	Finding	Due Date	Responsibility	Comments

14.0 Planning Activities to Support Software Goals

Software engineering goals are developed from organization and engineering goals. The MSG will analyze each of the software engineering goals and recommend the following activities in order to achieve the goals. When an activity supports more than one goal, it is described with the goal it primarily supports.

Describe activity

- Priority:
- Assigned to:
- Develop capability report and brief to program managers and marketing by [date]:

12.4.5 A Common Temptation: Trying to Run Before You Walk

When confronted with assessment results, some organizations start thinking about moving up several levels at once. They often do not understand, though, that part of what has to be changed is the culture of their organization, which needs the experience of performing an improved process multiple times for it to become second nature. Approaching improvement by trying to skip a maturity level almost never works: "When you are starting a long-term endeavor, the goal is not to finish. Rather, the goal is to start. Once you have started, the goal is to keep going, and if you get stuck, the goal is to start again. How do you start? Begin by understanding the relationship between the current state and the desired state... What are we doing now? What can we change now? And what can't we change yet?" [Caputo 98].

Continuous optimization means sustaining momentum for change, not necessarily changing everything at once. Progress is made one step at a time, which means accepting that some things can't be changed at this time but might be changed later.

Concentrate on what can be changed now. How much can be done in a month? Lay a foundation and come back in six months to make more improvements. Don't wait for perfection, or else you might end up writing nothing or writing useless processes: "Build momentum by achieving small, successful steps that add up to greater progress. Understand the direction you are heading and start moving in that direction" [Caputo 98].

12.4.6 Why Maturity Levels Can't Be Skipped

Process capability grows in stages. Processes are only effective after prerequisite processes are stabilized. Engineering processes, for example, usually do not improve before management stabilizes the way it makes decisions. If management changes working conditions every week, the best processes in the world do not have a chance to succeed.

Maturity Level 2 is largely concerned with management decision processes. As management discipline solidifies, so does a more general quality discipline [Humphrey 89].

Moving from Maturity Level 2 to Maturity Level 3 is concerned with developing an organizational discipline. Maturity Level 4 is concerned with managing by data and using statistical process control. And at Maturity Level 5, an organization has developed a continuous improvement discipline.

In technical terms, at Level 2, managers learn to prepare estimates with their team rather than by themselves and begin methodically to track actuals against estimates. These changes constitute an important increase in management rigor.

They also, however, involve changing perspectives. Managers are empowered by enhanced information to take corrective action early rather than late, and they get into the habit of doing so when they need to. When costly problems are found in reviews and then fixed early and easily, teams start to see the benefit of independent and methodical reviewing and begin to feel discomfort when consistent processes are missing.

12.4.7 Planning for Reiterated Assessments

A schedule of periodic assessments keeps an organization focused on what needs to be improved and on whether past improvements are really working. When assessments are conducted on a continuing basis, their effect becomes less disruptive, and they begin to instill an instinctive feeling for continuous improvement.

Kim Caputo relates Unisys's experience with multiple assessments this way: "Our initial assessment experience was like a shock to the system. When the assessors presented the list of major issues in five or six key areas, the managers were shocked by what they saw as bad news. They were not surprised by the contents of the list and they agreed that these were indeed the key major issues. But it wasn't very pleasant to see all the major issues all at once.

"The second assessment and subsequent assessments were slightly different. The expectations were higher, because improvement work was in progress. Even though there was a similar shock reaction to the issues, it was balanced by encouragement for the progress that had been made. So the shock was not as severe. It seems that the more an organization works on process improvements, the easier it is to accept the assessment of major issues objectively with fewer negative reactions. The report is simply information that you need to know in order to improve. You can't change what you don't know about; you can't change what you don't talk about" [Caputo 98].

Organizations have found that having frequent assessments is a very useful way to keep their eye on the improvement ball. Assessments signpost where an organization currently is, where its strengths lie, and what areas still need improvement. Periodic assessments allow this process to be conducted in a non-defensive way.

12.5 After the Plan: Managing the Introduction of Improved Processes

12.5.1 The Role of Senior Management in Implementing Improved Processes

12.5.1.1 Learning to Ask the Right Questions

As with post-assessment improvement planning, the role of senior management begins with learning to ask real questions and then expecting them to be answered.

If at monthly meetings senior management continues to ask only about profit and schedule, the organization will not change. The message such meetings send to middle management is: "Do whatever you have to do to meet the schedules. Quality isn't important." But quality *is* important—in fact, it is the best way to improve a company's predictability and its long-term profits.

"Executive questions provide insight into organizational priorities. It's nice that the process improvement sponsor asks process-related questions in the monthly steering committee meeting, but what kind of questions is the senior management team asking in project reviews... Some still growl things like:

- "Whose fault is it that the project's behind schedule?"
- "Who do I chew out/demote/fire to fix these problems?"
- "Given the state of the project, why didn't I see many cars here on Saturday?"

"Although these questions may reflect senior management's *real* concerns, the executives need to start asking questions that reflect their new and improved process-oriented view of the world. The kinds of questions that senior management should ask are things like:

- "How could the process be changed to avoid these problems in the future?"
- "How can issues like this be identified when they're still just risks, and subsequently mitigated?"
- "How do we communicate the painful lessons identified on this project to benefit others?"

"Admittedly, when faced with a crisis, senior management must act decisively to contain the situation. After all, when a man is drowning, it's no time to teach him to swim. But once the man is safely on the beach, rather than chastising his stupidity, it is usually more beneficial to explore how a similar situation might be avoided in the future—and then discuss how the efficiency of the rescue operation might be improved."

"Bottom line: senior management *influences* behavior based on the questions they ask. Furthermore, they change behavior when they insist on getting the answers. The executive question is a powerful tool that can be used to send a strong signal that expectations are changing...or it can be wasted getting answers like 'right Roger!'" [O'Toole 02].

12.5.1.2 Extending the Authority of Senior Management Without Diluting It

To be effective, structuring improvement requires systematic communication between senior management, the SEPG or process improvement group, and developers. Clear communication must establish how these groups will work together on the improvement plan and afterwards.

A viable management structure capable of introducing real process improvement might look like this one (in which all parts of the organization participate in process improvement and in which the entire organizational is linked back to senior management).

An **executive board** whose role is to review and approve potential improvements in any area of the organization.

An **overall process steering group** whose role is to manage, coordinate, and review activities across the organization.

Individual department process groups, such as engineering process groups, operations process groups, human resources process groups, etc., whose role is to coordinate the individual departments' improvement activities. These department process groups should include the managers of the appropriate department.

The activities for each group are reviewed periodically and monthly with senior management.

12.5.2 How to Create a Workable Ladder of Authority: An Example

Organization R, attempting to drive process improvement efficiently, created a process improvement structure tailored to its multi-disciplined matrix organization. The president extended his authority to drive the accomplishment of specific improvements, including in customer satisfaction, cycle time, defect reduction, and annual growth rate, to the VP executive staff and then to a board of overseers. Process steering groups were then established within each functional group.

Backed by the authority of executive management, the board of overseers (in fact a subset of the executive staff) coordinated the process steering groups and working groups beneath them. The board identified areas that needed to be changed and then defined and initiated process improvement initiatives in those areas. It made sure that coordination and cooperation occurred across functional boundaries. The board members became actively involved in the steering groups and ensured that continuous process improvement methodologies were implemented across all business processes.

The board of overseers thus became a coordinating body for the executive staff and a focal point of process improvement throughout the organization. The board met monthly to perform executive reviews of performance and process improvement. These reviews, when held in conjunction with monthly program reviews, made process improvement a part of project performance improvement, both of which were accountable all the way up the organization. Every month, every project manager had to show a chart indicating the red, yellow, or green status of process and product performance. Process group members became a part of each project, and the projects were required to maintain their awareness of process improvement.

The structure's principle function is to guarantee senior management's full involvement in the improvement process. In effect, it meant that the president presided over a standard "stoplight" reporting system for each project. If the status of a project was yellow or red, the project manager had to explain to the executive staff (president and executive VPs) at the monthly program reviews what was wrong and what he planned to do to bring the project under control. For each color, measurement limits were determined. If the project measurements exceeded the limit, the project moved from one color range to the next.

It is vital in the structure that the project manager rather than the software manager explain to the president why a particular area is yellow or red and provide quality measurements (in the form of defect charts) in the reporting. If this duty is assigned to a software manager (who often does not possess the authority to address the problem), the project manager is absolved of full responsibility, and the chain breaks.

12.5.3 The Role of Process Groups in Immature Organizations

In Watts Humphrey's words, process groups such as SEPGs "serve as a consolidating force for the changes that have already been made and should support the projects as they use new methods, standards, and technology. This support helps with the adoption of new practices and facilitates their retention in the working fabric of the organization. Without such guidance and support, lasting process improvement is practically impossible" [Humphrey 89]. Or, in Kim Caputo's words, SEPGs drive and facilitate the way an "organization learns from itself" [Caputo 98].

It should be kept in mind, however, that the foundations for efficient process group activity are not established before the changes in management structure the CMM/CMMI associates with Maturity Level 3. (The process group activities appear in organization process focus and organization process definition PAs/KPAs in both CMM/CMMI models at Level 3.)

Before that, process groups are useful but only up to a point. At Maturity Levels 1 and 2, process groups help project management and project staff members articulate their current procedures. The process group can also help organize working groups across projects when requested by project personnel. But before Level 3, process groups cannot be expected to develop organization-wide processes because at that level the organization is not capable of agreeing on what processes projects should use. The projects barely understand which processes work for them and which need improving.

The danger, then, of expecting Level 3 functions from a Level 1 process group is that the process group will try to impose activities that have no meaning to the people in the organization. The process group activities will be marginalized and seen as having no relationship to the projects and to delivering the products to the customers. Therefore it is important for the process group in a Level 1 organization to ensure that the projects understand that whatever activities the process group performs it is to assist the projects and not to dictate to or hamper them.

The appropriate use of a process group in a Level 1 company can be seen in the following example:

After a first assessment, Organization X began to implement its improvement program by creating a process group made up of the software project managers and one full-time process improvement manager. One of the SEPG's tasks was to design a template for a software project plan. Although each project in the organization had created some variety of such a plan, they all were different and all were missing pieces. The software managers decided that they should all work together to create a common template. They asked the process improvement manager to help make this happen. He formed a working group using software managers, whether they served on the SEPG or not. Eventually the template was tested and implemented, but only because the effort came from and took place in the projects. Had the template been entirely the product of an independent SEPG, the effort would never have worked.

A counter-example: The engineering director of another Level 1 organization set up an SEPG and assigned members of the SEPG to lead and participate in the working groups that were to write procedures for each area. There was little representation from the projects on the working groups. The procedures were written within a year, but the projects never used them. The year was wasted, and the process improvement program was set back many more.

This effort might have worked within a Level 2 organization moving to Level 3 because a Level 2 organization by definition recognizes the value of articulating and building on existing processes and how difficult it is to try to articulate new processes from scratch. It has also created a depository for measurement data and lessons learned. Without these foundations, projects view working groups as extraneous and distracting.

12.6 Creating, Tracking, and Implementing a Post-Assessment Plan for Process Improvement: A Step-by-Step Case History of How *Organization* Z Transformed Assessment Recommendations into Action Items, Implemented Improvements, and Conducted Subsequent Assessment and Improvement Cycles over a Four-Year Period

This section traces the history of how Organization Z after a multi-year plan of disciplined periodic assessments advanced from CMM Level 2 to Level 5 and improved its productivity by 47%.

12.6.1 Background

When Organization Z was assessed in 1998, it fully expected to be performing solidly at Level 3 on the CMM maturity scale. After an earlier Level 2 assessment, a team of long-term consultants helped write organization-wide processes and securely predicted a rating on the next assessment of Level 3. However, corporate headquarters insisted on an independent Lead Assessor for the next assessment, and the result was an unpleasant surprise. Although the new processes that the consultants had provided were on paper, few people in the organization understood them, and fewer still had begun to use them. More seriously, too few defects were being found before testing, with the result that the company (which aimed never to deliver defect-plagued products) was spending a huge amount of time and money on testing and retesting, and many products were over budget and schedule.

The initial reaction of senior management to the Level 3 assessment results was agitation and disappointment. The organization had been told it needed a Level 3 rating to keep a large contract. The brass was not happy.

The reason that the organization's response to the rating did not produce a general meltdown was largely due to an executive who in the wake of his superiors' anger voiced the staff view that the assessment showed no more than most of the organization's technical personnel already knew. The organization president, taken aback, then saw that his best course was to face into the truth and organize a real attempt to improve.

Even at that point, the president might have chosen to make a few quick changes and then look toward a Level 3 "certificate." He concluded, however, that "in for a penny, in for a pound": the most important thing for the health of the business was a program of sustained improvement. Showing real courage, he explained the results of the assessment to his sponsors and made a thorough case for addressing the organization's weaknesses. To his delight, the sponsors responded positively. They praised the president for his forthrightness and continued the contract.

12.6.2 A Summary of the First Assessment's Findings

The general results of Organization Z's 1998 assessment were not at all that unusual for a company just short of real organizational coherence. The organization's core problem was how to systematize, unify, and implement the first fruits of a sustained effort to introduce company-wide processes. Therefore, despite real strengths, the organization showed weaknesses, especially in managing and tracking the coordination of the new software processes and in convincing project management that the use of the processes was ultimately their responsibility and not the responsibility of their software managers.

12.6.2.1 Organization Z: Final Findings from the First Assessment

Table 12-5 presents the assessment's actual general findings and a specimen of one of the technical (KPA) findings. See also Figure 12-1.

Table 12-5 *Assessment's Actual Findings and Specimen of One of the Technical KPAs*

General Strengths
• Work ethic and technical competence of staff.
• President's visibility during employee meetings was taken as very positive.
• Senior management recognition of the need to improve.
• Company has developed a strategic view.
• Integrated teams are institutionalized and generally strongly supported.
• Tight coupling between different engineering disciplines in corporation.
• Software engineering directorate has taken the initiative in establishing a software engineering training program.
• Capital investment in PCs and tools has had a positive impact on engineers' ability to do their jobs.
• Recently hired employees were very enthusiastic about their assignments.
Critical Concerns
• Numbers of initiatives are not all tied together at company level.
• Since program managers are responsible for all aspects of a project, they must develop a greater understanding of existing key early warning indicators for the software portion of their project.
• Some individuals outside software engineering view software as something that other people do.

- The executive emphasis on process improvement has not percolated down to project management. Process improvement is viewed by some project managers as "just one more thing to do" rather than a way of gaining effectiveness in the way they do their job.
  - Some processes are perceived as burdensome with little perceived ROI.

General Concerns

- Employees perceive the management to be "too" accommodating to customers and therefore schedules are too aggressive.
- Managers perceive that engineers have too little consideration for business goals.
- Weak long-term career development path.
  - Limited conference attendance.
  - Limited planned project rotation.
- Not effectively using all the people.
  - People are stressed.
  - Long hours.
  - Critical work keeps going to the same key people.

Recommendations

- Executive staff needs to form a steering committee among themselves for process improvement. They are the only group that can fix the critical concerns. This responsibility cannot be delegated and still be effective.
- Company has set reasonable improvement goals. Software needs to be reviewed in the context of those specific goals. The company should transition its emphasis from means (CMM key process areas) to ends (defect reduction).
- All program reviews should include an emphasis on defect prevention (both software and hardware).

(continued)

Table 12-5 *Assessment's Actual Findings and Specimen of One of the Technical KPAs (continued)*

• Training (at a minimum, a three-day course) should be provided to program managers, their direct reports, and their key software staff to explain the importance of software early warning indicators and their effect on cost. • Each program manager should be responsible for intervening when software early warning indicators raise a red flag. • The use of metrics needs to be re-evaluated to determine which are useful and which can be consolidated.
Specimen Technical Finding: Organization Process Definition KPA (Level 3)
Strengths • Software process handbook established and on the web (easy to find). • Software metrics and historical databases available on the web.

Weaknesses
 	
• Structure of software process handbook does not always provide sufficient options.
  • Not structured as menu of all acceptable options for all types of projects.
• Tailoring guidelines difficult to use.
  • Should consist of rationale for choosing options.
• Web-sensitive configuration management needs to be in place.
• Software development methodologies not defined in the software process handbook.

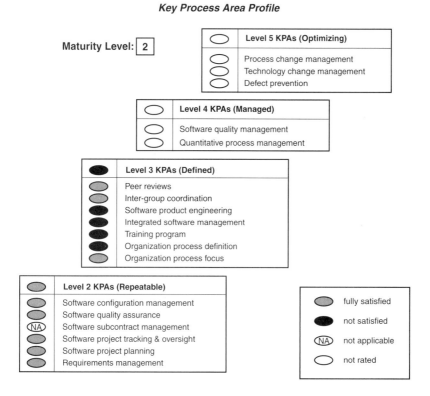

Figure 12-1 *Key process area profile from the first assessment.*

12.6.2.2 The Assessment Findings: A Summary

Table 12-5's set of assessment findings can be summarized succinctly. Organization Z had attempted to satisfy the letter but not the spirit of the CMM by imposing processes written by outsiders on themselves. They should have determined which of their own provisional processes worked best and then extended them across the organization through a process of horizontal and vertical cooperation.

The assessment findings not only registered the failures resulting from this shortcut—they also pointed out the reasons why it hadn't worked. Project managers were the only ones with the authority to require and supervise the assimilation of new processes, but they did not feel personal responsibility for the initiative's success, nor had they been given procedures to measure and report on the success or failure of the initiative. Also, a key instrument—a software process handbook—needed to inform and educate technical personnel about the new processes was deficient. Highly un-user-friendly, the handbook provided little real instruction on how to tailor the new processes for individual projects. Thus even when engineers realized that they were expected to update their processes, they had difficulty doing so.

Finally, the measures instituted by outside consultants had been so focused on *passing the assessment test* they had lost sight of the real purpose of software process improvement—the real-world business objective of improving quality, productivity, and predictability. For example, peer review procedures had been installed because the CMM required them rather than because they were a powerful tool to find defects early and save the company a huge amount of effort and cost. Not surprisingly, the peer reviews were implemented in letter but not in spirit.

The bottom line of the assessment findings was that Organization Z was not functioning *as an organization* with the efficiency of Level 3, nor could it hope to achieve the real benefits of Level 3 until it did.

12.6.3 Organization Z's Post-Assessment Efforts and the Difference They Made One and Two Years Afterwards

Organization Z organized a retreat, devised a post-assessment plan, and parceled out assignments for implementing it. In the following, we concentrate on a few significant parts of that implementation and correlate three of its most important concerns with the relevant findings of an informal CBA IPI (or health check) conducted one year after the original assessment and then with corresponding findings in a second CBA IPI assessment conducted two years after the original assessment and one year after the health check.

Concern #1 (Program Managers Need to Take More Responsibility for Software Issues and Process Improvement):

"Since program managers were responsible for all aspects of a project, they must have a greater understanding of existing key early warning indicators (don't need more) for the software portion of their project."

Initial Actions Taken:

1. Assignments were made to produce a plan to bring program managers up to speed on software early warning indicators by training and coaching them in how to integrate such indicators in the management of their projects.

2. Assignments were made to produce a plan to have all program managers present early warning indicators to the executive staff at monthly program reviews.

These actions were implemented within several months of the first Level 3 assessment.

One Year Later:

Within a year after these plans were implemented, program managers were including in their monthly reports to the president and executive staff quality, cost, and schedule information associated with software early warning indicators. (The indicators were graded red, yellow, and green for threshold target expectations that were being missed by a lot, missed by a little, or met.) The project managers were required to explain the measurements on which their reports were based and also to respond to each yellow and red indicator with a plan to put the projects back on track. No longer able to claim that software was entirely the responsibility of their software managers, they began to take a hands-on role in managing the software component of their projects.

Two Years Later:

Program managers are now:

- Participating in managing the software portion of their projects.

- Becoming comfortable with the use of early warning indicators to better manage their programs.

   Identify product and process problems earlier in life cycle.

   Improve vertical communication.

   Focus management attention on correct issues.

- Beginning to use quantitative management.

   Executive managers are also using early warning indicators to improve executive focus.

- Metrics make it easier to recognize problems early.

Concern #2 (Company-Wide Processes Are Not in Wide-spread Use):

In the area of process tailoring, the assessment had evaluated the organization's approach to standardizing and tailoring software processes on individual projects as inadequate because neither managers nor developers had sufficiently understood or implemented the processes the organization had formulated in the company handbook. Moreover, the assessment found that the company's process handbook did not contain options for all types of projects and was not easy to use, nor did it provide a set of rationales for choosing options.

Initial Actions Taken:

Assignments were made to produce a plan to restructure the organization's (web-based) process handbook to make it more user-friendly. It was recommended, for example, that it should be text-based instead of flow-chart-based, and that it should specify a set of options for each process and provide criteria for tailoring these options on different projects. The plan also specified that when undertaken all tailoring should be recorded in a project software development plan and that an SQA group was to monitor whether organization staff followed the processes they were assigned. (If not, why not?)

One Year Later:

One year after these plans were implemented, a health check determined that the new web-based handbook had made it much more effective. The health check determined that organization technical personnel had started to use the processes the new handbook contained, and that they were beginning to fulfill their obligation to inform the SEPG about which ones worked and which ones needed improvement.

Two Years Later:

The second assessment showed that the software process handbook was being accepted and used by even more people than during the first year and that process-tailoring guidelines were more widely accepted by the projects. These developments had also resulted in improvements in the quality of the processes that were being used.

Concern #3 (Defect-Detection):

In the area of early defect detection and defect prevention, the first Level 3 assessment recommended that instead of trying to "satisfy" individual CMM KPAs, the software division should focus on their real business goals: finding and fixing as many defects as possible before testing.

Initial Actions Taken:

Organization Z created a plan to make Fagan Inspection training required for all software and SQA personnel.

A plan was constructed to initiate Fagan Inspections on pilot projects and then to track their usefulness.

The software division created a plan to complete a certain number of Fagan Inspections per year. (This goal was then included in a software performance improvement plan and tracked monthly.)

Organization defect prevention teams were made part of a software performance improvement plan, and project defect prevention teams were made part of software development plans for each project.

A plan was made to train all teams in causal analysis and to track lessons learned.

One Year Later:

The software organization had been trained in Fagan Inspections, and these inspections had been made mandatory on all projects. Inspections were not required for all products but were required on select high-risk products.

Two Years Later:

"There appears to be buy-in by all levels on the value of Fagan Inspections."

"Defects are tracked by type and phase injected/detected. The numbers are analyzed and used by software managers."

"Quantitative goals on defects escaping to the field and defect detection prior to test have been established and progress toward the goals is being monitored."

"Most programs have defect prevention (DP) managers who coordinate project defect prevention activities and share DP ideas and status with other project DP managers."

Defect detection rates before test rose from 50% to 63%, resulting in a significant drop in testing cost and effort.

12.6.4 Two Years Later: Organization Z's Second CBA IPI Assessment

12.6.4.1 Organization Z's Second Assessment: Summary of Achievements

A second assessment, conducted two years after the first, rated Organization Z's maturity level at Level 3. The responses to the concerns raised by the first assessment already discussed in Section 12.6.3 were judged successful. As a result, the organization had made project managers accountable for the software and process improvement components of their projects, the software process handbook they had distributed had successfully disseminated information about company-wide processes, and the organization's strengthened inspection program had substantively increased the level of defects found before testing.

The results of these measures served not only to allow the organization to "pass" a Level 3 assessment but also to achieve difficult medium- and long-term business goals. Both the project managers and the organization president were given new visibility and control procedures, increasing their ability to understand and manage software development. Project personnel were able to make a more informed choice about software development processes. Projects were able to predict cost and schedule better; quality improved across the board. Finally, the organization needed to spend less time finding defects after testing.

As a result of these improvements, the organization started to see real improvement in efficiency, quality, and profits. By the time of the second assessment, at least 90% of the projects were delivering on time and on budget. Projects were finding 63% of their defects before test, producing marked decreases in development costs resulting in a 23% increase in productivity.

What part had assessments played in all this? The analytical power of the original assessment had demonstrated problems with the organization's information and authority structures. Beforehand, the software managers were sure that their engineers were using the company's software processes, yet during the assessment not one of the practitioners said they had properly understood them, much less used them. The assessment also pointed out that project managers had shirked a major part of their responsibility even though during interviews they said they thought they had their projects fully under control.

Meanwhile, it was the shock of the assessment that made not just the project managers but also the senior managers reevaluate the organization's management structure. Without that shock, it would never have been possible to reorganize the way one level of management reported to the next in such a dramatic and global way.

12.6.4.2 Organization Z's Second Assessment: Remaining Issues

The second Level 3 assessment showed that Organization Z was now capable of implementing company-wide processes and measuring their effect. Now able to more reliably produce high-quality products, the organization stood on the verge of exploiting the potentials it had unleashed. Their organization-wide effort to measure how processes worked, for example, began to give them the data to institute quantitative goals for improving process and product levels.

At this stage, however, senior management did not yet have enough experience with the new data to set the kind of realistic quantitative goals that could drive new improvements. Setting such goals constitutes one of the capability characteristics of a Level 4 organization.

A second area of concern reported by the second assessment involved creating a program to prevent defects from occurring. As a result of the improvements that had led to Level 3, Organization Z could now find more defects early, giving it for the first time sufficient data and expertise to set up a defect prevention plan using causal analysis techniques. This is one of the characteristics of a Level 5 organization.

The second Level 3 assessment recommendations suggested that the organization combine the implementation of these Level 4 and Level 5 initiatives into one improvement plan, and senior management agreed.

12.6.4.3 Organization Z Second Assessment Findings

The general findings of the second assessment are presented in Table 12-6. See also Figure 12-2.

Table 12-6 *General Findings of Organization Z's Second CBA IPI Assessment, Conducted Two Years After the First One*

General Strengths

- President and management staff continue to be actively involved.

- Program managers and their teams have become better at managing and meeting software commitments.

- A stronger process improvement culture exists now than at the last assessment.

- A more widespread understanding exists that process improvement is not a waste of time.

- Other disciplines have begun to see the improvements in software development as a model for themselves and to embrace process improvement.

- Staff members have begun to recognize the value of the feedback from frequent health checks and assessments.

- Early warning indicators are working.
  - Metrics have made it easier to recognize problems early.
  - Executive staff is now more focused on issues than individual blame.

- Staff morale is higher, and personnel are more willing to "go the extra mile."

- Training has improved and has been widely implemented.

- Fagan Inspections have been successful enough in software engineering that other engineering disciplines are looking into their use.

Continuing Weaknesses

- A continuous process improvement culture needs to be ingrained in the organization.
  - Personnel and management should be more willing to admit their own faults.
  - There should exist a more widespread awareness of the need for continuous process improvement.
  - Staff need to be more aware and more skilled in using measurement data.

Recommendations

- Establish quantitative organization-wide process improvement goals with visible senior management sponsorship.
  - Keep raising the bar.

(continued)

Table 12-6 *General Findings of Organization Z's Second CBA IPI Assessment, Conducted Two Years After the First One (continued)*

Recommendations (cont.)

- Establish a more structured integration of the individual process improvement initiatives across the organization directorates to ensure a single coordinated thrust.

  - Assign the best people.

  - Use software successes for leverage.

  - Continually monitor and adjust the program.

  - Continually monitor and adjust the program.

- Institute causal analysis for defects.

- Start implementing Level 5 process improvement technology

Key Process Area Profile

Maturity Level: **3**

○	**Level 5 KPAs (Optimizing)**
○	Process change management
○	Technology change management
○	Defect prevention

○	**Level 14 KPAs (Managed)**
○	Software quality management
○	Quantitative process management

●	**Level 3 KPAs (Defined)**
●	Peer reviews
●	Inter-group coordination'
●	Software product engineering
●	Integrated software management
●	Training program
●	Organization process definition
●	Organization process focus

●	**Level 2 KPAs (Repeatable)**
●	Software configuration management
●	Software quality assurance
NA	Software subcontract management
●	Software project tracking & oversight
●	Software project planning
●	Requirements management

●	fully satisfied
●	not satisfied
NA	not applicable
○	not rated

Figure 12-2 *Key process area profile from the second assessment.*

12.6.4.4 A Sample of Organization Z's Proposals After a Second Assessment and What Difference They Made One and Two Years Later

Concern #1 (Creating Organization-Wide Process and Product Goals):

The assessment recommendations advised that the organization needed to establish quantitative (organization-wide) process and product improvement goals. These goals must be viewed as the president's goals.

It also observed that, although the software organization had developed project defect detection goals and these metrics had been inserted into software development plans on pilot projects, management was not measuring progress in relation to these goals as a way of controlling the projects.

Initial Action Taken:

The president assigned the engineering division VP and his directors the job of developing quantitative goals for process and product improvement. They were, for example, to develop a plan to prescribe realistic numbers for increasing the organization's productivity. Such a plan might specify that the organization was each year to increase quality by x%, decrease cost by y%, and increase the business flow by z%, all based on the measures made available by the tools instituted in the previous improvement cycle.

The president also required project managers to start using already devised software quality goals.

Comment:

Managers in Organization Z tried to devise a set of general goals, but they were unsuccessful because they could not come up with a set of goals sufficiently clear to make sense to the entire organization.

Companies don't always manage to implement all of their improvement plans even when they make honest attempts to do so, and this is a good example of why improvements are sometimes delayed. The managers assigned to develop Organization Z's goals were middle managers and had only a partial view of the whole organization. They were too focused on details, and the goals they created were too complex. Every time they presented these goals to the president, he would send them back to the drawing board.

Nor was the organization's plan to utilize software quality goals successful because project managers had not been given training in the use of such metrics for planning and tracking.

One Year Later:

A health check carried out a year later highlighted the continuing lack of organizational goals and confirmed that existing software quality goals were not being used.

The health check recommended that the new goals, for example, should require x% productivity improvement for each program and should involve a statement of what percent of that figure was to be allocated to systems, software, hardware, production functions, and so on.

Concerning the software organization, the health check added that it needed to re-examine its progress in achieving stated goals and to establish whether the goals' assumptions and expectations were valid, and if not, to adjust them accordingly. The health check also recommended that existing software goals that required an x% improvement in productivity might be required to specify which part of this would come from technology, which part from reuse, which part from inspections, and so on.

Finally, the health check recommended that project managers should present to the next assessment team an account of how they had used Levels 4/5 quantitative management processes and a plan for achieving organization-wide goals.

The health check helped focus the entire organization on the notion of process improvement. It encouraged the president, for example, to think through a set of goals on his own. (The ones he came up with were clear and encompassing, and the organization rallied around them.) The health check also encouraged the president to motivate his project managers to start deploying quantitative measures in their monthly reviews.

Actions Taken Immediately After the Health Check:

After the health check, the president himself sat down with a small group from the engineering division and on a whiteboard sketched out four organizational goals that made sense to him. His guiding rules were to keep them simple, clear, doable, and measurable.

The president identified four organization-wide goals concerning quality, productivity, customer satisfaction, and business growth and required that they flow down to each of the vice presidents (engineering, programs, contracts, procurement, human resources, etc.). The vice presidents would then flow the goals down to the director level, and the directors down to the rest of the organization. These goals formed the basis of Organization Z's improvement initiative.

Two Years Later:

A third CBA IPI assessment, conducted two years after the second, reported the following:

"Clarity of strategic direction, which is the organization's goal, is greatly improved. Whole company more focused on goals."

Concern #2: Setting Up a Defect-Prevention Program

A second area of concern from the second assessment had to do with creating a software program for the causal analysis of defects (defect prevention).

Initial Actions Taken:

1. The president assigned the software director to create an infrastructure for quantitative management and defect prevention and to require that appropriate personnel focus on processes, procedures, metrics, and training for causal analysis.

2. The software director assigned a causal analysis manager to use data from a first round of Fagan Inspections to design a plan for quantitatively managing defect injection rates on the projects. Control limits were established, and a predictive model was created.

One Year Later:

A health check conducted one year later indicated the following improvements:

*   Defect prevention plans are in place on the pilot projects and are being used to manage the defect prevention activities.
*   Corrective action plans are being generated and are being tracked to closure.
*   Measurements on the effort involved in the corrective action process are captured using a standard method.
*   Software project leads not involved in the pilots already are recognizing the value of the defect prevention process.

The health check also indicated some continuing weaknesses:

*   Changes identified in the corrective action plan have not yet been flowed into the software development plan or, even further, into the software process handbook.
*   Early involvement of the program managers does not appear to be standardized.

Two Years Later:

A third CBA IPI assessment, conducted two years after the second, showed that:

"Most programs hold causal analysis meetings monthly, categorize root causes, and track corrective action proposals to closure."

"Software practitioners are kept informed of the results of causal analysis activities. Buy-in seems to have occurred."

12.6.5 Four Years Later: Organization Z's Third CBA IPI Assessment, Undertaken Two Years After the Second Assessment and Four Years After the First Assessment

12.6.5.1 Organization Z's Third Assessment: Summary of Achievements

A third assessment, conducted two years after the second, rated Organization Z's maturity level at Level 5. The responses to the concerns raised by the second assessment and the succeeding health check were, as Section 12.6.5.2 shows, successfully implemented. The president of the organization had found a way to set clear and quantitative organization-wide goals, and the company had rallied around them. Project managers were now using a quantitative predictive model to manage the software elements of their project and were able to see into (and report to the president) the impact of developments on the project. Projects could predict and prevent the occurrence of major unexpected problems later in the development cycle.

Also, because of the now successful operation of the project defect prevention teams and the organization defect prevention team, the number of defects inserted in products had been substantially diminished. Projects were not finding as many defects either before or during testing because there were fewer to find.

These improvements not only served to allow the organization to "pass" a Level 5 assessment but also allowed it to achieve real medium- and long-term business goals.

Bottom line: By now, projects were finding 75% of their defects before test and were producing less than .25 defects per thousand lines of code to the customer. Also, over 95% of the projects were delivering on time and on budget, increasing productivity by 24% over Level 3 figures. Customer satisfaction also increased by 9%, and the company doubled in size within two years of the time Organization Z achieved Level 5.

Looking back, the organization attributed much of their success to the steady cumulative improvements enabled by its program of reiterated assessments. The third assessment had also had a major positive effect toward integrating the organization. That is, the rethinking that the assessment required had helped transform the organization in a positive way, moving it not just toward individual improvements but also toward a vision of good practice that incorporated constant proactive practices and responded to risks before they became problems. Most importantly defects were being prevented before they occurred.

12.6.5.2 Organization Z's Third Assessment Findings

Table 12-7 describes the findings from Organization Z's third assessment. See also Figure 12-3.

Table 12-7 *Organization Z's Third Assessment (Chart of Findings and Recommendations)*

The Strengths: Organization Z Has Improved Significantly
 	
• There is less resistance to change.
 	
• There is more buy-in to process improvement.
 	
   • Those who didn't support the process years ago now see it working for them.
 	
   • Process improvement is seen as a big payoff when done correctly.
 	
• People like being in a company that is striving to be world-class.
 	
• Communication is stronger, with more open lines of communication.

Program and Executive Management Strengths • Program managers are now participating in managing software portion of project.

- • PMs are now understanding and using early warning indicators and quantitative management.
- Executive management.
  - • A real willingness to change and improve.
  - • Buy-in from the top.
- Executives modeling behavior for company.
  - • Clarity of strategic directions.
- Organization Z goals a great improvement.
- Whole company more focused on goals.
- Management listens to people.

Software Engineering Strengths

- Software group performance is more predictable.
  - • They can be depended upon to do as they say.
  - • They react to issues more quickly in a more disciplined manner.
- Day-to-day work life is better (easier to function, everything documented, organization running smoother).
- Great team spirit.
- Good to have process in place; something to fall back on.
- Software engineering is being used as a model of how to do process improvement for the company.
- Improved productivity.
  - • Fewer working weekends.
  - • Meeting milestones.
- Although we were told some projects were "in trouble," they discovered their problems earlier and in more quantitative manner.

(continued)

Table 12-7 *Organization Z's Third Assessment (Chart of Findings and Recommendations) (continued)*

Remaining Issues:
Level 4 and 5 Processes Are Very New

- Quantitative Management is the foundation for predictability.

  - Establish well-understood baselines so that you understand the important characteristics of the processes.

  - Bring in a consultant with expertise in applying statistical techniques to software process improvement to assist the QM manager in the improvement of process baselines.

  - Meet with other Level 4/5 QM managers to gain insight from other organizations.

  - Use and adjust these baselines at the project level.

  - Expand quantitative management beyond defect data.

- TCM and PCM processes are not clearly being driven by strategically looking at the capability baseline.

  - Strategies should be based on data and results quantitatively evaluated.

  - Some tool evaluation has been driven by opportunity instead of analysis and measurement.

  - More discipline and control is needed.

  - The rationale for conducting pilots needs to be captured in the SPI plan.

  - The benefits of completed pilots were not quantified.

Systems, Hardware, and Program Management Issues

- Organization needs to understand what parts of the CMMI apply (e.g., integrated product and process development IPPD).

- Not everyone understands how each area works today (what is good and what needs to be improved).

- Processes are not consistent across projects.

- Although measurements have begun, until you know what your processes are, it's hard to measure.

- Company pyramid goals do not appear to be flowed down to program managers' performance evaluations.

- Although the pyramid goals are great at a company level, each area needs to eventually better understand how they contribute to these goals.

- Some disciplines believe that their processes cannot be measured. This is a symptom of a cultural change that is still needed.

Recommendations:
Transition from CMM to CMMI

- The organization needs to understand which part of the CMMI will provide the greatest benefit at this time.

- CMMI is a major initiative that should not be underestimated in terms of the time and effort to get there.

- A full-time CMMI manager reporting to the executive level is recommended to push this effort forward.

  - Level 2 looks at 10 generic practices in 7 process areas, as well as 55 specific practices (125 total practices).

- Well postured to do it, but a long way to go!

- Need an overall plan, as well as a plan for each process area, for each program, and for each practice not currently established today.

(continued)

Table 12-7 *Organization Z's Third Assessment (Chart of Findings and Recommendations) (continued)*

Watch Out for Conditions That Can Disturb Process Improvement

- Growth at a rapid pace.

- Change in management.

- Being too impatient.

  - Asking for the right things too early.

Key Process Area Profile

Maturity Level: 5

	Level 5 KPAs (Optimizing)
	Process change management
	Technology change management
	Defect prevention

	Level 4 KPAs (Managed)
	Software quality management
	Quantitative process management

	Level 3 KPAs (Defined)
	Peer reviews
	Inter-group coordination
	Software product engineering
	Integrated software management
	Training program
	Organization process definition
	Organization process focus

	Level 2 KPAs (Repeatable)
	Software configuration management
	Software quality assurance
	Software subcontract management
	Software project tracking & oversight
	Software project planning
	Requirements management

	fully satisfied
	not satisfied
NA	not applicable
	not rated

Figure 12-3 *Key process area profile from the third assessment.*

12.6.6 The Payoffs for a Level 5 Organization

Probably the best way to conclude this book is to review the benefits of a program of software process improvement assisted by a program of reiterated assessment. Let us consider the case history of Organization Z that we have just concluded.

12.6.6.1 *The Bottom Line: Productivity and Performance Improvements in Organization Z*

To sum up: In the year of Organization Z's first Level 3 assessment, the organization reported its projects delivering on time and on budget 72% of the time, at an Earned Value Cost Performance Index of .72. The percent of defects detected prior to test was 50%, and the percent of defects detected during test was 49%.

In the two years between Organization Z's first and second Level 3 assessment, the figures for projects delivering on time and on budget had risen from 72% to 91%, and the Earned Value Cost Performance Index had improved from .72 to .89. Software productivity had climbed in the two years by an average of 11.5% a year. Projects were now finding 63% of their defects before test and 36% during test (instead of 50% before test and 49% during test).

Then between a second and third assessment these figures went up again. At the time of the third assessment, 96% of the projects were delivering on time and on budget, the Earned Value Cost Performance Index had climbed from .89 to 1.02, the software productivity rate had increased by an additional 24% in the two years (an average of 12% per year), and projects were now finding 75% of their defects before testing, leaving only 24% to be found during testing.

The gains collectively indicated by these figures are clear and substantial (see Figure 12-4). All in all, over the four years from 1999 to 2003, Organization Z reported a gain in software productivity costs of 47% and an increase in customer satisfaction of 9%. These increases can be attributed most directly to an improvement in early defect detection practices, which had markedly reduced the organization's costly integration test periods.

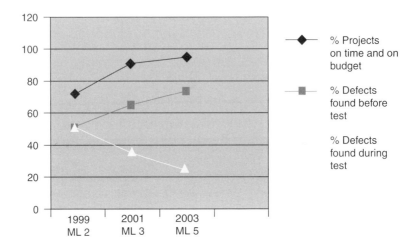

Figure 12-4   *Organization Z's schedule and quality improvement between Maturity Levels 2 and 5.*

But perhaps the clearest way to state Organization Z's savings is in dollars, and the clearest measure is in relation to the increased number of defects that Organization Z's software process improvement program was able to find before testing.

For many years the rough industry rule of thumb for the cost of finding defects is this. It costs approximately $100-$200 to find and fix a defect before testing, approximately $1,000-$2,000 to find and fix a defect during testing, and $10,000-$20,000 or more to fix a defect after delivery [Bush 2002].

Organization Z is a company that produces approximately 300,000 lines of code per year. Of this, approximately 16% (50,000 lines of code per year) is relevant because it constitutes either new or modified code. (The rest of the code is reused and therefore does not figure into these computations.) According to its internal figures, Organization Z injects 125 defects per thousand lines of code into new or modified code: 50 requirements defects per thousand lines of text, 50 design defects per thousand lines of text, and 25 code defects per thousand lines of code. Based on Watts Humphrey, this is as good or better than the industry average [Humphrey 02].

By increasing the defects it found before testing from 50% in 1999 to 63% in 2001 and to 75% in 2003, then, Organization Z should have saved about $4.5 million dollars minus the cost of quality improvements. ($4.5 million works out to something less than $812,500 per year for the first two years plus about $1.57 million dollars a year for the second two years, remembering that the savings for the first year of the two-year cycles would be smaller than those for the second year.)

This was remarkably close to what Organization Z in fact reported. Their figures show that they saved $4,542,000 in development costs over the period 1999-2003 (not including the positive ripple effect into other departments).

What were the costs of these savings? Organization Z spent a total of $3,138,000 for software improvement costs over the four years, including training, assessments, and new software improvement measures. ($1,956,000 of this in fact went for the cost of administering Fagan Inspections. Only $237,000 was for assessments.)

This works out to a total return on investment of software improvement costs of $1,404,000 over four years—$350,100 per year—or in percentage terms, a return of 44.6% per year.

In a larger picture, as a percentage of Organization Z's total software development budget of $14,000,000 per year, the same figure represents a net increase in profit of 2.5%.

Finally it should be said that Organization Z was, at the beginning of its software improvement efforts, an example of a better-than-average company, producing high-quality software to its customers even though sometimes behind schedule and over budget. Companies with more problematic records might expect to benefit even more dramatically from software improvement efforts.[2]

[2.] For other reports on the payoffs of a program of software process improvement driven by assessments, see [Krasner 98], [Vu 00], and [Waina 02].

12.6.6.2 The Benefits of Reiterated Assessment in Company Z: Analysis, Positive Change, Transformation, and Education

How can we sum up the structural benefits of Organization Z's regular assessment and improvement program? Let us return to the list of the four principal functions of an assessment with which we began this book.

Analysis

The *analytical* power of the original Level 3 assessment had demonstrated real gaps between Organization Z's perception of its own processes and the way those processes really operated.

The first assessment revealed, for example, problems with the organization's information and authority structures that involved both project managers who had in effect absolved themselves of responsibility for software issues and software managers who were unaware that their engineers were not using the company's software processes. When these problems were addressed and rectified, a second assessment showed that Organization Z was organized to exploit the power of quantitative management to create incentives for new improvements and establish a feedback loop for continuous improvement.

The force of these analyses, meanwhile, derived not just from the assessment's power to probe objectivity into issues that the organization could not realize or confront, but also from the global vision of how software operations ought to work. This global vision was provided by the assessment's reference model, in this case the SEI CMM, which kept a picture of the whole enterprise in mind, not just a catalogue of individual good practices.

Initiation of Positive Change

Meanwhile, it was the shock especially of the first assessment that made both project managers and executives reevaluate the organization's management structure. Without that shock, it would never have been possible to reorganize the way one level of management reported to the next in such a dramatic and global way. After the first assessment, the president of

Organization Z was moved to use his own authority to redress a version of the organization's problems, which during the assessment had been articulated by the assessment team and then ratified by the organization's ladder of personnel, middle managers, and executives. Many of these people already knew what was wrong before the assessment, but it was the assessment itself that consolidated their energies in the direction of positive change.

Positive Transformation

The beginnings of the structural transformation involved in this reorganization, moreover, can be located in the procedures of the assessment itself. Conducted in a way that related each project to the organizational and administrative capabilities of the entire organization, the assessment launched Organization Z into a full rethinking of how its different parts and functions related to each other. The efforts launched by the president and senior management after the assessment were only the logical extension of the kind of rethinking that began to occur during the course of the assessment itself.

Education

None of these advances would have proceeded, of course, without the artificially intense education that the organization had received during the assessment—an education that synthesized and transmitted the current state of software practice. The company chose to change when they recognized the deficiencies of their own operation in relation to other, more successful software operations around the world. They had been shocked, and their ways of thinking had been transformed, but ultimately it was the lure of increased success that motivated them to improve.

A Continuous Program of Assessment and Improvement

These results, finally, were facilitated not only by a single assessment but also by the organization's decision to begin a cyclical program of assessment and improvement. The innovations introduced after the first assessment were confirmed and encouraged by the health check that followed a year later, and then by the second assessment, the next health check, a third assessment, and so on.

In this process, the second and each subsequent assessment and health check functioned not as wake-up calls but rather as exercises in course-correction. All of them reinforced the improvements already under way at the same time that they communicated a sense that new improvements would extend initiatives undertaken in the first cycle.

By the time the organization had begun to incorporate the improvements recommended by the second assessment, the practice of rigorous analysis—previously avoided because of its potential for disruption—had become just an ordinary way of doing business.

References

[Armstrong 02]   Armstrong, J.; Barbour, R.; Hefner, R. and Kitson, D. *Standard CMMI^SM Appraisal Method for Process Improvement (SCAMPI^SM): Improvements and Integration.* Systems Engineering 5, No. 1, 2002, pp. 19–26.

[Averill 93]   Averill, E.; Byrnes, P.; Dedolph, M.; Maphis, J.; Mead, W. and Puranik, R. *Software Capability Evaluation (SCE) Version 1.5 Method Description.* (CMU/SEI-93-TR-017), Pittsburgh, PA: Software Engineering Institute, Carnegie Mellon University, 1993.

[Bamford 93]   Bamford, R. C.; Diebler, W. J. *Comparing, Contrasting ISO 9001 and the SEI Capability Maturity Model.* IEEE Computer, October 1993.

[Besselman 92]   Besselman, Joe. *A Collection of Software Capability Evaluation Findings: Many Lessons Learned.* Presented at NSIA, March 1992.

[Boyett 98]   Boyett, Joseph H. and Boyett, Jimmie T. *The Guru Guide—The Best Ideas of the Top Management Thinkers.* Boyett & Associates, 1998.

[Bush 02]   Bush, Marilyn. "Applying the S/W CMM and the CMMI: Unlocking the Hidden Logic of Process Improvement." SEPG 2002. February 2002.

[Byrnes 96]   Byrnes, Paul and Phillips, Mike. *Software Capability Evaluation Version 3.0 Method Description* (CMU/SEI-96-TR-002). Pittsburgh, PA: Software Engineering Institute, Carnegie Mellon University, 1996.

[Caputo 98]   Caputo, Kim. *CMM Implementation Guide: Choreographing Software Process Improvement.* Reading, MA: Addison-Wesley, 1998.

[Cheung 03]   Cheung, Sally. "Transforming Appraisal Findings into a Process Improvement Plan." SEPG 2003. February 2003.

[Chrissis 03]   Chrissis, Mary Beth; Konrad, Mike; Shrum, Sandy. *CMMI—Guidelines for Process Integration and Product Improvement.* Reading, MA: Addison-Wesley, 2003.

[CMMI Product Team 02]   CMMI Product Team. *CMMI for Systems Engineering/Software Engineering/Integrated Product and Process Development/Supplier Sourcing, Version 1.1 Staged Representation* (CMU/SEI-2002-TR-012, ESC-TR-2002-012). Pittsburgh, PA: Software Engineering Institute, Carnegie Mellon University, March 2002.

[CMMI Product Team 01]   CMMI Product Team. *Appraisal Requirements for CMMI^SM, Version 1.1 (ARC, V1.1),* (CMU/SEI-2001-TR-034). Pittsburgh, PA: Software Engineering Institute, Carnegie Mellon University, 2001.

[CMMI Product Team 00]   CMMI Product Team. *SCAMPI^SM, V1.0, Standard CMMI^SM Appraisal Method for Process Improvement: Method Description. Version 1.0.* (CMU/SEI-2000-TR-009). Pittsburgh, PA: Software Engineering Institute, Carnegie Mellon University, 2000.

[Crosby 79]   Crosby, Philip B. *Quality Is Free—The Art of Making Quality Certain.* McGraw-Hill, 1979.

[Deming 82]   Deming, W.E. *Out of Crisis.* Cambridge, MA: MIT Center for Advanced Engineering Study, 1982.

[Dunaway 01a]   Dunaway, Donna K. and Baker, Michele. *Analysis of CMM®-Based Appraisal for Internal Process Improvement (CBA IPI) Assessment Feedback.* (CMU/SEI-2001-TR-021). Pittsburgh, PA: Software Engineering Institute, Carnegie Mellon University, 2001.

[Dunaway 01b]   Dunaway, Donna K. and Masters, Steve. *CMM®-Based Appraisal for Internal Process Improvement (CBA IPI) Version 1.2 Method Description.* (CMU/SEI-2001-TR-033). Pittsburgh, PA: Software Engineering Institute, Carnegie Mellon University, 2001.

[Dunaway 01c]   Dunaway, Donna K. *CMM®-Based Appraisal for Internal Process Improvement (CBA IPI) Lead Assessor's Guide V1.2.* (CMU/SEI-2001-HB-002). Pittsburgh, PA: Software Engineering Institute, Carnegie Mellon University, 2001.

The Lead Assessor's Guide was not made available to the public. It was distributed to registrants in the SEI's offerings of CBA Lead Assessor Training. Because this training course is no longer provided at the SEI, some of the instructive parts of the Guide have been included in this book with appropriate citations.

[Dunaway 99] Dunaway, Donna K.; Berggren, Ruth; des Rochettes, Gilles; Iredale, Paul; Lavi, Itzhak. *Why Do Organizations Have Assessments? Do They Pay Off?* (CMU/SEI-99-TR-012). Pittsburgh, PA: Software Engineering Institute, Carnegie Mellon University, July 1999.

[Dunaway 96a] Dunaway, Donna K. and Masters, Steve. *CMM-Based Appraisal for Internal Process Improvement (CBA IPI): Method Description.* (CMU/SEI-96-TR-007). Pittsburgh, PA: Software Engineering Institute, Carnegie Mellon University, 1996.

[Dunaway 96b] Dunaway, Donna K. *CMM®-Based Appraisal for Internal Process Improvement (CBA IPI) Lead Assessor's Guide V1.1.* (CMU/SEI-96-HB-001). Pittsburgh, PA: Software Engineering Institute, Carnegie Mellon University, 1996.

[Eickelman 03] Eickelman, Nancy. *An Insider's View of CMM Level 5.* IEEE Software, Vol 20, No 4, pp. 79–81, July/Aug 2003.

[GEIA 01] EIA, EPIC, and INCOSE, EIA/IS 731-2, Systems Engineering Capability Model Appraisal Method, GEIA (Government Electronics and Information Technology Association). Washington, DC: 2001.

[Gremba 97] Gremba, Jennifer, and Myers, Chuck. *The IDEAL^SM Model: A Practical Guide for Improvement.* Bridge, Issue Three. Pittsburgh, PA: Software Engineering Institute, Carnegie Mellon University, 1997.

[Hammer 96] Hammer, Michael. *Beyond Reengineering—How the Process-Centered Organization Is Changing Our Work and Our Lives.* Harper Business, a division of Harper Collins Publishers, 1996.

[Hayes 04]   Hayes, Will; Miluk, Gene; Ming, Lisa; Glover, Margaret; and Members of the SCAMPI B & C Project. *Handbook for Conducting SCAMPI B and SCAMPI C Appraisals.* SEI Draft Document for Community Review, August 2004.

[Humphrey 02]   Humphrey, Watts S. *Getting Executive Support.* Proceedings, SEPG 2002. Phoenix, Arizona, February 2002.

[Humphrey 92]   Humphrey, Watts S. *Introduction to Software Process Improvement* (CMU/SEI-92-TR-007), Pittsburgh, PA: Software Engineering Institute, Carnegie Mellon University, 1992.

[Humphrey 89]   Humphrey, Watts S. *Managing the Software Process.* Reading, MA: Addison-Wesley Publishing Company, 1989.

[Humphrey 87]   Humphrey, W. and Sweet, W. *A Method for Assessing the Software Capability of Contractors* (CMU/SEI-87-TR-23). Pittsburgh, PA: Software Engineering Institute, Carnegie Mellon University, 1987.

[ISO 87]   International Organization for Standardization, Quality management and quality assurance standards— Guidelines for Selection and Use ISO 9000, Geneva, 1987.

[Juran 88]   Juran, J. M. and Gryna, F. M. *Juran's Quality Control Handbook, 4th Edition.* New York: McGraw-Hill, 1988.

[Kanter 02]   Kanter, Rosabeth Moss. "Leadership in Turbulent Times: Coping with Change in Business, Technology, Communities and the World." Willis M. Tate Distinguished Lecture Series, Southern Methodist University, November 2002.

[Kanter 01]   Kanter, Rosabeth Moss. *eVolve! Succeeding in the Digital Culture of Tomorrow.* Boston, MA: Harvard Business School Press, 2001.

[Kasse 02]   Kasse, T. *Action Focused Assessment for Software Process Improvement.* Cambridge, MA: Artech House, 2002.

[Kitson 01]   Kitson, David, et al. Document presented at SCAMPI Lead Appraiser Upgrade Training. March 16, 2001.

[Kotter 96]   Kotter, John P. *Leading Change.* Boston, MA: Harvard Business School Press, 1996.

[Krasner 98]   Krasner, Herb. "Using the Cost of Quality Approach for Software," *Crosstalk*. November 1998.

[Kuvaja 94]   Kuvaja, P.; Simila, J.; Krzanik, L.; Bicego, A.; Koch, G.; Saukkonen, S. *Software Process Assessment and Improvement: The Bootstrap Approach*. Oxford: Blackwell Business, 1994.

[Masters 95]   Masters, Steve and Bothwell, Carol. *CMM Appraisal Framework, Version 1.0* (CMU/SEI-95-TR-001). Pittsburgh, PA: Software Engineering Institute, Carnegie Mellon University, 1995.

[Members of the AMIT 01]   Members of the Assessment Method Integrated Team. *Standard CMMI^{SM} Appraisal Method for Process improvement (SCAMPI^{SM}), Version 1.1: Method Definition Document.* (CMU/SEI-2001-HB-001). Pittsburgh, PA: Software Engineering Institute, Carnegie Mellon University, 2001.

[Olson 89]   Olson, T. G.; Humphrey, Watts; Kitson, D. H. *Conducting SEI-Assisted Software Process Assessments.* (CMU/SEI –89-TR-7). Pittsburgh, PA: Software Engineering Institute, Carnegie Mellon University, 1989.

[O' Toole 03]   O'Toole, Patrick. Do's and Don'ts Article 13, "Lead by Example." Personal Communication to the Author: 27 April 2003.

[O'Toole 02]   O'Toole, Patrick. Do's and Don'ts Article 10, "Do Ask Different Questions." Personal Communication to the Author: 12 February 2002.

[Paulk 94]   Paulk, Mark; Weber, Charles V.; Curtis, Bill; Chrissis, Mary Beth. *The Capability Maturity Model: Guidelines for Improving the Software Process*. Reading, MA: Addison-Wesley Publishing Company, 1994.

[Paulk 93a]   Paulk, Mark; Weber, C.; Garcia, C.; Chrissis, M.; Bush, M. *The Capability Maturity Model for Software Version 1.1.* (CMU/SEI-93-TR-024). Pittsburgh, PA: Software Engineering Institute, Carnegie Mellon University, 1993.

[Paulk 93b]   Paulk, Mark; Weber, C.; Garcia, C.; Chrissis, M.; Bush, M. *Key Practices of the Capability Maturity Model, Version 1.1.* (CMU/SEI-93-TR-25). Pittsburgh, PA: Software Engineering Institute, Carnegie Mellon University, 1993.

[Rifkin 03]   Rifkin, Stan. "Why New Processes Are Not Adopted." *Advances in Computer*. Marvin Zelkowitz, editor, vol. 59, 2003.

[SEI 01]   SEI Agreement, License Agreement Between CMU SEI and {transition partner company name} for the CMMI Product Suite, Candidate Lead Appraiser Selection Criteria.

[SEI 03]   SEI, Standard CMMI Appraisal Method for Process Improvement: Team Training: Module F Assigning Assessment Ratings, from SEI SCAMPI Kit, 2003.

[SEMA 03]   Software Engineering Measurement & Analysis Group. *Process Maturity Profile of the Software Community.* April 2003. www.sei.cmu.edu/sema. Pittsburgh, PA: Software Engineering Institute, Carnegie Mellon University, 2003.

[SPICE 95]   SPICE: Baseline Practices and Process Assessment Guide, Version 1.01, January 1995.

[Vu 00]   Vu, John Du V.; Griffin, Scott. *Process Improvement Journey (From Level 1 to Level 5).* Keynote Address, SEPG 2000 Conference. Seattle, Washington, March 2000.

[Waina 02]   Waina, Richard. *Capability Maturity Model Benefits.* Multi-Dimensional Maturity, Celina, Texas, http://www.mdmaturity.com/reference.html, 2002.

[Wiegers 2000]   Wiegers, Karl E.; Sturzenberger, Doris C. "A Modular Software Process Mini-Assessment Method." *IEEE Software*. January/February 2000.

[Zubrow 03]   Zubrow, Dave. *CMMI Appraisal Results*, SEPG 2003. Software Engineering Institute, Carnegie Mellon University, February 25, 2003.

[Zubrow 94]   Zubrow, Dave; Hayes, Will; Seigel, Jane; Goldenson, Dennis. *Maturity Questionnaire* (CMU/SEI-94-SR-7). Pittsburgh, PA: Software Engineering Institute, Carnegie Mellon University, June 1994.

Index

SEI Partner

Carnegie Mellon

The SEI Series in Software Engineering

ISBN 0-321-18613-3

ISBN 0-321-11886-3

ISBN 0-201-73723-X

ISBN 0-201-54664-7

ISBN 0-321-15496-7

ISBN 0-201-70372-6

ISBN 0-201-70482-X

ISBN 0-201-70332-7

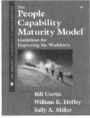
ISBN 0-201-60445-0

ISBN 0-201-60444-2

ISBN 0-201-25592-8

ISBN 0-201-54597-7

ISBN 0-201-54809-7

ISBN 0-201-18095-2

ISBN 0-201-54610-8

ISBN 0-201-47719-X

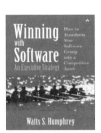
ISBN 0-201-77639-1

ISBN 0-201-61626-2

ISBN 0-201-70454-4

ISBN 0-201-73409-5

ISBN 0-201-85480-5

ISBN 0-321-11884-7

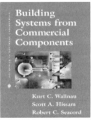
ISBN 0-201-70064-6

ISBN 0-321-15495-9

ISBN 0-201-52577-1

Please see our Web site at http://www.awprofessional.com for more information on these titles.